The new protectionism

The new protectionism

Protecting the future against free trade

Tim Lang and
Colin Hines

Published in the United States by The New Press, New York
Distributed by W.W. Norton & Company, Inc., 500 Fifth Avenue,
New York, NY 10110

Originally published in the United Kingdom by
Earthscan Publications Limited
120 Pentonville Road, London

Library of Congress Cataloging-in-Publication Data
Lang, Tim.
The new protectionism: protecting the future against free trade /
Tim Lang and Colin Hines.
p. cm.
Includes bibliographical references and index.
ISBN 1–56584–135–2
1. Protectionism. 2. Free trade. I. Hines, Colin. II. Title.
HF1713.L32 1993
382′.73—dc20 93–28024
CIP

Established in 1990 as a major alternative to the large, commercial publishing houses, the New Press is the first full-scale nonprofit American book publisher outside of the university presses. The Press is operated editorially in the public interest, rather than for private gain; it is committed to publishing in innovative ways works of educational, cultural, and community value that, despite their intellectual merits, might not normally be "commercially" viable. The New Press's editorial offices are located at the City University of New York.

Printed in the United States of America.

93 94 95 96 9 8 7 6 5 4 3 2 1

Typeset by The Castlefield Press Ltd, Wellingborough, Northants

Contents

List of Tables

Foreword
Jim Hightower

In recent years, strange sounding acronyms — GATT, NAFTA, and so on — have filled the newspapers and the airwaves. While these terms have never really been explained to the American public, we have repeatedly been told, 'Don't worry, it'll be good for you.' Tim Lang and Colin Hines rolled up their sleeves and set out to decipher this alphabet soup. They found out that 'GATT' really means 'Gotcha again!'

While GATT negotiations stalled — thanks to grassroots pressure here in the US and throughout the world — American corporate interests started drawing up a free trade scheme for their own backyard. 'NAFTA,' they call it, the North American Free Trade Agreement.

With the global pact running into trouble, they got together with their corporate buddies from Canada and Mexico to set up a regional zone to unleash the flow of goods and capital across the North American continent. The deal was cut quickly, and now it's before the 635 members of the U.S. Congress, awaiting their 'yea' or 'nay' — and it's up to us to bring a dose of reality and common sense to their decision making.

These two Brits have put together a war chest of arguments against these free trade scams for those of us farmers, workers, consumers, and environmentalists fighting in the trenches. Here's a book you want to keep in your back pocket as Washington and Wall Street prepare to sell us a pig-in-a-poke.

In their book, *The New Protectionism*, Hines and Lang give voice to those of us who sense that something rings hollow in the cries for 'free' trade. The notion of 'free trade' begs the question — 'free' for whom? and 'free' from what? Hines and Lang wrestle these questions to the ground in the first three sections of this book — a necessary and laudatory task given the exaggerated and overestimated theoretical virtues generally attributed to free trade.

The theory of free trade may have worked well and good in Adam Smith's day, but those days have gone. Adam Smith did not envision the global mobility of capital; he expected capital to remain in the home country while goods would be traded according to the law of 'comparative advantage.' Smith believed that a country would produce what it was best at producing and then trade its surplus goods for whatever goods it was unable, or less able, to produce itself.

But according to Hines and Lang, today's trading game follows the rules of 'absolute profitability' instead of Smith's comparative advantage. Nowadays, when a multinational conglomerate has the monetary muscle to uproot and transfer operations to low-wage, less regulated countries, free trade theory doesn't work well at all.

A case in point: In 1985 Zenith employed 4,500 Americans making TV sets in Evansville, Indiana and another 3,000 in Springfield, Missouri. Workers made about $9.60 an hour — hardly a fortune, but enough to raise a family. Today, all of Zenith's jobs are gone from Evansville, and only 400 remain in Springfield. No, Zenith hasn't gone out of business — it's gone to Mexico, where it pays Mexican workers only 64 to 84 cents an hour. And it's not just Zenith. It's General Motors, Motorola, and AT&T — hundreds of U.S. brands have moved production to Mexico, taking 500,000 of our jobs with them. Adam Smith could have used a lesson or two from Thomas Jefferson, who said, 'The selfish spirit of commerce knows no country and feels no passion or principle but that of [its own] gain.'

'Free trade' would be better explained as a means whereby global corporations are 'freed' from the community (local and global), responsibility for human rights, environmental protection, and economic fairness. Multinational corporations are 'free' to flee from countries with strong and worthy regulations for protecting human health, worker safety, and the environment to countries with less stringent — and less stringently enforced — regulations. They are 'free' to relocate plants and production to parts of the globe where the going manufacturing wage is $1.85 an hour. They are 'free' to produce and sell chemicals that were banned from use in one country to farmers in a less developed country and produce food for export to the country that banned the chemical in the first place. Multinationals are 'free' to export food products even if it means that those who grow the food go hungry.

Most disturbing is that under these free trade proposals, global companies would be 'freed' from democratic government oversight. Our own laws would be subject to compliance with new global rules. And if our laws were stronger than the international standards, our laws would be subject to challenge and possible trade retaliation. For example, while the U.S. has some of the strongest regulations on pesticide residues in foods, the international body responsible for setting the international standards, called the Codex Alimentarius, sets standards ten to fifty times more lax than our own. The Codex allows fifty times the amount of DDT residue on bananas as does our own Food and Drug Administration. Under GATT, we'd have to eat our DDT bananas because Codex would be standing guard at the border instead of the FDA. We could still legislate higher standards within our borders, but the importation of less regulated food would likely exert a downward pressure on FDA standards.

According to the authors, the Codex would relieve us of our role as 'citizens' and put us in our place as passive, powerless 'consumers.' The Codex is hardly a democratic decision-making body. Most meetings are held behind closed doors with agrochemical conglomerates warming most of the seats. A study cited by Hines and Lang reports that in the 1989–1991 session of the Codex, only twenty-six participants represented public interest groups while 660 participants represented industry giants such as Monsanto, Nestlé, and DuPont. And public interest groups don't even have a say — they hold positions as 'observers.'

We already have proof of the way in which global rules can cut us out of the democratic decision-making process. The Marine Mammal Protection Act was amended in 1988 to set conditions for the harvesting of tuna. The MMPA banned the importation of tuna harvested by the encirclement method, which unintentionally kills dolphins. Mexico challenged the law as 'unfair trade rules,' and a three-person GATT panel upheld its objection. The panel deemed the MMPA illegal and set a precedent that threatens a country's right to use trade measures as a way to protect the environment.

Hines and Lang provide us with a blaring wake-up call, warning that if we aren't careful, we'll lose our stand as citizens, surrendering our authority to a passive and powerless global agency called the Multilateral Trade Organization, which will set and enforce global trade rules for us. The MTO would have a legal personality, unlike that of GATT, and would ensure that all nations take the necessary steps to bring domestic law into compliance.

At a time in our political history when voting numbers are at an all-time high and when citizen participation in the 1992 elections swept in over one hundred new members to the U.S. House of Representatives, most of whom ran on anti-NAFTA platforms, we are about to be shut off from exercising our democratic rights. We face losing the right to determine our own food safety laws and environmental protections. The New World Order would set in place global rules — designed by an unelected, unrepresentative body — that supersede those of our own congress.

The authors look at 'both sides of the coin,' as they say, and concern themselves with who's really getting the free lunch and who's left to pick up the tab. This book delves into the impact of free trade in three important areas: the environment, economics, and equity.

Most importantly, *The New Protectionism* forces us to consider the true 'cost' of free trade. There is very little about it that is 'free.' Free traders and economists laud the virtues of breaking down the barriers of trade in order to increase global trade and benefit us all. Hines and Lang warn us that 'increased global trade' can also be translated to mean increased pressure on natural resources for the production of cash crops for export instead of domestic consumption, increased toxic pollution due to more manufacturing in areas with less environmental control, and increased displacement of workers and unemployment compensation in the countries that companies will leave for cheaper havens.

We already have a glimpse of what's to come through the experience of the Maquiladoras. Take for example, Matamoros, Mexico, just across the bridge from Brownsville, Texas. Matamoros is one of the most polluted cities in the world — polluted by U.S. corporations that pay Mexican workers 63 cents an hour to make everything from chemicals to cosmetic brushes, which are all exported back to the United States. The soil, air, and water of Matamoros are badly contaminated with various toxins, and people there suffer a startling array of ailments, from cancers to severe birth defects. Free trade in Matamoros has come with a very high price tag. This is repeated in towns all along the southern side of the U.S.-Mexico border, where two thousand foreign-owned factories stretch from Matamoros to the Pacific. This is the real-life embodiment of the North American Free Trade Agreement, which would multiply this horror a hundred times. What a deal for both sides: We get to export our factory jobs to Mexico and import cosmetic brushes. They get 63-cents-an-hour jobs and babies born without brains.

Hines and Lang do not mince words. They make a bold and courageous attempt to redefine the meaning of 'protectionism' and liberate the word from its nasty reputation. The authors make a strong and clear distinction between the protectionism of the past, or 'Old Protectionism,' and the kinds of protective laws they believe we need today. 'Protectionism,' as we have known it, has meant the sheltering of lethargic industries — in effect, companies that want to grow bananas in Utah. The Old Protectionism is about writing the rules in the interests of the holder of the heaviest moneybags.

The proposed free trade agreements of GATT and NAFTA are plain-as-day rules to 'protect' multinational corporations from paying decent wages, and from complying with workplace safety laws and environmental rules. But mostly this is about protecting profits. You need only look at who's *for* this deal to know who'll be awash and who'll get hung out to dry.

The USA-NAFTA lobby is a coalition of corporate hucksters headed up by the main man at Kodak — the same fellow who earlier this year announced another two thousand 'involuntary layoffs' of Kodak workers in our country. The group is made up of hundreds of U.S. corporations and big-business lobbies, including AT&T, Proctor & Gamble, Motorola, and American Express. And the Mexican government had even gone so far as to set up an investment fund (now disbanded because it played poorly politically) specifically to buy U.S. companies and move them down to Mexico to take advantage of cheaper labor. As Yogi Berra once said: 'You can observe a lot just by watching.'

Going beyond simple observation, the *Wall Street Journal* recently confirmed our suspicions. The Journal's survey of 455 top executives found that 55 percent of the biggest employers say they're planning to shift production to Mexico if NAFTA goes through.

These same men in alligator shoes and $1000 suits say we just don't understand the new 'global economy.' By moving, they say, Mexico's wage levels will rise, making it possible for their workers to buy American consumer products, thereby creating more jobs here. Now I was born at night, but it wasn't last night. The average manufacturing wage in Mexico is $1.45 an hour. U.S. companies operating in Mexico pay, on average, 63 cents an hour for the Mexican workers they hire. They're not raising Mexican wages — they're depressing them. How's a Mexican worker going to buy a Buick on 63 cents an hour? Our companies aren't creating consumers in Mexico — they're creating serfs.

The real purpose behind the NAFTA is not to help Mexican workers, but to use their low wages as a machete to whack our high wages down. The *Wall Street Journal* even found in their survey that one-fourth of U.S. executives admit that this is what they've got in mind. Like Sam Houston said about one of his political opponents, these guys have 'all the characteristics of a dog — except loyalty.'

Hines and Lang articulate what many of the farmers, environmentalists, workers, and consumers in this country have been saying for a long time. We're not in favor of the Old Protectionism, which only protected the profits and power of the minority elite. What we need is a New Protectionism, a reassertation of priorities such as protection of the environment, economic fairness, and equity among nations.

The New Protectionism offers us a bold and courageous (and possible) alternative to world trading rules. The authors want to rearrange the alphabet soup to GAST — the General Agreement for Sustainable Trade — and NASTA, the North American Sustainable Trade Agreement. It's time to replace the Old Protectionism with the protection of citizens' rights, protection of the environment, and protection of the poor and disadvantaged from the greed and indifference of the global conglomerates.

Preface

Many people have encouraged us to develop our thoughts into this book, have corresponded with us while writing the book and, most onerously of all, have read lengthy drafts. We set out to articulate an alternative vision for trade, drawing on the experience and world view of the movements we have worked with and for: the environment, consumer, public health and development movements. This meant we had to express what we dislike about the current belief in trade liberalisation, exemplified by the General Agreement on Tariffs and Trade (GATT) Uruguay Round. We have tried to represent the fears and hopes raised by the debate among this group of people about the impact of trade. All across the world, broad alliances are being made by groups which do not normally work together, having previously had different interests, but who are brought together because of emerging common themes, which we have called the three 'Es' in this book – the case for social and global equity, a sane economy and a sustainable environment.

We think that a humane, progressive alternative to free trade *is* quietly emerging, which not only deserves a wider public but has to be the property of the public worldwide. It is crucial to contest the virtually unchallenged view that free trade is good, generates wealth and helps the poor. Changes to the world trading system are being proposed which will fundamentally alter the relationship between citizen and state – reason alone for there to be a debate about trade, rather than the one-sided perspective so often dished up to and by politicians. The free trade vision distorts the potential to make the world a better place, where co-operation rather than ruinous competition rules. Articulating such a broad vision means that we range widely. Lastly, we wish to make it clear that this book was written in our personal capacities and the views expressed in it are ours.

Tim Lang and Colin Hines
London, April 1993

Acknowledgements

An especial thanks to Kevin Watkins, Simon Festing, Martine Drake and Charlie Clutterbuck for help on early drafts, and to the long list of friends and colleagues who have read bits or whole drafts or answered early morning or late night queries. They include Charlie Arden-Clarke (WWF-International, Switzerland), Natalie Avery (Essential Information, USA), Lara Baker (Parents for Safe Food), David Baldock (Institute for European Environmental Policy), Michael Barratt Brown (TWIN Trading), Clive Bates (Greenpeace UK), Stewart Boyle (Greenpeace International), Rudi Buntzel (Protestant Farmers Group, Germany), Liz Castledine, the Central Statistical Office, Helge Christie (GATT campaign, Norway), Tracey Clunies-Ross (*The Ecologist*), Charlie Clutterbuck, Herman Daly (World Bank), Barbara Dinham (Pesticides Trust), Martine Drake (Consumers Network on Trade), Joyce d'Silva (Compassion in World Farming), Cameron Duncan (Greenpeace International), Richard Eglin (GATT), Paul Ekins (Birkbeck College), Michael Finger (GATT), David Gee, Susan George (Transnational Institute, Amsterdam), Sir James Goldsmith, Teddy Goldsmith, Nick Hildyard and Simon Fairlie (*The Ecologist*), Mayer Hillman (Policy Studies Institute), Tim Jackson (Stockholm Environment Institute), Mike Jellicoe, Robin Jenkins (Food Commission, UK), Mandy Jetter (New Consumer), Jeremy Leggett (Greenpeace International), Peter Madden (Christian Aid), Ed Mayo (New Economics Foundation), Pradeep Mehta (Consumer Unity and Trust Society, India), Melanie Miller (SAFE Alliance), Erik Millstone (Science Policy Research Unit, University of Sussex), Caroline Mulvihill (formerly Parents for Safe Food), Jonathon Porritt, Robin Murray (Institute of Development Studies, University of Sussex), Hugh Raven (SAFE Alliance), Geof Rayner (Public Health Alliance), Mike Rayner (Coronary Prevention Group), Mark Ritchie and Kristin Dawkins (Institute of Agriculture and Trade Policy, USA), Steve Shrybman (Canadian Environmental Law Association), Alistair Smith (Farmers' Link), Richard Tapper (WWF-UK), Ronnie Taylor (Friends of the Earth, England, Wales and N Ireland), Jesper Toft (NOAH, Denmark), Ann Wainwright, Lori Wallach (Citizen Tradewatch, USA), Kevin Watkins (Oxfam), Tony Webb (Food Policy Alliance, Australia) and Karen West. Our thanks to all these long-suffering colleagues and friends is heartfelt; may the GATT-watching circles grow ever wider. Thanks, too, to our marvellous editors Kath and Geoff Tansey, and to the team at Earthscan: Jonathan Sinclair Wilson, Jo O'Driscoll and Lisa Day.

PART ONE
Confronting the Myth

'Free trade is heart-breaking nonsense.'[1]
George Bernard Shaw

'Free trade is foreign trade not subject to regulation by the nation's government.'[2]
J Cuthbertson

I Introduction

How can a situation emerge where:

- countries are forced to accept laxer controls on pesticide residues in food?
- a country's ban on asbestos can be undermined?
- dolphins cannot be properly protected from tuna fishing?
- poorer countries cut back on social expenditure to boost exports?
- local industry and jobs go, but imports of similar goods come in?
- people sell food they previously ate?

The answer, as we will show for all these examples, is when economies bow the knee to the demands of free trade. Whatever the problem – the recession, regional decline, unemployment, poverty in the Third World or Eastern European crises – the same phrase crops up in the answers of Western pundits: free trade. The more free trade principles are applied, it is asserted, and the fewer the barriers to trade, the greater will be economic activity between nations and therefore the more wealth there will be to accelerate away from the problems which worry the world. This book questions that logic. It argues that free trade is a misnomer for deregulated commerce. Trade liberalization hopes to bring more international trade, yet more trade brings more of the problems the world needs less of: threats to the environment, uneven spread of employment, and widening gaps between rich and poor, both within societies and between societies.

It is ironic that free trade theory, which places such emphasis on choice and freedom, brooks no opposition to itself. There is a choice, however, and this book maps out what that could be. Free trade holds out the prospect of continued job losses and endless ruthless competition, growing power of unaccountable transnational corporations (TNCs), more distant government and painful economic restructuring bringing the human crises that follow from instability. In the other direction is the goal of protecting everyone's future, not just the future of the few, which is what free trade and old style protectionism offer.

The New Protectionism, as we have called this orientation, aims to protect the environment by reducing international trade and by reorienting and diversifying entire economies towards producing the most that they can locally or nationally, then looking to the region that surrounds them, and only as a last option to global international trade.

Free trade is traditionally described as being at the opposite end of a continuum to protectionism. Our argument is that *both* free trade and what we call the old protectionism have been approaches to trade and markets which have benefited the powerful. In contrast, our New Protectionism sets out to protect and heal the environment, to reduce economic inequalities and to meet basic social and human needs for all, not just the privileged few or few countries. These three 'Es' – the economy, environment and equity – are the core of today's global challenge, so we try to map out an approach to trade which meets them. This new approach would replace the present destructive situation, which gears entire economies to being internationally competitive regardless of the adverse effects of this fixation.

Our assertion is that *protection is good*. The very word *protect* has been made a dirty word by the free trade ideology, but look to your everyday life, and judge honestly if protection is not a key motive in much that you do. Ask yourself if you would pay taxes to the state if it did not do some things for you in return that protect everyone's interests.

Free trade usually brings with it a package of ideas, which we explore throughout this book. Many of these ideas have become familiar over the last two decades as the new generation of free traders have obtained political power. They are often obsessed about lowering taxes – 'getting the state off our backs' – to allow companies and enterprises to outdo their competitors, but in reality, this merely sets citizen against citizen in a dehumanising scramble to come out on top of the heap. Often this process of competition is not even visible, as it occurs between people and environments across the world. In the past, perhaps ignorance of these processes was an excuse, but now most people know they live in one world. Present institutions and ideas often block the capacity to tackle local or national problems, let alone global ones.

There is nothing intrinsically wrong, indeed there is lots good, about protection. One of the first challenges is to rescue the *language* of protectionism. Peasants are lampooned as 'protectionists' for resisting trade liberalization and for trying to preserve an 'inefficient' way of life. Workers and businesses are described as 'standing in the way of progress' if they express worries about their trades being undercut by imports. Consumer and environmental organizations are criticized as 'green protectionists' for raising the thorny issue of not allowing free trade to roll back hard won environmental or product safety regulations or the introduction of more stringent measures.[1] But if we look at the meaning of protection, interesting questions follow. Protection of what? For whom? For what ends? To whose benefit? In answering these questions, we map out why the New Protectionism is needed and what its key principles are.

The world's population is expected to double from today's 5.4 billion by the middle of the next century. The world is already brutally divided.

Introduction

Those one billion or so of us living in the affluent North live on the backs of the South's hidden labour and at the expense of the environment. Anyone's environmental degradation eventually affects everyone, which is why free market solutions ultimately do not work. They create problems for everyone but only benefit the minority and short term ends.

What is needed, then, is a vision which meets all the goals which qualify for a civilized society: a good quality of life for all, secure employment, minimal environmental damage, diverse regional economies, decent homes, food and social support for hard or unhealthy times. The market's only approach to these goals is to put a price on everything. Health and the environment become commodities like everything else, to be bought, sold, exchanged and bet on. Commodification restricts access. An alternative to the free trade package is sorely needed. The present free market driven political and social system is, as even its proponents admit, faltering in its heartlands of the North. Free trade promises more than it can deliver and like all junkies when faced with failure, its only solution is to repeat the dose. In contrast, the New Protectionism, with its emphasis on sustainable local and regional economies, is the route to a better, more equitable, more environmentally friendly future.

In Part One of this book, we confront the ideas in the free trade package, and introduce the New Protectionism. In Part Two, we look in more detail at who has the power under the present trading system, and in particular the working of the General Agreement on Tariffs and Trade (GATT). We detail the deleterious effects of the free trade package in Part Three. Finally, in Part Four, we discuss present trading alternatives and flesh out the mechanisms and how to pay for the New Protectionism.

1. The Challenge

To begin with, we must clarify:

- what free trade really is and what ideas come with it;
- why the free trade package is an inappropriate goal for running economies;
- the challenges any alternative has to address.

Free trade is, in theory, a system where traders are allowed to exchange money and goods without any concern for national barriers. There should be few legal constraints, no artificial protection or subsidies influencing the freedom to exchange. Traders, the theory goes, need to be free to do what they like. The presumption is that the traders know what they are doing and that markets will sort out any problems to emerge, whether these problems are the relative decline of the British or US economy, threats to the environment from wasteful energy policies or inappropriate systems sold to the Third World. Problems will be resolved by determining by how much somebody is willing to *pay* to get them sorted out. Free traders argue that their primary concern is to increase the size of the world's economic cake, and that once this has happened, there will be more to share around and some of it will 'trickle down' to the poorest. The analogy is that wealth creation is like the icing flowing down the sides of a giant cake.

There is no realistic competing ideology to free trade, say its proponents. But when a country is uncompetitive, they warn, it can easily slide into protectionism, and attempt to protect its home industries from foreign products. It may amongst other things introduce:

- tariffs, which impose a duty on goods entering the country, thus making them more expensive;
- embargoes, which prohibit the import of particular commodities or goods of particular countries;
- quotas, which limit imports of particular goods, or imports from particular countries, to a permitted amount by volume or value;
- technical specifications, which deliberately exclude foreign goods, or demand modifications or adjustments, which increase costs and delay the impact of the foreign competition on the home-produced market.

Free trade proponents dislike all of these measures. We, however, make a distinction between two uses of the word protectionism. The historical practice of protectionism we call the old protectionism because it was used by big and powerful interests to pursue *their* goals. The second we call the New Protectionism because it seeks to protect *public* interests, like health or the environment or safety standards or reduction of poverty, against the interests of unrestrained trade. Our argument is that *neither* free trade *nor* old protectionism is up to the awe-inspiring challenges which face the world in the 21st century.

Since the 1970s, free trade thought has gradually dominated Western economic and social thinking. In North America and Europe, politicians have introduced new laws and encouraged their industries to promote new working practices in the name of *efficiency* and *competition.* Gearing their economies to export dominates internal national and business policies. Workers and business alike have to become 'lean and efficient' in order to compete in global markets despite the fact that such policies will usually mean more unemployment and environmental degradation. Throughout this process of change, free trade is promoted as: the most efficient route to sustained economic growth; the best long-term ideology for creating wealth and avoiding economic stagnation; and the only route out of today's world recession and economic malaise.

As the 21st century approaches, the world's economic rules are being restructured to remove barriers to trade both at home and internationally through GATT. The best way to make sense of this restructuring is by realising who sets and seeks to benefit from the rules. The world economy is being dominated by a relatively small number of giant TNCs and three regional superblocs – centred on the USA, Japan and Europe – which we discuss in Part Two. But even within the new world top class there are squabbles and disagreements over world trade such as those over steel, cars, farm products and public procurement contracts.

Meeting the three 'Es'

We argue that the three 'Es' – the economy, environment and equity – are the core of today's global challenge, and that neither free trade nor old protectionism offer any long term way out. Trade is not an end in itself and economic activity should be shaped to meet human needs and to sustain the environment on which life depends.

The economy

Clearly in Britain and all over the world, economies are in trouble. Even the miracle economies such as Germany and Japan which have been held up as the models for other 'old' economies to emulate have seen unemployment rocket and recession hit living standards. Everywhere, pundits have indulged in soul-searching, asking what is wrong and what should be done to get economies moving again. Pessimists remind us that the Roman Empire, too, declined. A mood of resignation hovers not so far beneath the cultural surface. Politicians are blamed for being out of touch. Social evils are sought to explain economic failings. Victorian fears about the underclass, crime and insecurity are modernized.

Optimists about the economy admit that the length of the economic downturn took them by surprise, but still conclude that people need to work harder and become better trained, and companies and sectors need to get leaner and fitter, so that *our* national economies can compete more efficiently against everyone else's. An *us and them* economics is promoted. Meanwhile, other countries are being encouraged to do the same. There is also a global increase in the numbers of people who are unemployed, under-employed or quasi-employed on government schemes designed more to take numbers off the unemployment statistics than to create life-enhancing skills.

As the 1990s recession has worn on, and the search for the 'green shoots of recovery' (in the UK Chancellor's memorable phrase) has got tiring, the economy dominates the public's concerns. Who is going to be next to lose their job? But besides economic concerns, two other crises should demand attention: the equity crisis – the gap between rich and poor between and within nations; and the environmental crisis.

Equity

Between 1960 and 1990, global inequality worsened. According to the United Nations Development Programme (UNDP), the richest fifth of the world's population, by nation, today earns over 60 times more than the poorest fifth.[1] The equitable and rational goal of enabling people to have more power over their lives and to earn enough from work to live a fulfilling life gets more distant for huge numbers of people. Trade has brought wealth to those who benefit from it, but a welter of books and reports in the 1990s argue that global inequality is growing or being accentuated due to current terms of trade.[2]

Developing nations' share of global wealth fell from 22 per cent to 18 per cent between 1980 and 1988. Only in Asia did per capita incomes outpace this drop. For sub-Saharan Africa, the decline in its income from primary commodities in real terms was 50 per cent.[3] In practice, for the fisherfolk of Kerala state, India, for example, this translates into a stark choice: export or eat. Their waters have been overfished as a result of a combination of factors – modern trawlers, subsidies, abandoning of traditional methods and a rise in numbers of fisherfolk.[4] They are under pressure to sell food they previously ate and suffer as a result (see Chapter 12).

A similar paradox has been documented in the Philippines – home to the Green Revolution's International Rice Research Institute. By 1990 the Philippines was importing 600,000 tonnes of rice, 18 per cent of its production needs, and malnutrition is one of the top ten causes of child death in the country.[5] Average food consumption figures continues to decline *despite* increases in productivity. Francisco Lara of the Philippine Peasant Institute reports:

> 'The greatest irony is that the worse off children are those in regions which figure prominently as the country's food basket areas: Southern Mindanao, where rice is grown abundantly and where the huge banana and pineapple plantations are situated and Central Luzon, the country's rice granary. (. . .) 70 per cent of our population are 40–60 per cent deficient in energy food intake.'

The developed countries of the world (the North) with around a quarter of the world's population consume 70 per cent of the world's energy, 75 per cent of its metals and 60 per cent of its food. If we just look at energy consumption per capita, North America's is far higher than any other region with Western, Central and Eastern Europe next.[6] Within the developing world (the South) there are tremendous income disparities too. In Brazil, for example, the top 20 per cent of people receive 26 times the income of the bottom 20 per cent.[7]

The environment

In the last 20 years the world environment has deteriorated dramatically for such a short space of geological time. Examples include the destruction of the ozone layer and rain forests, widespread contamination of the seas and accelerating air pollution and global warming. The good news is that most organizations and governments now claim to be environmentally aware or involved, but the bad news is that often their practices do not match their promises.

Free trade proponents usually argue that only when the economy is back in good shape (through 'growth') will there be enough wealth and political space to address the environment and world equity.[8] In contrast, we argue that the only way to tackle any of the three 'Es' is together. Indeed, today's economic crisis is here, in part, because free market forces have failed to include the costs of environmental damage and have ignored the needs of a vast slice of humanity.

Free trade economics has meant the pursuit of wealth and consumption for the world's richest 1.1 billion inhabitants only. This is to the detriment of the rest and to the environment. Alan Durning of the USA-based Worldwatch Institute rightly argues that a new ecological global class system has emerged. The richest ecological class should actually be called the consuming class, as it consumes a disproportionate share of the globe's resources and takes 64 per cent of the world's income.[9] Using mainly United Nations (UN) data, the Worldwatch Institute calculates that the industrial countries consume the vast majority of the world's resources (Table 1). Broadly speaking, an average citizen in the industrial countries, for example, consumes 18 times as many chemicals, ten times as much energy and three times as much grain as an average citizen of a developing country.

Table 1 *Consumption of selected goods, industrial and developing countries, late 1980s*

Good	Industrial countries' share of world consumption (%)	Consumption gap between industrial and developing countries (*ratio of per capita consumption rates*)
Aluminium	86	19
Chemicals	86	18
Paper	81	14
Iron and steel	80	13
Timber	76	10
Energy	75	10
Meat	61	6
Fertilizers	60	5
Cement	52	3
Fish	49	3
Grain	48	3
Fresh water	42	3

Source: Durning, 1992[10]

The explosion of consumption by the world's rich consuming class is a major feature of today's environmental crisis. The Northern way of life depends on the use of energy, chemicals, metals and paper, the profligate use of which now threatens that very way of life. These consumption patterns have put the green movement into a conundrum: on the one hand it wants mass public support in the North, yet on the other hand it desires to change radically the lifestyle and production style of those populations.

The ecologically threatening lifestyle has also had contradictory social effects. Despite labour-saving devices in the home, US and UK studies suggest that women, for instance, still spend as much time on domestic labour as they did 30 years ago.[11] Unless social relations change, technology fails to deliver the advertised promises.

Free trade and GATT

Free traders are poised to gain their greatest triumph: a new set of trading rules favouring them in the GATT. The GATT Uruguay Round, so-called because the process of negotiating these rules was launched in Punta del Este, Uruguay in 1986, represents an extraordinary extension of trade liberalization – precisely the economic policies which we argue in this book are wholly inappropriate. Free traders see this new GATT as the way out of the recession, but the GATT proposals are a dramatic extension of the same policies that helped get the world into the mess in the first place. Their vision for saving the world is more trade, more deregulated commerce.

The New Protectionism

The state of the world demands another vision for the future. A frame of reference from which to question the future being mapped out for the next century by the world's new, unrepresentative, baronial class: the TNCs, the trade superblocs and the GATT. We believe that the ends to which an economy should be organized should be different. The goal should be to protect the future through restrictions on international trade and by reorienting and diversifying entire economies towards producing the most that they can nationally, then looking to the region of countries that surrounds them, and only as a last resort to international trade. Our vision is for less trade and, where it happens, for trade to be more local, more equitable and to meet higher standards. More long-distance trade will only intensify the damaging trends which are already bringing the world to its current sorry state.

This is the New Protectionism. Our goal is to initiate debate about the case for protecting the *public* good, in place of the current policies' success in protecting the *elite's* good. By elite, we refer to what Professor JK Galbraith, former adviser to President Kennedy and grand old man of Keynesian economics, has recently called the *contented*, the two thirds in rich countries who live well compared to their society's disenfranchised and poor one third,[12] and globally, what Alan Durning calls the *ecological consuming class*, the world's affluent one billion or so consumers.[13]

The heart of the matter is what sort of world, what methods of production, what patterns of consumption, and what legacy will we leave our children and future generations. In the consumer, environment and world development movements, there are those who argue that progress in environmental protection will best be served by arguing the benefits to business. There can be benefits to business from toughened environmental standards, but it is short-sighted to sell those advantages as coming without disadvantages to business too. The big challenge for the future is to develop policies which meet the needs of the economy, the environment and equity – stopping and reversing the alarming growth of poverty everywhere. All the soul searching and anxiety over slowing of Western growth is a diversion from the basic political challenge, which is to win more people to policies which stop being tokenist about the far-off poor, which make the environment a priority (not just when it suits) and which distribute work and rewards more rather than less fairly.

Left-wing political parties cannot decide what they stand for. They support market theory for business, but don't like its social consequences. The Right is similarly disoriented – Thatcherism and Reaganomics are discredited, but there is no populist replacement yet – and in the UK, despite trying to project a caring image for the 1990s, the government is preparing for another period of trade-oriented deregulation.[14]

Outside conventional party politics, there is also some confusion about trade policy though there are now excellent analyses of how current policies penalize the world's poor.[15] One reason is that trade is pretty low on domestic political agendas, but another is that people who like to think of themselves as progressives often feel as nervous about the old protectionism as they do about free trade. There are some excellent prototypes of more equitable trade, which we discuss in Chapter 11.[16] In the short term, we have no doubt that alternative trading represents a significant gain for producers in developing countries, but our concern is the long term implications, and to promote shifts in whole economies, not just niche markets.

Other thinkers about trade, such as Egyptian-born economist Samir Amin, have argued similarly but from very different starting points. The only way for the South to get out of the cycle of dependency upon the North, Amin says, is to reduce the export mentality. External trade should be subjected to *domestic* priorities. Amin calls this vision for the world 'polycentrism', to indicate a world unlike the present, which is centralizing power and trade rapidly.[17] He argues that trade should result in less dependency upon the North and more national and regional (within a country, what we call local) development.

The word 'sustainability' is much in vogue, but it perhaps begins to lose its meaning when even giant chemical companies use it. We prefer the phrase *self-reliance*, not in the sense used by some Third World economies in the 1960s, which led to dependency upon a few commodity markets for foreign capital and crazy attempts to be self-sufficient, but self-reliance in the sense of celebrating and aiming for diversity of production, diversity of economic activity, and retaining control over capital, rather than letting it flow around the world in search of the highest interest. The South has to avoid the twin myths of self-sufficiency behind national barriers or that it can gain by adopting free trade policies – both spell underdevelopment.

Theoreticians about global development and equity cannot agree completely about what form inequity takes.[18] Some argue that the world is dividing into a 'core' of powerful nations and a 'periphery' which is a kind of underclass. Others argue that rich and poor countries are mutually dependent, though unequal. Still others argue a catch-up theory, which says that the middle ground is growing and that the Newly Industrialized Countries (NICs) are in transition to full industrialized affluence. And finally, others argue that the world is still a pyramidal social structure, with power and control serving those at the top.

The great irony about this theoretical debate is that to the poor of the South its nuances are academic. The North controls almost all the capital that fuels development. And as economist Michael Barratt Brown, Chair of Twin Trading, an alternative trading organisation, reminds us, only a third of the $1,200 billion debt the Third World owed the banks of the First World in 1990 was the orginal debt. The rest was accrued interest and capital liabilities.[19] Given the South's continued reliance upon exporting raw commodities, whose real value is unlikely to rise and whose market access may be further restricted, less developed countries will have to develop regional trade policies to survive. The goal of these regional policies should not just be to foster South–South trading relations, but diverse, *local* economies. The question should be asked: foreign exchange for what?

Southern economies dependent on trading in primary, unprocessed commodities such as jute or coffee have seen declining returns in recent decades. They are on a treadmill – having to sell more to get less in return. Another problem with specialized economies is their vulnerability to new inventions. An example is cane sugar, already threatened by artificial sweeteners and maize-derived sugars, but now additionally threatened by the impact of biotechnology. Cocoa is also under threat from a new biotechnology-derived substitute. Southern economies have got to prepare for such changes and need to jump off rather than speed up their efforts on the treadmill. Selective import controls can certainly be justified to keep luxury cars out, but to allow machine tools in, for example. One is gas guzzling for the elite while the other can serve a wider citizenry. Selective import controls can also be used to buy time to develop local infrastructures.

These arguments are equally valid to ensure a more diverse and equitable future for the North – and the former communist countries of

Eastern Europe. Internal redistribution of power and wealth is urgently needed. In the short term, small producers, on and off the land in both North and South, but particularly in the South, need to get a higher percentage of the money that consumers pay for processed commodities.

A new political agenda

The political challenge is to *make* the era of free trade close, yet most politicians are frankly at sea about trade issues. They may believe that free trade is a good thing, but when pressed, most have never read a word of GATT documents. The huge task we offer them is to begin to redirect the world's economies. In the short term, we want politicians to work towards the following long term goals:

- A shift in politics away from promoting the free trade package (see chapter 2) to giving priority to equity and the protection of the environment.
- A new trade policy. The world needs less, not more international trade. Much trade is ecological madness with ships and wagons traversing the globe passing others carrying similar goods, or goods which could be produced more locally, going the other way.
- Promoting regionalism. Every region, by which we mean both localities within countries and regional groupings of neighbouring countries, should be economically diverse and production organized on a local level, rather than the current tendency to globalize production. The long term goal should be to achieve as much regional self-reliance as possible, to minimize the distance goods travel unnecessarily.
- A new competition policy. Global intervention to control TNCs is a priority. This is unlikely to come through the UN which in 1992 downgraded, *de facto* gutted, its own centre for studying TNCs,[20] but it is more likely to come from local or regional groupings of nation states bent on protecting the economic health of their areas.
- New trade mechanisms to control and monitor trade should have as a goal the need to protect the environment adequately and to reverse the growing inequality of the world. We'd like GATT to become GAST, the General Agreement for Sustainable Trade.
- Research on developing transitional strategies to move trade into the new regional patterns.

The task may be formidable, but the movement for such a new vision for trade is already emerging. The GATT talks have generated opposition from an unparalleled global network of public interest groups – a coalition of environment groups, public health workers, citizens, farmers and others. In Chapter 2, we now go on to look at the reality of present world trade, the theory behind free trade, and some of its critics.

2. Reality and Myths of the Free Trade Package

There have been four major phases of development in trade.[1] The first was associated with a *mercantile* division of labour, where a surplus of commodities was generated through the accidents of geography, climate, and the spread of plants and animals. While merchants were swapping these goods, they began to organize labour, in particular as plantation workers and slaves. Plants such as potatoes, cotton, tea, sugar, rice and rubber were moved round the world to make better use of supplies of labour.

The second phase came with the *industrial* division of labour as machines began to be used in the production and processing of tropical commodities. Europe drew in labour from farms to factories in the towns. Workers were increasingly dependent on wages. Some countries with a shortage of labour pulled in workers from elsewhere – the USA pulled in over 35 million peasants from farms in Europe. Infrastructures such as international canals, roads and rails were built. These developments gave rise to the first strikes and workers' protests.

These conflicts lessened as money from the home countries moved to colonies where sufficient profits were produced to fund modest improvements for workers at home. This is often called the *imperial* division of labour. Workers in European colonies grew food and dug up materials which were exported to Europe and Europe's new working classes made the manufactured goods that were exported throughout the world. Peasant proprietors in the colonies became cash crop producers tied to the world markets, and European trade unions slowly became partners in the process.

The world is now in a fourth phase, the transnational phase, characterised by a *transnational* division of labour, where power has centred on the USA, Europe and lately Japan. This leaves in place many previous trading relationships, but has restructured industrial production in the developed countries, imported migrant labour to those countries, and internationalized key sectors such as the oil giants, car companies, and electrical goods. Most recently there has been a shift of manufacturing to Southeast Asia.

World trade today

In 1990, the total value of world trade in goods was US $3485 billion, with an additional $810 billion in commercial services. That is an awful lot of products flying, steaming, trucking and occasionally being walked across the world's surfaces. The goods are physical – things which have been mined or grown or manufactured, but services are more intangible – insurance, legal advice, banking and ownership of ideas. Every time these goods or services move about the globe, someone takes a cut. Sometimes, as in the futures markets, people bet on whether the price of commodities will go up or down.

One of the most striking features of world trade markets is how relatively *few* companies or countries dominate any one sector. For instance, six countries – USA, USSR, France, UK, Germany and China – have 90 per cent of the world's arms trade. The grain trade is dominated by a handful of companies, and in 1988 just one country, the USA (home to all but one of those companies), accounted for 60 per cent of net exports.[2]

World trade in primary goods, such as food, raw materials, minerals and energy, as well as manufactured products, has grown on average 5.4 per cent a year since 1950, according to the world trade statistics laboriously compiled by the GATT secretariat in Geneva from national statistics and estimates.[3] This growth has regularly exceeded the expansion of global output as a whole. Thus as a percentage of the natural resources used or extracted, or the manufactured goods produced, the amount traded internationally is increasing faster than that produced for domestic use. Trade in services and direct investment in foreign countries are also growing rapidly.[4] However, over the last 20 years, the proportion of trade in goods to trade in services has remained remarkably constant: four to one.[5] This is interesting because for the last 20 years there has been a continuing debate among economists about whether developed countries can afford to see their manufacturing bases decline on the promise that there will be compensatory growth in service employment.[6] The Thatcher government, for example, strongly rejected criticism of the decline in UK manufacturing in the early 1980s using this argument. The rate of growth in both goods and services has actually been slowing from over 8 per cent in 1960–70, to 5 per cent in 1970–80 and down to 4 per cent in 1980–90.[7]

Unequal trade

World trade is hopelessly unequal. Developed countries account for 71.5 per cent, developing economies 21 per cent and China, plus centrally planned Asia, Central and Eastern Europe and the USSR, a grand 7 per cent. Three quarters of world trade and investment takes place between industrialized countries.[8]

The Third World countries are net exporters of food, raw materials, minerals and fuels to the industrialized world and these primary products tend to dominate their total exports – for example more than 98 per cent for Bolivia, Ethiopia, Ghana and Nigeria compared with 24 per cent of US exports and 2 per cent for Japan.[9] Although the industrialized world is responsible for most exports of manufactured goods, some forms of manufacturing – textiles, leather, iron and steel production and chemicals – are increasingly concentrating in developing countries. Developing countries' share of manufactured exports increased from 4 per cent to 19 per cent between 1955 and 1989 and the NICs of Southeast Asia have been expanding exports of manufactured goods rapidly. But most developing countries still maintain their high dependence on primary goods[10] and therefore their economies (and living standards) are highly dependent on the prices paid for these goods.

Although traditionally, international trade is seen as something carried out between nations, the expansion of world trade was underpinned by the burgeoning overseas investment of TNCs. This accelerated in the 1980s when information technology and deregulation of foreign exchange markets in the industrialized countries allowed TNCs to increase their competitiveness by manufacturing in the most advantageous places. International trade is in fact dominated by trade within TNCs. In 1985 the combined sales of the world's largest 200 TNCs was more than $3 trillion, equivalent to nearly one third of global Gross Domestic Product (GDP). Deregulation and takeovers have since increased the dominance of these huge conglomerates, whose control stretches from production and processing to banking and transport.[11]

Trade in goods is dominated by Western Europe, with just under half, Asia (mainly Japan) at 22 per cent, North America at 15 per cent, Latin America at 4 per cent and the whole of Africa at just 2.5 per cent. Again, we see how unbalanced world trade is. And what of the goods? Agricultural goods are 12.5 per cent, mined products 14 per cent, and manufactured goods 70 per cent, with 35 per cent of this being just on machinery and transport equipment.[12]

When we look at which countries do the trading, a remarkable pattern emerges. The biggest importers are the biggest exporters (see Table 2) but not all big trading countries balance their books. At the top of the trade tables, some were making more money from exports than spending on imports: Germany (+ $55.8 billion) and Japan (+ $52.2 billion), but other big traders were in deficit: USA (– $123.4 billion), UK (– $37.6 billion), France (– $17.8 billion), Italy (– $11.7 billion).[13]

Lower down the tables, Brazil exported $31.4 billions worth and imported $22.5 billion (+ $8.9 billion) but this apparently positive figure in

Table 2 *Top 15 exporting and importing countries, 1990*

Top exporters	Top importers
Germany	USA
USA	Germany
Japan	Japan
France	France
UK	UK
Italy	Italy
Netherlands	Netherlands
Canada	Canada
Belgium-Luxembourg	USSR
USSR	Belgium-Luxembourg
Hong Kong	Spain
Taiwan	Hong Kong
Korea	Switzerland
Switzerland	Korea
China	Singapore

Source: GATT, 1992[14]

fact excludes Brazil's debt burden. Mexico was near parity, exporting $41.1 billion and importing $41.6 billion (– $0.5 billion). Half a billion US dollars might sound small – it's only 0.01435 per cent of total world trade in goods – but to Mexico, half a billion dollars of debt is the equivalent of an awful lot of welfare spending. So for a country such as India with a balance of payments in deficit to the tune of – $5.6 billion, the trouble trade brings is immense. Governments exhort workers to take cuts in wages and a ruthless cycle of international competition ensues, with those at the bottom of the social and global heap taking the brunt of the suffering.

Trade puts countries into an unequal gladiatorial contest. For the winners, it may be fine but for the losers it's a haemorrhage. In 1989, for instance, Niger's export trade in goods collapsed by 40 per cent on 1988 exports, Nepal's by 17 per cent, Burkina Faso's by 47 per cent, and Burundi's by 41 per cent. Samoa, which exported $12 millions worth of merchandise in 1989, saw that figure offset by a worrying $67 million of imports in the same year.[15] Shifts such as this pose terrible strains on poor countries. Before criticising these countries, remember that the UK and USA balances of payment in recent years have had deficits in billions of dollars, not the millions of Samoa. Under Presidents Reagan and Bush, the USA – home to the World Bank and International Monetary Fund (IMF) – was allowed to build up staggering deficits, with no outside intervention.

It helps if you control the purse-strings.

In the trade in commercial services (banks, insurance etc) almost the same countries dominate and the same ones are at the bottom. Here, the USA and UK pull back some of their losses on goods, the UK by + $11.2 billion, the USA by + $31.5 billion, but Brazil goes into deficit on services by – $2 billion, and India by – $1.6 billion.[16]

So what happens if a country's balance of trade goes awry? To paraphrase Keynes on debt, if you owe a little it is your problem, whereas if you owe a huge amount it is the banks'. Large debts give some leverage to debtors in that non-payment of huge sums can inflict considerable damage, as they threatened to when Latin American states refused to pay debt interest in the 1980s. Small debts, however, allow banks to be ruthless, so poorer countries are doubly exploited – neither being able to borrow large sums, which they need more than anyone, nor being able to pay back their debts easily. In practice, both large and small debtor countries are encouraged to trade their way out of debt. We explore whether this works, and what its impact is on the environment and the poor in Chapter 8 when we describe the so-called Structural Adjustment Programmes of the World Bank and the IMF.

Trade trends

World trade is concentrating. Certain regions dominate and increasingly trade with each other: North America, dominated by the USA; Western Europe, dominated till unification by West Germany; Asia, dominated by Japan. Africa and Latin America are losing ground. For example, Western Europe's internal trade grew by an annual 8 per cent from 1980–90[17]; its trade with North America grew 10 per cent and with Asia 11.5 per cent, but with Latin America only 1.5 per cent and with Africa, Europe's trade shrank 0.5 per cent a year.[18] North America's internal trade grew by an annual 8 per cent from 1980–90; with Asia trade grew 8 per cent, with Western Europe 5 per cent, but with Africa it shrank by 1 per cent a year and with the Middle East by 0.5 per cent.[19] Japan is another winner. In 1992, Japan's trade surplus grew by 37.6 per cent, and, as the *Financial Times* put it, 'the politically sensitive' surpluses in trade with the USA and EC each rose by 14 per cent.[20]

The free trade package

The idea of free trade doesn't come alone. It is part of a package of positions, which include the following assertions:

- Some countries are more suited to doing some things than others, therefore let them find their *forte*. This is the theory of 'comparative advantage'.

- The private sector is always better than the state sector, because the dead hand of bureaucracy quickly stifles initiative and wastes money. Therefore, argues the free trader, get the nanny state off the people's or industry's backs.
- Living standards rise under free trade. Even though there may be inequalities in wealth as a result of entrepreneurial activity, some wealth will trickle down to the poorest, so even they ultimately benefit.
- Free trade gives consumers more choice and more information to enable them to make choices.
- Free trade promotes the most efficient use of resources, people and capital.

Protectionist measures – such as tariffs, embargoes, quotas and exclusionary specifications or regulations – are said by free traders to reduce the international specialization of labour and to decrease global wealth. They are seen as perpetuating production in uneconomic areas and preventing maximium economies of scale and efficiency. It is claimed that this results in a lower standard of living for the people of the protected country, since protectionist measures mean more expensive goods or services. Inefficient, uncompetitive domestic industry is allowed to survive and any pressure on them to become more productive that would arise in the free market is lessened. Such industries will lobby to ensure their continued protection from international competition.

Free trade theory dates back to the writings of classical eighteenth century economists such as Adam Smith and David Ricardo. The theory of free markets describes how trade occurs under conditions of perfect competition and full information. Individuals choose what to buy and through the price mechanism supply and demand are balanced, leading to an efficient allocation of resources.

The theory of comparative advantage

Economists claim that all nations benefit from trade because of this principle of 'comparative advantage'. Each country specializes in what it can produce most cheaply and has an advantage in. As producers vie with each other to improve production and sell their goods, they become more efficient. Efficiency and competition thrive off each other. The trader ensures that goods get to where there is the most appropriate market. Goods are exchanged for those produced elsewhere and everyone is better off. The nature of comparative advantage for a country may alter completely through long term planning, education and investment. Japan has made its wealth on manufactured goods, despite being poor in natural resources and energy. But for poor countries, *as their economies now stand*, free trade would mean condemning them to continue their role as low cost producers of primary goods for Western consumption.

One historical basis for this theory lies with Adam Smith, who wrote that prosperity was dependent on specialization, which made workers more productive. Since one worker produced one thing more efficiently, there were more total goods to go around. This requires a market for the goods. But the more specialized the production, the larger the market needed to assimilate it. This division of labour is thus limited by the extent of the market, as is the prosperity which can be generated. Smith argued that the case for specialization and large markets does not stop with national boundaries. The same advantages gained by trade among free citizens within the nation would apply unchanged to exchanges between citizens and firms in different nations. The ideal, according to the theory, is a completely open global market in which goods and services pass freely over all national boundaries.

Thus, the basic thesis of free trade is that, instead of a country being self-sufficient, each one should specialize and produce what it is best at and can produce most cheaply, ie the things in which it has a 'comparative advantage'. It would then exchange its goods for what could be produced more cheaply elsewhere. As everything would be produced more cheaply, everyone would be better off. The 'invisible hand' of market forces would direct every member of society and every nation, using the dynamo of self interest, to the most advantageous situation for the global economy as a whole. This theory runs into difficulty where one country can produce products more cheaply than others and has no incentive to trade, or where a country has little or no comparative advantage in anything.

Ricardo used a semi-fictitious example to illustrate how the theory of comparative advantage works to everyone's advantage. Say, Portugal is capable of producing both wine and cloth with less labour (hence less cost) than England. However Portugal can make the most money by transferring all efforts to the production of its most profitable commodity, in this example wine, and importing cloth from England. This comparative advantage would be big enough to overcome the fact that Portugal can produce cloth cheaper than England can. From England's perspective, although it has to give up producing wine in order to produce enough cloth for its exports, the cost differences between the two products internally, when compared with the cost advantage of ceasing wine production and just trading cloth, mean that England also enjoys a 'comparative advantage' by engaging in this trade. Both countries appear to gain.

Today, Ricardo's example would be upset by the capacity of capital to move, since many economies have deregulated controls on capital, especially internationally. Now Portuguese capital would at first flow to wine, increasing its productivity and output and the price would drop. Capital would therefore flow to cloth where Portugal also has a comparative advantage. The result would probably be such a drop in the price of Portuguese cloth that the English cloth producers would eventually be forced out of the market, due to cheaper Portuguese imports. English capital would also flow to Portugal to supplement Portuguese capital, making even more inevitable the situation where both wine and cloth are produced in Portugal. Under the European Community (EC), English labour might also move to Portugal, thus reducing labour costs even more because of the competition for jobs involved.

The problem of capital

The free flow of capital and goods, and not just of goods as was basically the case in Smith's and Ricardo's time, means that investment is now governed by absolute profitability and *not* by comparative advantage between countries. Neither Ricardo nor Smith thought that capital would be so mobile. They assumed that it would remain in the country of its owners. Ricardo felt it would be the force of the community that would keep capital at home. Smith, in the famous 'invisible hand' passage, took it for granted that it is in the personal interest of capitalists to invest at home:

> 'By preferring the support of domestic to that of foreign industry, he intends only to his own security; and by directing that industry in such a manner as its produce may be of the greatest value, he intends only his own gain, and he is in this, as in many other cases, led by an invisible hand to promote an end which was no part of his intention.'[21]

The world of the 1990s by contrast is dominated by the political interests of powerful nations, cosmopolitan money managers and TNCs. These latter two have largely transcended the control of individual governments. They may make reference to a 'world community' in which they operate, but since no such entity in reality exists, they have escaped from most of the restraints and responsibilities that could have been put upon them in their home base community.

Herman Daly and Robert Goodland of the World Bank's Environment Division argue that the theory of comparative advantage no longer fits, because it depends upon each country having control over its capital and finance, but the post World War II period has seen an unprecedented international mobility of capital.

> 'As capital leaves a country in pursuit of greater absolute advantage, then that country loses both capital and jobs and becomes worse off. (...) There may be good arguments for free trade, but in a world of

international capital mobility, comparative advantage *cannot* be one of them' (their stress).[22]

The moral dimension

Free trade theory sells a social and moral vision which argues that responsibility is atomized and individualized. This is nothing particularly new, but the sad thing is that rich historical traditions of rejecting it have temporarily been forgotten. The case for intervention in the market is once again having to be made. Markets are not miracle mechanisms that somehow act on their own, or inevitably to the general good, which is why in the past corrective controls, regulations and institutions have been put in place.

At its nastiest this free trade morality encourages traders to trample on others less fortunate or powerful. Any success that life brings is wholly or largely due to themselves, they believe. Even in softer forms, the free trade approach undermines social responsibility. Having got what they want from others, rich people or rich nations can always protect themselves behind high gates and pull up drawbridges. It is your fault and your responsibility, the argument goes, if you have not got there too.

The moral dimension to the debate about trade deserves fuller and wider debate. Is it right individualistically to pursue economic ends whatever the costs to society? Is it right for institutions to take no account of their social and environmental effects? Currently that debate is restricted to the churches or aid organizations, when it should be occuring in wider, secular society too. Today, many unelected institutions are being spawned which determine people's lives – not just the GATT and its offshoots which we discuss in Chapter 5 but at local level too, which we discuss in Chapter 10, highlighting the appointment of new unelected powerful bodies such as, in the UK, the Training and Enterprise Councils with huge budgets. These new appointed bodies operate at such rarified levels that ordinary citizens are understandably either unaware of them, relatively powerless before them or, in the case of world bodies, even in awe of them as *world* bodies. And in the 1990s more and more new global institutions are being created.

Writers such as Susan George of the Transnationals Institute in Amsterdam, who has worked on hunger, debt and corporate control, and Graham Hancock, who has trenchently criticized the UN and World Bank, have shown how world bodies can be corrupt or cause institutional damage.[23] Recently, the UN Food and Agriculture Organisation (FAO) has been vehemently criticized by ecologists for perpetuating a model of agriculture which suits the trader and which dislocates the poor.[24] The track record of bodies such as the World Bank and the IMF is poor and the secretiveness of the IMF in particular is scandalous.[25]

World bodies

It would be tempting to argue that world bodies are either so corrupt or corrupting that it would be better to have none. This would be foolish. There *is* a need for world bodies, for example, to monitor and enforce environmental standards or those for worker health and safety. The problem is that so often such bodies are underfunded and dominated by free trade logic. There are three issues here: how can world bodies be made effective? To whom should they be responsible? How can trade interests be prevented from taking priority over other considerations?

World bodies do and could play a vital role in matters such as ozone depletion or climate change – issues which cross borders and are in everyone's interest. New agreements, institutions and mechanisms for regulating the impact of economic activity are urgently needed – a theme we return to in Part 4. But free traders want to keep the goal of environmental protection seperate from that of trade liberalization; it is up to government, not trade, to protect the environment, they argue. The World Bank, the GATT itself and eminent economists are all opposed to environmental protection through unilateral trade measures.[26] But the difficulty is their own creation, by promoting an environment-damaging approach. Lawrence Summers, formerly of the World Bank but now a member of President Clinton's administration, fulminates against keeping products produced to lower environmental standards out of any country as being 'counter to accepted principles of international trade'.[27] He is also unhappy about harmonizing environmental standards, let alone worrying about harmonization stopping standards rising. He argues that it is up to governments to set their own standards – an interesting argument given that free traders ostensibly want to *limit* the power of governments. In practice, they want governments to do what *they* want them to do!

World agreements such as the Montreal Protocol on ozone depletion have come into existence as a result of a combination of public pressure, scientific evidence and political support. Now the challenge is to ensure that trade does not undermine them. We believe – unlike free traders – that where there is conflict between exising agreements, priority should go to protection of the environment and social justice.

State intervention and privatization

Reducing state intervention in industry has taken three basic forms: firstly, governments have sold off industries they owned; secondly, they have promised to reduce taxes on industry, a stop which requires minimizing state expenditure and with it the need to raise taxes and/or cut social services; and thirdly, they have tried to cut out regulation altogether or to replace it with self-regulation.

In the 1980s, privatization was seen as the permanent solution to rolling back bureaucracy and state intervention. All over the world, state assets were sold off. But despite privatization, many Western economies have been unable to reduce public spending significantly. Many of the industries and services transferred to the private sector were economically viable (or close to it) before the sell-off – otherwise why would anyone buy them? In the UK, some of the former public utilities – gas, water and telecommunications – are now the economy's most profitable and capital-rich companies. Their sale asset-stripped the public. Governments, however, are still spending vast amounts of money on areas such as social security, health, defence and education. These are areas of social infrastructure where, in the language of the market, the state is spending as an investment in human capital.

The first wave of privatization was in areas where assets could be profited from quickest – telecommunications, water, energy. In the areas which are harder to privatize, the state's new role has been to introduce the language and management systems of the private sector into areas where different styles and cultures used to rule. Thus, public health, social services, transport and education are being forced to operate in a different way – introducing inappropriate business methods which hinder their ability to provide proper services. Form-filling and tests now take preference over service delivery. For all the rhetoric of freedom and deregulation, the state is being used in an authoritarian and centralizing manner.

Although free trade proponents argue for deregulation on most occasions, at other times they promote regulations. Their rationale for world bodies is always the golden words: harmonization of world standards. Standardization is presented to the consumer as an advantage because it removes the 'burden' of industry having to meet different national standards. We discuss the problems in this approach in Chapter 9.

Deregulation

Free traders often argue that deregulation is needed to 'get the nanny state off their backs'. The implication is that bureaucracy stifles innovation, is anti-democratic and means tax-payers' money is working against their interests. They argue that freedom flourishes if bureaucracies are minimized. It's an attractive line, but often wrong. Far from being anti-bureaucratic, free traders merely *reorganize* the bureaucracies; they make the state and international state machinery work either directly for corporate interests, for example through giving them contracts, or indirectly by removing democratic accountability and the likelihood of awkward questions from local and elected personnel. The GATT, as will be seen in Chapter 5, provides an excellent and topical example of this process.

The indomitable former US Trade Representative, Mrs Carla Hills, who spoke for the USA under President Bush, put it thus: 'I would like you to think of me as the US Trade Representative with a crowbar, where we are prying open markets, keeping them open so that our private sector can take advantage of them.'[28]

Economic growth

In his review of the role of the EC, Japan and the USA in today's world economy, Professor Thurow of the Massachusetts Institute of Technology's (MIT) Sloan School of Management points to the declining rate of economic growth. The growth rate of the non-communist world was 4.9 per cent in the 1960s, 3.8 per cent in the 1970s and 2.9 per cent in the 1980s. For the 1990s the prognosis is currently lower. Professor Thurow summarizes the problem:[29]

> 'Capitalism has its virtues and vices. It is a wonderful machine for producing abundant goods and services, but it is hard to get started. Third World failures far outnumber First World successes. The Second World, the formerly communist world, is finding it very hard to get capitalism started. Free markets also tend to produce levels of inequality that are politically incompatible with democratic government. Witness rising inequality and homelessness in the United States, and note the need for large social-welfare income-transfer payments systems in every major industrial country.'

Yet proponents of trade liberalization respond to the South's crises of debt, unemployment and malnutrition by arguing for more Western-style growth to promote wealth, which would then be used to clean up the social damage caused in the process of growth. The World Bank makes much of the growth rates of some Asian countries as the way forward. But this argument is madness. If the world's equity, environment and social stability are already being threatened by unfettered growth to benefit only an estimated one fifth of the world, there is absolutely no way that a similar path of growth is environmentally supportable for the other four fifths. As Richard Douthwaite argues in his powerful book, *The Growth Illusion*, the growth process of the last hundred or so years has already threatened both environment and social justice by perpetuating gross inequalities.[30]

Yet mainstream pundits – whether hardline free traders or more moderate Keynesians – want their governments to continue encouraging past patterns of growth. People like Professor Thurow and Professor Reich, now President Clinton's Labour Secretary, argue that the US government needs to invest in skills training and education to enable the

USA to compete in the global market. In the UK, this is the line of both parliamentary opposition parties; they see the role of government as spotting new growth areas with which to corner global markets and to act as a base for 'friendly' or national TNCs.

Professor Reich also argues that the technological transformation of the labour process means the nation state of the past is over:

> 'There will be no *national* products or technologies, no national corporations, no national industries. There will no longer be national economies, at least as we have come to understand that concept . . . Each nation's primary assets will be its citizen's skills and insights.'[31]

The role of government, he argues, is to invest in education and training, transport infrastructure (to move all those goods about) and in communications (to do the deals). Reich's argument is seductive, and it will be interesting to see if the Clinton administration puts it into practise. The model may be more humane than free market arguments at their most brutal, but underneath it is the same, invoking the same pressure to exploit, compete and undercut in order to trade. Ironically, Reich's argument might be just the kind of fillip big business needs – bright and not distracted by the old obsessions about trades unions and nanny states. If Reich's and Thurow's policies are implemented, it wouldn't be the first time that in straitened economic times, business conveniently buried – whether reluctantly or willingly – its antipathy to the state sector in favour of a period of economic reconstruction and state-funded investment – for example, during the New Deal in the USA and in wartimes.

While Professors Thurow and Reich do acknowledge structural problems with today's trading system – its failure to meet everyone's needs, or to train and educate everyone appropriately, or to their abilities – others more hard line claim that everything is really all right: the recession will end, the green shoots shoot, and later the economic downturn will look like a blip. The free market conservative revolution has further to run, they argue; there is no alternative to free market capitalism.[32]

Free trade critics

Criticism of free trade over the years has come from a broad range of opinion and experience. Keynes, the great economist, changed his view on trade at least twice in his life, from free trader to protectionist, and thence to multilateralist, culminating in the Bretton Woods agreement of 1944 which created the post-war economic system. In the early 1920s he originally regarded free trade 'not only as an economic doctrine which a rational and instructed person could not doubt, but almost as part of a moral law.' He was later to realize the full implications and deficiencies of free trade:

> 'I sympathise, therefore, with those who would minimise, rather than with those who would maximise, economic entanglement between nations. Ideas, knowledge, art, hospitality, travel – these are the things which should of their nature be international. But let goods be homespun whenever it is reasonably and conveniently possible; and above all let finance be primarily national.'[33]

By 1933, he was writing in support of national self sufficiency:

> 'It does not now seem obvious that a great concentration of national effort on the capture of foreign trade, that the penetration of a country's economic structure by the resources and the influence of foreign capitalists, that a close dependence of our own economic life on the fluctuating economic policies of foreign countries are safeguards and assurances of international peace. It is easier in the light of experience and foresight, to argue quite the contrary . . .. Advisable domestic policies might be easier to compass, if, for example, the phenomenon known as "flight of capital" could be ruled out. The divorce between ownership and the real responsibility of management is serious within a country when, as a result of joint stock enterprise, ownership is broken up between innumerable individuals who buy their interest today and sell it tomorrow and lack altogether both knowledge and responsibility towards what they momentarily own. But when this same principle is applied internationally, it is, in times of stress, intolerable – I am irresponsible towards what I own and those who operate what I own are irresponsible towards me.'[34]

Eventually Keynes was:

> 'doubtful whether the economic cost of self sufficiency is great enough to outweigh the other advantages of gradually bringing the producer and consumer within the ambit of the same national, economic and financial organisation.'[35]

Another critic of free trade from the last great era of debate on the subject was that formidable proponent of national sovereignty, Mahatma Gandhi. Gandhi had a jaundiced view of the realities of free trade for weaker countries over 50 years ago:

> 'Free trade for a country that has become industrial, whose population can and does live in cities, whose people do not mind preying upon other nations and, therefore, sustain the biggest navy to protect their unnatural commerce, may be economically sound (though, as the reader perceives, I question its morality). Free trade for India has proved her curse and held her in bondage.'[36]

For Keynes' or Gandhi's generation of free trade critics, the brake on the worst excesses of trade had to be national. Today, the theory of free trade has taken on almost mythical proportions. Jeremy Seabrook, a writer on social affairs with an especial interest in India, has called it International Monetary Fundamentalism.[37] Seabrook's assessment of the religious elements in free trade is worth quoting in full:

> 'Because we understand "fundamentalism" to be a purely religious phenomenon, it is easy to misperceive the same processes in seemingly secular institutions. The west's economic ideology has become more rigid, even as the inflexibilities of communism have yielded. The west, once inhibited by the communist threat, now feels free to disseminate its truths across the world. This is International Monetary Fundamentalism: the imposition of identical prescriptions on all countries that come under its tutelage no matter what conditions prevail locally. Whether it is Peru, Poland, the Philippines, Nigeria, Ghana, Venezuela, Algeria, the advice, exhortations and orders are always the same; and the consequences, for the poorest, identical.
>
> But here is a problem. The amassing of the west's wealth depended for centuries on the occupation of other people's lands, and the tribute exacted by their conquerors. These conditions are simply not available to those now being urged to follow the western path. It is becoming ever clearer to people in the third world that western promises are disingenuous and unrealisable; are, in fact, prescriptions for subordination, the maintenance of western privilege, and have little to do with lifting the mass of suffering humanity out of hunger and despair.
>
> Since 1945, western prosperity continued to be founded on the flow of wealth from poor to rich, by means of adverse terms of trade, the import of third-world raw materials to feed their industrial economies. The rawest material of all was human – the large numbers of Turks, Indians, Afro-Caribbeans and Indonesians brought in to keep wages down. Latterly, the south's enormous debts have become another means of transferring wealth to the rich, to such a degree that it has been estimated that the net flow from south to north – if we include the effects of debt servicing, brain drain, resource transfers – is up to US $200 billion a year.'

We now need to consider in Part Two *who* today is behind the proposals to extend trade and why.

PART TWO

The Powers Behind the Free Trade Package

'Under the broad and benign cover of laissez faire and the specific licence of the market, there are forces that ravage and even destroy the very institutions that compose the system, specifically the business firms whose buying, selling and financial operations make the market. This is a striking development of modern capitalism; the particular devastation is of the great management-controlled corporation. Such destruction has become especially severe in the years of contentment.'[1]

Professor JK Galbraith

3. Transnational Corporations

Even the most cursory observer of trade matters soon encounters TNCs. These are the big companies which straddle the world's economies, like leviathans. As with powerful people, TNCs are shrouded with myth. According to some, they are a modern conspiracy, the evil players behind every dastardly deed. According to others, the might of TNCs gives them a fabulous potential to right any wrongs quickly and efficiently once they are discovered. Precisely because they are so large, the argument goes, they have to keep on their toes. TNCs have featured heavily in the promotion of free trade. The International Chamber of Commerce, a club of giant corporations, has been one of the most consistent lobbies in and for a new GATT, on occasion writing to papers, expressing a view, always acting behind the scene and at Geneva.

The economic might of TNCs is staggering, as we'll see in this chapter. A seasoned economist such as Professor JK Galbraith has said 'the self-destructive tendency of modern capitalism begins with the large corporation'.[1] But equally it is right to remember that TNCs are run by people who have an interest in ensuring that the corporation stays around.[2] However, TNCs are hardly likely to be a motor force for ushering in the New Protectionism; they are too wedded to international competition, seeking new markets and global reach.

The US industrialist Rockefeller said in the early 1960s that:

> 'what we people in the Western Hemisphere really need is a more efficient division of labour, one of the tried and true economic principles that will be valid in the future as it was in 1776 when it was first spelled out by Adam Smith. The less developed countries will also gain. With abundant supplies of labour and wage levels well below those in the West, they could export processed food, textiles, apparel, footwear and other light manufactures.'[3]

Thirty years on, this benign view needs drastic revision. Even though international trade is conventionally analysed in national terms it is almost all carried out by companies, many of which have outgrown their home states and become transnational. One of the ideological successes of trading companies is how they blur the distinction between themselves and the national interest. When a company proclaims its nationality, this can mean that it is getting or about to get its home state to act on its behalf

– as has happened with the US and UK textile industries' arguments for the Multifibre Arrangement (MFA), the textile agreement under negotiation at the GATT.

Free trade or TNC trade?

The TNCs have gained an increasing share of world trade. According to Dr Kevin Watkins of Oxfam:

> 'Traditionally, international trade is seen as an activity carried out between nations. In reality, trade flows are dominated by powerful corporations located overwhelmingly in Western Europe, North America and Japan. In 1985, the combined sales of the world's largest TNCs exceeded $3 trillion, equivalent to one third of the world's Gross Domestic Product.'[4]

The number of branches, subsidiaries, and affiliates of TNCs from the industrialized countries is estimated to be around 100,000. Smaller TNCs do exist but the larger ones dominate. At least 65 million people are directly employed by TNCs, 43 million in the home countries and 22 million in host countries,[5] representing about 3 per cent of the total estimated workforce throughout the world of over 2000 million. According to the World Bank, TNCs control 70 per cent of world trade. In 1990, the world's largest 350 TNCs accounted for almost 40 per cent of world merchandise trade which then totalled US $3485 billion.[6] The top 500 TNCs control two thirds of world trade.[7] In addition over 40 per cent of international trade is carried out *within* TNCs.

The amounts of money involved are staggering. More than 35,000 TNCs now account for $1.7 trillion in foreign direct investment and global sales totalling $4.4 trillion.[8] The 15 largest global corporations today, including names like General Motors, Exxon, IBM, and Royal Dutch Shell, have a gross income larger than the GDP of over 120 countries, including almost all Third World countries except for the very largest. In 1970, over half the 7,000 TNCs tracked by the UN were based in the USA or UK. In 1990, just under half the 35,000 TNCs it found were from four countries: USA, Japan, Germany and Switzerland, with the UK now seventh most popular TNC base.[9] Excepting South Korea, all the top 500 industrial companies listed in the US business magazine *Fortune*'s Fortune 500 are headquartered in the North with the USA home to 167, Japan to 111, the UK to 43, Germany to 32, and France to 29. The combined wealth of the top 500 manufacturing and top 500 banking and insurance companies amounts to US $10 trillion, twice the USA's GDP.[10]

Concentrated power

Within trade sectors, a similar picture of global concentration emerges and this has devastating effects. According to UN figures, almost all primary commodities are each now marketed by fewer than six multi-commodity traders.[11] For example, Cargill – a family-owned Canadian corporation – has a greater sales turnover in coffee alone than the GDP of any of the African countries in which it purchases coffee beans. Cargill also accounts for over 60 per cent of world trade in cereals. According to Christian Aid, the low prices of world primary commodities, produced by Third World countries overwhelmingly, is in part due to the existence of so many commodity producers but so few commodity buyers, ie companies. And it is right. The top five companies have 77 per cent of world cereal trade; the biggest three companies in bananas have 80 per cent of world banana trade; the biggest three cocoa companies have 83 per cent of world cocoa trade; the biggest three companies have 85 per cent of tea trade; and the biggest four companies have 87 per cent of world trade in tobacco.[12]

Consumers may be bedazzled for choice when they go food shopping, but behind the many products and brands are often relatively few owner companies with enormous power. For instance, one US company, Sara Lee, owns coffee brands in Europe which have 74 per cent of the Netherlands market, 27 per cent of Denmark's, 21 per cent of Spain's and 15 per cent of France's.[13] A large study in the 1980s for the UN found very high levels of TNC control in the world's food markets. And of 189 TNCs which had turnovers of above $300 million in 1976, all but one were based in the developed world – the exception, Bunge and Born was one of the world's giant grain traders. One hundred of these TNCs had revenues of over $1 billion and five above $10 billion, even then. This food power was being used to diversify into other sectors – shipping, tobacco, finance, pharmaceuticals. Only a sixth were not diversifying.[14]

High levels of concentration are not just the preserve of primary commodities. By 1989, the world's top 20 agrochemical companies accounted for 94 per cent of world trade – nine of these were companies from Europe, six from the USA and five from Japan.[15] The top 14 car companies produce four out of five of the world's cars; of these, three based in the USA produce 33 per cent; six based in Japan produce 25 per cent; and Europe's companies produce 21.5 per cent.[16] The same concentration and disparity between the industrialized world and the developing world is happening in one of the world's fastest growing sectors – telecommunications. Western Europe (the EC and the European Free Trade Area (EFTA) combined) is the largest world market, at 47 per cent of the overall world market. North America has 32 per cent, Asia 11.5 per cent and South America only 2 per cent.[17] Ten TNCs control 66 per cent of the world semi-conductor industry and nine telecommunications TNCs control 89 per cent of that market. In computing, IBM owns more than 60 per cent of the world main frame computer market. TNC capital is the source of these big corporations' power.

We could go on, but the big question is whether this level of concentration matters. We think it does for three reasons. Firstly, it hands over power to unelected and unaccountable people. The top 87 finance companies in the world for instance are valued at US $1,300 billion,[18] a concentration of power which gives a relatively small number of boards of directors extraordinary control over a high proportion of the world's liquid capital upon which investment (which can either improve or threaten people's standards of living) depends. Secondly, concentration means that power gets more distant from the ordinary consumer. When consumers shop, they face many products, but few owners, and decisions about their local market may be being taken on the other side of the world. Thirdly, concentration affects standards of production which affect the quality of life.

It is sometimes argued that concentration can lead to improved standards as companies operating in highly concentrated sectors are more vulnerable to pressure.[19] Companies could use their market power to push environmental standards upwards, either to steal a marketing march on competitors if consumers are calling for tougher standards or to squeeze out smaller competitors whose budgets cannot finance the investment needed for new clean-up equipment or technologies. TNC power, it is argued, could be benign as well as damaging. Alas, experience suggests that TNCs are more likely to use their global reach to squeeze prices and costs to *their* advantage rather than anyone else's.

Christian Aid has analysed where the cost the consumer pays for a banana goes. The TNCs control the processing, transport and marketing and sometimes the actual growing of the crop. Ripening and shipping to the consumer country takes 37 per cent; further ripening and advertising in the consumer country takes 19 per cent; wholesalers and retailers take 32 per cent; the grower's costs for fertilizer and transport take 5 per cent; the grower's other costs and profits another 5 per cent; and just 1.5 per cent is left for the fieldworker's wages.[20]

Another enormous advantage for TNCs is that they can globe-trot to where standards and markets are most congenial for them, ignoring environmental effects. European TNCs produce and market in the Philippines pesticides long banned in Europe; US car or furniture manufacturers relocate to Mexico to escape the costs of domestic environmental legislation, poisoning Mexican ground waters and rivers in the process; Japanese logging companies deforest Pacific rim countries in a manner which would be unthinkable at home.[21]

Beyond national control

In the main, the growing number of TNCs have escaped the control of individual governments and are no longer based in their national communities. When TNCs seek out the lowest labour costs and environmental standards it can result in appalling environmental destruction and worker exploitation. As Herman Daly and John Cobb say:

> 'Free traders, having freed themselves from the restraints of community at the national level and having moved into the cosmopolitan world, which is not a community, have effectively freed themselves of all community obligations.'[22]

What can control TNCs awe-inspiring power? The UN set up its Commission on Transnational Corporations in 1973, and asked it to draft a UN Code of Conduct to establish a system of accountability for TNCs. Nearly 20 years on, the Code exists, but drastically weakened from successful lobbying by TNCs in the lengthy drafting stages. The Code calls on TNCs to become more accountable, to respect host countrys' economic priorities, to end pricing policies which deprive countries of revenue (by returning profits to the parent TNC's base country and by what is called 'transfer pricing'), to protect the environment and to promote international consumer and environmental standards. But these calls are hollow when the GATT rules on free trade take precedence (see Chapter 5).

The growth of TNC power ultimately matters because of their financial muscle and because there is no counterbalancing democratic constraint on their activities. Their needs come before the needs of the poor. Leslie Sklair of the London School of Economics, summarises the emergence of TNCs and their role in the global system. He contrasts their worth to that of whole countries, arguing that many of the largest TNCs have assets and annual sales far in excess of the Gross National Product (GNP) of about half of the countries of the world. In 1986, according to World Bank figures, 64 out of 120 countries had a GDP of less than $10 billion. UN data for 1985–6 show that 68 TNCs in mining and manufacturing had annual sales in excess of $10 billion and all the top 50 banks, the top 20 securities firms, and all but one of the top 30 insurance companies had assets in excess of this.[23] With such financial muscle, to do what they want rather than what the poor or the majority need, the TNCs cannot be seen as a benign force. They may shelter behind free trade logic, but its effect is plain to see.

Britain in a global market

Britain under the Thatcher Government makes an interesting case study of one political formula for a TNC-dominated national economy. Although the UK economy has become relatively weak among developed nations in the post-war period, it is still a home base to formidably powerful TNCs. In retrospect, the Thatcher revolution was mainly oriented to turning Britain into a docile base for incoming TNCs wanting assembly points for goods to sell in Europe, and for domestic TNCs wanting a financially sympathetic home base to sell, not just to Europe, but to the globe.

Although as we saw, the UK's total TNC rank has fallen from 1970 to 1990, among the world's 1,000 largest companies UK companies are the third largest group with 110, worth a staggering $777 billion – twice the value of Germany's or France's TNCs in the world's top 1000.[24] UK companies in the *Financial Times* FT500, Europe's top 500 companies, in 1993 were calculated to be worth $712 billion and their capitalization is nearly three times greater than either Germany's or France's.[25] The UK is base to 25 of Europe's top 50 companies. The UK, in fact, has a two track economy – one part made up of big global players, and the other part a tottering domestic economy.

4.

The Superblocs

The emergence of the three regional power blocs – Europe, North America and Japan – has been much commented on in recent years.[1] US pundits decry European and Japanese superior efficiency and their pundits do likewise.[2] The economic and political power of these blocs is awe-inspiring, and to outsiders intimidating, yet numerically they represent only a seventh of the world's population. Table 3 gives some key indicators for the three power blocs. Compare these to the fact that, according to the World Bank, in 1990 total world GNP was $22,192,380 billion and the world average GNP per capita was $4200 per person.[3]

Table 3 *Superbloc key indicators, 1991*

	EEA([a])	**NAFTA([b])**	**Japan**
Total population[c]	379	360	123
Total GNP[d]	7087	6568	3140
GNP per capita[d]	18700	18300	25400
Exports[d]	1700	576	339
Imports[d]	1773	645	255
Exports-imports[d]	−73	−69	84

Notes:

[a] European Economic Area (EEA) = the EC: Belgium, Denmark, Eire, France, Germany, Greece, Italy, Luxembourg, Netherlands, Portugal, Spain, UK plus EFTA: Austria, Finland, Liechtenstein, Norway, Sweden, Switzerland.

[b] North American Free Trade Agreement (NAFTA): Canada, Mexico, USA. Note NAFTA has yet to be ratified; Canada and the USA ratified the Canada–USA Free Trade Agreement (FTA) in 1989.

[c] Million

[d] US $ billion

Source: Janssen, 1992[5]

Although not strictly speaking a bloc, Japans' economic pre-eminence in Asia, means that it is usually mentioned in the same context as Europe and North America. The population of the Asia–Pacific region is 20 times that of Japan's, yet the total GNP of the region is only 1.5 times that of Japan. Despite rapidly rising output, the 2.5 billion inhabitants of Asia produce only half the Japanese GNP.

A power imbalance

There is an enormous imbalance in the economic power of the superblocs compared to the rest of the world. One camp of observers see this inequity as evidence of a new world class system. Within this camp, opinion is divided about whether this class system is fluid or setting like concrete.[4] Some argue the structure is pyramidal; that countries can climb up the pyramid and that rich countries, ie the superblocs, *need* the poor – for resources, as a reserve source of labour, and as markets. Others argue that the gap between 'core' and 'periphery' is so wide that great areas of the world are *de facto* separate from the core, and the issue for them is whether there is *any* fluidity of movement between those classes.

There is much debate about whether the emergence of the NICs, such as Korea and Taiwan in Asia, indicates the existence of genuinely independent, 'new' capital, or merely the use by Japanese capital of cheaper but still local labour. The optimists view the emergence of NICs with relief, banishing fears from the 1960s and 1970s that the Third World would erupt in a wave of anti-Western separatism. The demise of the USSR has helped put paid to that fear, though it has been replaced by other moral panics and threats such as Aids and famine and fears about rapidly rising population.

In the second camp are those who acknowledge this global gap, but for whom the key question is different. As one European industrialist, Baron Janssen, Chair of the Belgian chemical company Solvay et Cie, has put it: 'The great question is whether the three trade areas (NAFTA, EEA and Japan) will be protectionist or open to liberal trade.'[5] This second group of observers differ from the first camp not so much in their analysis, but in how they intend to exploit the imbalance between superblocs and between the superblocs and the rest of the world. Some industries are content to work behind the protection and influence superbloc residence gives them. Others know that they need better Third World bases to exploit, for example, cheap labour and laxer standards.

Whichever camp you support – the critics or exploiters – all agree that countries outside the three superblocs are put into a difficult situation by the trade power of the superblocs. They could choose to 'go it alone' in a modern version of what some African countries tried to do in the 1960s or Cuba has done since the 1950s, but realistically those days are past. The only course of action appears to be willingly or unwillingly to accomodate their economies to the trade patterns being dictated by the superblocs and their free trade ideologies. Third World examples of this process are well documented.[6] What is less frequently realised is that rich countries are also affected. In Scandinavia, for instance, both the food and chemical industries are adapting their standards, marketing and cross border ownership of subsidiaries to the emerging might of the EC.[7]Norway is systematically and speedily harmonizing its food standards to those of the EC, which itself has internally harmonized its 12 member states' standards under the single market programme.

There are serious issues raised by such harmonization, not just for food quality and health standards, but for democracy and accountability. Decisions which were local are now far removed from small producers, let alone consumers. Large companies can afford to pay for global liaison independently, in trade associations and in sector 'clubs'. In Europe, for example, one such club is the Senior Advisory Group on Biotechnology, which includes six of the world's top ten drug companies, chemical companies such as Dupont, ICI and Monsanto, as well as food giants such as Nestle and Unilever.[8] Small companies and consumers can only lobby regionally or globally on a shoe-string, if at all.

For TNCs, the three trading superblocs are natural ground. For medium or small national companies, however, they often seem impenetrable and the source of bewildering flurries of new rules. To companies, traders and governments of the South, the superblocs are often just a threat, intent on increasing Northern companies' share of the world or Third World markets.

Regional free trade or protectionism?

The superblocs promote a more efficient internal market, but retain some aspects of the old protectionism in order to make their corporate giants more effective in the global market. To the pure free trader, this policy looks a lot like hidden protectionism. Indeed it is. In the late 1970s and 1980s – the period of supposed trade liberalization – there was an increase in this kind of protectionism through the rise of non-tariff barriers, voluntary export restraints and orderly marketing arrangements.[9] Third World countries bitterly complain about these hypocrisies.

According to the World Bank, today's US manufacturing sector's nominal tariffs of 6 per cent are in fact bumped up to a real tariff of 23 per cent by a collection of anti-dumping measures, notably dumping duties on imported steel, cars and textiles. In the 1940s when the GATT began, tariffs averaged 40–50 per cent across the world. Although the GATT's apologists often claim that significant reductions have occured due to the operation of its rules, its own data shows the number of cases being brought against such hidden tariffs rose in the 1980s.[10]Public and political accusations against farming subsidies and tariffs are widespread. Yet, when seeking re-election 'free trader' President Bush made available new subsidies under the Export Enhancement Programme and a $1.15 billion food aid package to Russia. France also complained about an estimated $1.1 billion farm subsidy package proposed by President Bush.[11]

When the blinkers of free trade theory are taken off, the reality looks different. Superbloc practice looks like the development of economic 'safe havens' not free trade. Most free trade purists would agree with this assessment, and look to the GATT to deliver one large trading agreement to reduce barriers to a wide range of trade in one fell swoop. We think – as we will amplify in the next chapter – that this would be folly. But not all free traders want to go the whole way so rapidly. They fear that a rush to global free trade could backfire. One articulate case has been made by Professor Dornbusch of MIT in the USA. He argues that the Uruguay Round's expansion of the trade sectors to come under GATT rules – agriculture, services, intellectual property, etc – is too ambitious and that there is no rush. World free trade could be introduced at some later date when regional free trade has settled down, he argues.[12] The pure free market argument against this gradualist position is that regional free trade blocs are residual mercantilism – internal free trade, with protection at the borders.[13] It remains to be seen how this debate among free traders works out.

Meanwhile, the figures suggest a high degree of internal trade within the existing powerful trade blocs – 41.4 per cent of world trade in 1988 according to the World Bank. The EC's link with Eastern Europe and the USA and Canada's links with Mexico would take this up to nearly half.[14] According to the IMF, 71 per cent of the EC's and EFTA's exports are within their borders, 31 per cent of Japan's and East Asia's within theirs, and 42 per cent of NAFTA's within theirs. Eighty per cent of Mexico's exports, for instance, go to the USA whereas Africa sends 95 per cent of its exports beyond the continent.[15]

Other trading blocs

Besides the three superblocs, other smaller or less well-known trade blocs in discussion or in place include: Latin America's Southern Cone Common Market Treaty (MERCOSUR),[16] one in Central Asia, another in Central America, and the potentially formidable Asia Pacific Economic Co-operation (APEC) which would include Japan, already *de facto* a superbloc in its own right, due to its regional and global economic power. Table 4 lists some key trading blocs, their members and date of inception.

Table 4 *Various trading blocs and their members*

Trade bloc	Members	When founded
Andean Pact	Bolivia, Chile (now left), Columbia, Ecuador, Peru, Venezuela	1969
Asia–Pacific Economic Co-operation (APEC)	Australia, Canada, China, Hong Kong, New Zealand, Japan, Korea, Taiwan, USA + 6 ASEAN ccountries	first met 1989; secretariat 1992
Association of SE Asian Nations (ASEAN)	Brunei, Indonesia, Malaysia, Philippines, Singapore, Thailand	1991
Central American Common Market (CACM)	Costa Rica (1962–92), El Salvador, Honduras (1961–76), Guatemala, Nicaragua	first agreed 1961; new agreement 1992
East African Community (EAC)	Kenya, Tanzania, Uganda	1967–77
European Community (EC)	Belgium, Denmark, Eire, France, Germany, Greece, Italy, Luxembourg, Netherlands, Spain, UK Portugal	first signed 1957; new agreements 1987 and 1993
European Economic Area (EEA)	EC + EFTA	1992
European Free Trade Area (EFTA)	Austria, Finland, Leichtenstein, Norway, Sweden, Switzerland	1960
North American Free Trade Agreement (NAFTA)	Canada, Mexico, USA	1992 initial signing
Southern Cone Common Market Treaty (Mercosur)	Argentina, Brazil, Paraguay, Uruguay	1992

Table 5 *Share of regional trading schemes in intra-regional exports and world exports, 1990*

Scheme	Share in intraregional exports[a]	Share in total world exports[b]
Australia–New Zealand closer Economic Relations Trade Agreement	7.6	1.5
European Community	60.4	41.4
European Free Trade Area	28.2	6.8
Canada–US Free Trade Area	34.0	15.8
Association of South East Asian Nations	18.6	4.3
Andean Pact	4.6	0.9
Central American Common Market	14.8	0.1
Latin American Free Trade Area/Latin American Integration Association	10.6	3.4
Economic Community of West African States	6.0	0.6
Preferential Trade Area for Eastern and Southern Africa	8.5	0.2

[a] Intraregional exports as percentage of the region's total exports.
[b] Region's exports as percentage of total world exports.

Source: de Melo and Panagariya, 1992[19]

Even in the matter of trade blocs there is clear global inequality – see Table 5. The EEA, for instance, when the merger comes into force will account for about 50 per cent of world merchandise trade and its *internal* trade will account for 35 per cent of total world trade. At the other end of the scale, Southern attempts to trade with themselves are small and can easily falter. Trade between Andean Pact members, for instance, represents only 5–15 per cent of the members' total foreign trade. Of the Southern trade blocs, only the CACM had any significant internal trade.[17]

The East African Community (EAC) between Kenya, Tanzania and Uganda collapsed, in part because most foreign investment in the bloc was funnelled into Kenya, which already had the best infrastructure. Jasper Okelo of the Kenyan Consumers Association and a professor at the University of Nairobi, has argued that: 'the EAC collapsed (in 1977) because of the strong feeling that Kenya was taking the rest of the EAC for a ride.'

A structural reason for Southern trade blocs being difficult to maintain – shown both by Kenya and the EAC and economies such as Chile – is that many Southern economies have been structured by their colonial past. Chile, after President Allende was overthrown by the Pinochet dictatorship, has been oriented to service the North, and has now left the Andean Pact; 75 per cent of its exports now go to the USA, EC and Japan.[18] In Chapter 12, when we discuss the New Protectionism, we will explore how a more diversified and local economy could be a better model for the South.

On the surface, regional free trade seems enticing. Regional trade blocs promise more local control and the great social advantage of being large enough to over-ride petty nationalism. They also have a potential for diversity. But the pure free traders are right. Regional blocs *do* undermine the global removal of barriers to trade. It is this which makes them so interesting to us from a New Protectionist perspective. The regional emphasis in such trade blocs could be a step in the right direction. However the danger is that in the form they are being prepared, they are more likely to accentuate threats to the environment, give disproportionate emphasis to the interests of large companies and do little to tackle inequality internally, let alone internationally.

If our fears are realized, the superblocs will merely accelerate already worrying trends and enable the world's already most powerful companies to become more powerful. For this reason alone, we are wary about an excessive enthusiasm for the single European market. Like the TNCs, our eyes are on the GATT. For TNCs, the GATT is an opportunity to continue to expand globally while retaining regional home bases, and for us it is another step in the wrong political direction. We look at this in more detail in the next chapter.

5.

GATT – A Charter for the Powerful

The GATT is a fundamental pillar underpinning present trading arrangements. The Uruguay Round of GATT talks is now attempting to 'liberalize' trade even further, but this will work in the interests of those already powerful. The GATT was formed in 1948 with 23 countries as signatories, an organisation that had originally been conceived to be an International Trade Organisation (ITO). It was the brain child of the USA, forming a part of its efforts to extend the US economic model of high volume, standardized production and aggressive expansion of markets to the rest of the world, particularly those whose industrial economies were in tatters after World War II.

Originally the USA envisaged the establishment of an ITO within the UN system to complement the IMF, which lends money to sovereign states, and the World Bank – the International Bank for Reconstruction and Development, to give it its formal name – which finances international projects. But in 1950, agreement on the ITO was defeated because the US Congress opposed the transfer of sovereignty on trade matters to such an organisation. Instead the GATT was left to set up and develop a contract between sovereign states providing for a set of mutually agreed rules on the conduct and co-ordination of international trade. Its purpose was to reduce tariffs and increase the volume of world trade. Between 1948 and today, official tariffs on manufactured goods have fallen from 40 per cent to 5 per cent and world trade volume has increased fourfold.[1] There have been seven rounds of GATT negotiations since 1948 and it is supposed to have been a major contributor to economic well-being. However, many independent critics have begun to dispute this rosy view.[2]

The present Uruguay Round negotiations, started in 1986 (and still not finally agreed as we write), are the eighth since the GATT began. The previous rounds were aimed at encouraging international trade through reduction of tariff (taxes and duties) and non-tariff (eg quotas and import licences) restrictions on imports. The Uruguay Round is fundamentally different from previous rounds, the most complicated of any postwar multilateral agreement. It goes far beyond just tariff cutting and incorporates new areas such as agriculture, services, foreign investments and intellectual property into the GATT framework.

Proponents claim the Uruquay Round aims to create a 'level playing field' in which traders could gain equal access to all markets, many of whom have restricted access at present. Negotiations have dragged on for seven years now, with agriculture often (but erroneously) portrayed as the main stumbling block. The election of the Clinton US administration has fuelled the anxiety of those pushing for a GATT completion, as they fear President Clinton will be more protectionist than his predecessors.

What is GATT?

At present, GATT is a set of regulations on world trade, which 108 countries had signed by 1993, with more following all the time. China, the last major economic force outside GATT, began formal negotiations to join in 1993. Russia, too. Most trade between countries of the 'free world' is theoretically governed by GATT – around 90 per cent of world trade. It is one of three enormously influential global institutions, along with the World Bank and the IMF. Technically, GATT is an agreement and not an organization so it has not had a significant formal standing body. But in December 1991, the new draft set of GATT rules was published which proposes to change that.[3] The fruit of five years of negotiation, it is known as the Final Act – its internal GATT reference name on all documents – or the Dunkel Draft, after GATT's then Director General, Arthur Dunkel.

Three central principles underpin the GATT. The most fundamental is 'non discrimination', whereby if a 'contracting party' to GATT wants to impose a duty on the imports of one country, it has to apply the same duties to all other sources. The only exceptions allowed under GATT are customs unions and free trade areas, whose members are allowed to enjoy preference over external trade partners. Regional and multilateral arrangements have always been conceived as two elements of the GATT, which should co-exist and both contribute to the longer term objectives of free trade.[4]

The second GATT principle is 'reciprocity', whereby if one country lowers its tariffs on another's exports, it can expect the other to lower its tariff in return. The other GATT members are required to make the same concessions, thus creating a 'virtuous circle' of liberalization. Finally, the principle of 'transparency' advocates the replacement of non-tariff barriers, such as quotas on imports, with tariffs. These are relatively easy to monitor which is important since GATT membership involves a commitment to fix tariff ceilings, which are then to be negotiated down.[5]

A new Multilateral Trade Organization

Critics have accused GATT of being undemocratic and dominated by the influence of TNCs,[6] a concern which has been heightened by the insertion into the Uruguay Round in 1991 of proposals for a new and powerful governing body to regulate world trade – the Multilateral Trade Organisation (MTO).[7] The MTO would be a permanent secretariat (subsuming the current GATT staff) with a ministerial conference every two years. Member nations in the MTO (GATT signatories) will have one vote each. This new global commerce agency will, unlike the current GATT secretariat, have a legal personality, placing it on a par with and separate from the UN and existing UN bodies which consider trade-related issues, such as the United Nations Conference on Trade and Development (UNCTAD) and the United Nations Conference on Environment and Development (UNCED).

The MTO proposal is singularly vague about how the MTO would co-operate with UN bodies, but it does specifically mention the need for 'greater coherence in global economic policy making' with the IMF and World Bank, the two Bretton Woods institutions. The IMF is already on record as expressing a 'special interest' and concern that provisions under the GATT to allow differential interest for developing countries – already criticized as not strong enough by development non governmental organizations (NGOs)[8] – should be weakened.[9] The GATT signatories will be required to 'take all necessary steps, where changes to domestic laws will be required to implement the provisions . . . to ensure conformity of their laws with these agreements.'[10]

The MTO will 'co-operate, as appropriate' with the IMF and the World Bank. These two institutions are already under attack for their handling of environment and development issues. Its task will be to put into effect the GATT treaty. Unlike the original 1947 proposal for an ITO, the MTO proposal makes no provision for controlling restrictive business practices or protecting labour rights, let alone more recent concerns such as the protection of the environment or improving trade rules for the Third World.[11]

Reaction to the MTO proposal from NGOs has been swift and hostile. The MTO could easily be a tool for the rich and powerful nations to promote their version of free trade. The MTO does not even have a commitment to sustainable development or environmental protection or allow an adequate process of democratic consultation. An independent legal interpretation of the text by the Foundation for International Environmental Law and Development at King's College, University of London, was that it: 'limits consultation and co-operation to those non-governmental organisations which are concerned specifically with the conduct of trade relations between states in matters dealt with by the original GATT and its related agreements.'[12] So if an organization is not already being consulted, there will be no legal right for it to be consulted in the future, unless there are changes to the MTO. Environment, development and public interest NGOs which currently have no consultative status with the GATT will lack any status in the future.

Like the growing army of GATT watchers around the world, we were first interested and then alarmed by these proposals for an MTO. The MTO would allow for cross-retaliation between sectors – so if a country did not comply with the MTO on services, for example, another country harmed by this could be approved by the MTO to cross-retaliate in trade of goods, a threat to which Third World countries would be much more vulnerable. In trade disputes, the burden of proof would be on the defendent rather than the other way round. National governments would be required to force lower-level government to comply with the standards set by MTO-approved bodies. In short, the MTO would be a new world body with extraordinary intervention and regulatory powers over international trade and for arbitrating in trade disputes, which it is being introduced by the back door and to by-pass existing bodies. There has been little public discussion, even at parliamentary or congressional level, about the implications of this global centralization. In each country, political attention about the democratic implications of trade is still fixated upon the national level, or, as in Europe over the Maastricht treaty or the USA over NAFTA, upon regional decision-making. Global centralization is less commented upon even though the centralization of decision making leaves the citizen and the nation state relatively powerless. All in all, many independent observers believe the MTO will do more harm than good.

In 1992, around 160 NGOs from 60 countries wrote an open letter of protest to their heads of government[13] and began alerting national elected representatives to the fact that a major leverage they have over matters of vital import in their economies was being quietly removed. When presented with the implications of the MTO for their own roles in parliament or congress or wherever, even initially concerned representatives got a little nervous sensing that they are walking into political 'no go areas'. It is one thing to chip away at the local minutiae, another to question the global edifice. Even so, belated hearings have been arranged in the German and European Parliaments in 1993. In the UK, every MP was written to by a coalition of ten environment and development agencies in December 1992. Whatever the outcome of lobbying about the MTO, the proposals got the balance between globalism and localism hopelessly out of kilter. Such bodies suit TNCs not individuals. Indeed, why pay taxes to your home state or country if it only has one vote in such a distant but more powerful forum?

A poisoned chalice for the Third World

Although an Organisation for Economic Co-operation and Development (OECD) study is often quoted to indicate that the new GATT would lead to a $200–300 billion increase in trade, little if any of this would benefit the Third World. According to Jean-Claude Paye, the Secretary General of the OECD, the study was 'highly theoretical' and he has added that the media under-reported the fact that the putative gains would take place over ten years and that some developing countries would be hurt by a GATT deal.[14] According to Chakravarthi Raghavan, Chief Editor of SUNS, a Third World news service, and author of the first assessment of the new GATT from a development perspective:

> 'in theory, all contracting parties to GATT are equal, and GATT's consensus decision-making process appears to be democratic. But in practice when the weaker trading countries have tried to assert themselves, they have been ignored or told that the countries with the largest share of world trade have more at stake in the trading system and its rules, and so their views should prevail.'[15]

If the GATT Uruguay Round is completed and free traders succeed in their project, Third World countries (the South) will have to open up or liberalize their national economies more than ever and open up their agricultural sectors too, threatening their food security and opening the possibility of increased food dependency on the USA and EC. This economic liberalization will give TNCs sweeping rights not simply to export to, but also to set up mining and manufacturing bases in these countries and to be treated as locally-owned companies. The GATT negotiations also cover service sectors such as banking, insurance, transport, communications and professional services, which will also be opened up to Northern companies and institutions. The Third World will be placed at a further disadvantage by the Round's attempt to narrow access to industrial technology and information through new rules on intellectual property rights which favour the TNCs. Under penalty of retaliatory measures against their exports, governments would have to introduce laws protecting and enhancing patents and other intellectual property rights of TNCs.

The likely result of both of these would be that a sizeable proportion of people in the Third World would become even poorer, as will their (and the world's) environment. Concurrently, the large companies, international banks and other vested interests in the developed countries will extend and expand their control over the world economy. The Third World has not yet been able to organize effectively to block these developments.[16]

There is opposition, however. In India there is much hostility to the

GATT's proposals on intellectual property rights.[17] Over 250 eminent Indians – members of all parties in the Indian Parliament, jurists, scientists, academics and others – signed a statement of deep concern at GATT's threat to the 1970 Indian Patents Act.[18] 'Home Rule is better than GATT rule' was one assessment of the underlying issue.[19] There is also widespread dismay in the Indian consumer movement about rising drug prices, about the textile agreement and the farm deal.[20] There has been no satisfactory answer to this protest. Weaker countries, though, are expected to fall in line with their powerful trading partners.

From the South's perspective, another criticism of the existing GATT is that it has not removed old style Northern protectionism. The South's markets have been opened up, but the North's have not, for example in textiles. The MFA is a GATT approved 'transparency' agreement set up in 1974, which by 1990 covered $136 billion worth of textile trade (but not intra-EC textile trade).[21] The MFA enables Northern textiles companies to operate behind tariffs and to stop Southern producers from adding value to their own material – ie turning cotton into clothes. The Uruguay Round, although setting out to supercede the MFA, has approved a package which gives another 10 years or so to Northern textile companies to hide behind the MFA. Yet the answer does not, we believe, lie in Europe dismembering its own textile industry – see Chapter 12.

Environmentally unfriendly

The word 'environment' does not appear in the Dunkel Draft GATT text. For most of the world, trade practices determine the scale and character of resource exploitation and this greatly affects the environmental crises facing people and the planet. The current GATT negotiations aim to achieve the fullest liberalization of trade in natural resource-based products, which includes the reduction and ultimate elimination of export controls. Governmental negotiators have solicited and received input from large corporations and trade associations only, and the shroud of obscurity and secrecy which surrounds trade negotiations allows the TNCs' interests in profit maximisation through deregulation to be advanced without regard for their effects on the environment.

GATT makes it more difficult for countries to maintain or implement tough environmental standards and protect the competitiveness of their domestic industry. In theory, a government wishing to do this can establish import tariffs to offset pollution control costs, so that domestic producers will not be at a disadvantage when competing with imports from countries without similar environmental regulations. Or, a country could subsidize the costs of environmental protection with general revenues by underwriting pollution control costs. Neither of these options are likely to find favour under GATT, since it limits the right of governments to implement tariffs or use subsidies. Any nation that decides to do so may face retaliation for creating a 'restraint on trade'. Under the proposed new rules, much of the authority to protect the environment or food or jobs or small businesses will be taken away from national and local governments and the community and transferred to trade ministers, TNCs and the MTO.

For example, if California attempted to set higher standards for pesticide use, or to restrict the import of food contaminated with pesticides now banned in the United States, foreign governments, at the behest of corporations that consider themselves disadvantaged, could sue the USA for establishing non-tariff barriers to trade. A similar fate could meet the UK's rules on labelling irradiated food, Denmark's ban on PVC food containers and Germany's laws requiring beverage containers to be recycled and paraquat to be banned. Countries could also lose the ability to restrict the imports of goods, such as hazardous waste, simply because they apply higher environmental standards than other countries.

The results of many trade-related disputes so far is disturbing. For example, a GATT dispute panel ruled that Canada's export ban on unprocessed herring and salmon as part of its west coast fisheries conservation and management scheme was not allowable under GATT. Japan has also claimed that a US ban on exporting logs from the ancient forests of the northwest USA breaches GATT rules. It has not, however, pursued this complaint formally, although in the course of the Uruguay Round negotiations it had sought to weaken environmental exemptions in the GATT which might in future aid such a challenge. Furthermore, if the GATT does remove the North's barriers to agricultural imports from the South, then countries desperate to obtain hard currency to repay their debts might clear even more massive areas of forests to grow, for example, sugar or beef.[22]

Perhaps the most worrying part of the proposed expansion of GATT's powers is the threats it could pose to international agreements for protecting the environment. The Montreal Protocol for the elimination of ozone-depleting substances such as chlorofluorocarbon (CFC) emissions, for example, contains provisions for trade sanctions against states which do not comply with the Protocol. These measures have not yet been invoked, but they would conflict with GATT; countries breaking the Montreal Protocol could claim GATT protection. Efforts to halt global warming could also be threatened because any treaty to limit emissions of carbon dioxide involving trade measures could fall at the same free trade hurdle.

Overall, the main beneficiaries of GATT reforms will be TNCs and the main losers will be the environment and the world's poor. Trade negotiation and dispute resolution processes would be far less public and democratic than the procedures of the elected bodies and administrative agencies which would otherwise deal with important environmental matters. Standard-setting processes would be transferred to institutions which are less accountable to the community and more amenable to corporate influence and control. There is already international concern about the Codex Alimentarius Commission (Codex), the intergovernmental food standards committee to which the GATT Dunkel Draft gives considerable new powers; in Chapter 9 we outline how this 'neutral' committee draws excessive participation from the business community, but no environmentalists.

The GATT's Response

Aware of the rising concern that the growth in trade sought by the proponents of GATT would bring trade into deeper conflict with environmentalists, the GATT secretariat began in 1991 to produce a number of studies, culminating in a position paper on trade and the environment in 1992.[23] This paper was an attempt to defuse the environment as a potentially embarrassing and politically effective source of opposition to continued trade liberalization.[24] It argued that free trade will enhance environmental protection by increasing wealth which then can be used to clean up the environment, which was necessarily damaged by the first 'burst for growth'. This argument is clever nonsense. Why first dirty your backyard, only to trumpet the virtues of cleaning it up? It also ignores the fact that the North's capacity to industrialize, grow and become wealthy was given an unprecedented historical boost by the colonial period, in first the Americas and then in the Far East and Africa. Environmental limits will make such levels of growth impossible, but pursuing such a path will ensure that the potential conflict between trade expansion and environmental damage still looms large.

Disputes between the EC and USA

One area where well-organized sections in developed countries *have* seen GATT to be against their interests has been a large proportion of the farming lobby in Europe. The USA and the Cairns group of 14 mainly Southern agricultural exporting countries originally wanted a 75 per cent cut in internal farm support and a 90 per cent cut in export subsidies by the EC. However, EC negotiators, under pressure from the powerful agricultural lobby, did a deal in 1992 which only cut allowable farm subsidies by around a third. The US–EC farm trade deal in 1992 lowered the value of EC cereal subsidies by 29 per cent, reduced exports by 21 per cent and settled the long running oilseeds dispute – to much fanfare and subsequent farmers' riots in France. As soon as it was completed, other sensitive trade issues began to emerge to public view. One is the film and TV industry, where US companies want a slice of Europe's $30 billion a year industry and feel kept out;[25] others include steel, pharmaceuticals, construction machinery, medical equipment, paper, non-ferrous metals, textiles, glass products, electronics, fish, alcoholic drinks, and government procurement contracts.[26] In all these sectors, either the USA or the EC wants to defend its industry from the other, or seeks access to the other's.

Patents and services

GATT's proposals for patenting are much more important than farm commodities to some top TNCs. In GATT-speak, patents are Intellectual Property Rights (IPR), which matter hugely, particularly for expanding sectors such as biotechnology. The new rules will allow almost anything to be patented in an internationally harmonized way. They assume that private investors will only invest in biotechnology if they can be assured they will own the end-product. As the Consumer Society and Unity Trust (CUTS), an Indian consumer NGO, says: 'the objective of intellectual property protection is to create incentives that maximise the difference between the value of the intellectual property that is created and used and the social cost of its creation, including the cost of administering the system.'[27]

Many chemical companies are fast diversifying into biotechnology even though the US Office of Technology Assessment (OTA) reported in 1991 that 'to date, most US biotechnology companies have been losing money since their inceptions.'[28] Former Vice President Dan Quayle's Council on Competitiveness Report estimated the world market for biotechnology products to be $50 billion by the year 2000. No wonder the large and well-funded pharmaceutical and chemical companies are entering this market. Of 15 biotechnology-based drugs and vaccines approved for sale in the USA up to mid 1991, no fewer than nine were owned directly or indirectly by TNCs.[29] Mergers, licence deals, strategic alliances and acquisitions have been growing, according to the OTA.[30]

Against this backdrop, the GATT section on Trade-Related Intellectual Property Rights (TRIPs) can be seen to promise staggeringly profitable chances to companies to *own* what was previously common: genes, species and combinations of the two. Already plants and animals are being bred with totally foreign genes: a tomato with a fish gene to give it longer shelf life;[31] a laboratory mouse with a gene to predispose it to develop cancer;[32] sheep that excrete a human protein into their milk; and pigs to produce 30 piglets in a year.[33] Such inventions might be sources of wonder if they were not using common human inheritance – genetic diversity – and making it private property.[34] Biotechnology is a further twist in the privatization of common inheritance. Seeds, for example, are almost always covered by national patent laws, but the TRIPs represents an expansion of this, by the internationalizing and harmonizing of patent laws.

With its experience of being a test bed for Western science (such as the Green Revolution[35]) it is no accident that India is the site of so much resistance to the GATT's proposals on seed patents. In December 1992, for instance, more than 500 farmers from the Karnataka Farmers Union ransacked the Bangalore offices and burned files of Cargill Seeds, the US TNC's Indian subsidiary company, in protest against the GATT's TRIPs proposals. Their demands included the presentation of the Indian Patent Act 1970 which excludes patents on all life forms and they called for a ban on TNCs entering the Indian seed sector.[36] Awareness about what is being seen as 'gene theft' is rapidly rising, with 40,000 farmers from the national coalition of farmers organisations demonstrating against the GATT in Delhi on March 3, 1993.[37]

GATT also opens up the service sector. 'Clean' industries such as banking and insurance are licences to print money, if the rules are right. They are also opportunities to lose large sums, as Northern banks did with Latin American loans in the 1980s, though they got their money back by making other customers pay.[38] The risks in financial sectors are a reason GATT's proposed rules on trade in services, the Trade-Related Investment Measures (TRIMs) section, are so important. Under the TRIMs proposals, previously closed national financial markets will be opened up to external competition. A Third World country will no longer be able to keep powerful Western banks out of its financial markets. Good news for Western banks, but bad news for developing countries which want to control their investment in more self-reliant directions. As we argued in Chapter 2, this internationalization of capital undermines the intellectual basis of the theory of comparative advantage, which applies only if capital is national and can be controlled.

Will GATT resolve trade problems?

With the world economy in recession, the powerful are looking to GATT to push forward their interests. As we noted earlier, the OECD Development Centre study which promised a $200–300 billion growth in trade from a new GATT is often quoted suggesting urgency for completion of the GATT. Sir Leon Brittan, Vice President of the EC, put the figure differently, saying 'failure to agree (the GATT) would deprive world trade of almost $1 billion a day.'[39] Already there are doubts that this growth will happen. The OECD study in fact promised total growth of $19.5 billion a year over ten years, hardly staggering in conventional terms. In truth, no-one can be sure what benefits the GATT Uruguay Round would bring. Even Professor Jagdish Bhagwati, economic adviser to the Director General of GATT, has stated:

> 'Nobody really knows. I mean that's basically ballooning up estimates . . . I think the $200 billion figure you keep hearing all the time, that relates to the extent of incremental trade, which, according to some models, we expect to get. But I have been in this game long enough to know that, you know, if – it's almost astrological to try and forecast specific numbers. What economists are really better at is rules and devising principles.'[40]

The US Economic Strategy Institute (ESI), after a wide-ranging review of the Dunkel Draft's likely impact on the US economy, has calculated that President Bush's administration's earlier claim that the USA alone would benefit to the tune of $125 billion *in the first year alone* is impossible. Also using the Dunkel Draft as a guide, the ESI calculated in 1992 that the USA could see net annual GDP *losses* of between $36.3 billion and $62.4 billion.[41] The ESI estimated that US losses in manufacturing will be an annual $37.7 – 43.7 billion, $13 billion of that total from a possible ending of the MFA.

The reality is that the GATT is being sold to a public on the basis of a misleading and weak study using an inappropriate economic model. Meanwhile, in the real world, more and more people are being consigned to a future of either no work, or badly paid part-time work or for those in full-time work, a life of deep insecurity, wondering when their job will go.

Our thesis is that the ceaseless pressure to increase trade is often at the root of current concerns. India, for instance, has long been concerned that its pharmaceutical industry's cheaper generic drugs will be halted by the TRIPs patenting agreement. Canadians are bruised by their experience of the Canada–USA FTA which preceded NAFTA, with many Canadians blaming the USA–Canada deal for the collapse in Canadian manufacturing employment. In Europe, political anxiety is growing and, since 1992, EC attention has been on the GATT externally and the Maastricht Treaty internally.

In Eastern Europe, the imposition of privatization at a rapid pace is leading to a collapse in the number of jobs and a savage erosion of the social infrastructure. And in Japan, where unemployment in the past has been minimal or hidden, job losses are rising, almost as fast as the positive balance of trade figures. There, too, trade is becoming contentious with concern about rice, pesticide standards, and protectionism against their consumer goods and cars. Consumers groups have allied with farmers to defend local production of rice and the exclusion of cheaper US imports –

remembering only too well the suffering of the post war period when there was little home production.

With the election of President Clinton, it is tempting to argue that there may be change. And these are sorely needed. The USA in recent years has used existing GATT measures to wave the big trade stick at a long list of countries, including: India, Brazil, China, the EC, Japan, Mexico, Venezuela and Thailand.[42] What these disputes suggest is that GATT or no GATT, trade is a source of tension. A set of rules made by and for the powerful players, will do little to stop these tensions. We now move on in Part Three to look in more detail at the effects of free trade.

PART THREE

The Effects of the Free Trade Package

'A few years ago, I was eating at a restaurant in Saint Paul, Minnesota. After lunch I picked up a toothpick wrapped in plastic. On the plastic was the word 'Japan'. Now Japan has little wood and no oil. Yet in our global economy, it is deemed efficient to send little pieces of wood and some barrels of oil to Japan, wrap the one in the other and send them back to Minnesota. This toothpick may embody 50,000 miles of travel. Meanwhile, in 1987, a Minnesota factory began producing millions of disposable chopsticks a year for sale in Japan. In my mind's eye, I see two ships passing one another in the northern Pacific. One carries little pieces of Minnesota wood bound for Japan; the other carries little pieces of wood from Japan bound for Minnesota. Such is the logic of free trade.'[1]

David Morris

6.
On the Environment

To free trade further now would be to add insult to environmental injury. Trade already directly damages the environment and further deregulation would be an incentive to greater harm. Examples of such damage are discussed in this chapter.

Increased transport

The dramatic post-war increase in international trade means that more materials and goods are transported round the globe with a resulting increase in energy use and pollutants. The transport involved in international trade is estimated to account for one eighth of world oil consumption.[1] The four billion tonnes of freight transported on ships in 1991 used up as much energy as was used by Brazil and Turkey combined, – the equivalent to 4.2 billion 60 watt lightbulbs left on continously for a year. The 17 million tons of freight sent by plane used the equivalent of a year's energy consumption of the Philippines. Air freight is much more energy intensive – it takes 47 times as much energy to carry a ton of goods a kilometre by air as it does by boat. To these figures have to be added the energy consumed in the road and rail transport of these internationally traded goods.[2] Extending such trade will increase energy consumption unless there are fantastic leaps in energy saving transport.

More global trade creates waste and pollution by the very act of transporting goods over greater distances. There are considerable differences in which kind and how much pollution different modes of transport cause.[3] But if it is cost effective to keep bringing citrus fruits 10,000 miles from Latin America to Europe while Mediterannean countries dump fruit, there is something wrong with the costings system. The same problem arises *within* the European single market. Take croissants, for example. In a grocer's shop in North London you can find, neatly packaged on the shelf, a box of croissants from Alicante, Spain. Across the road is a bakery which makes croissants on the premises. It may be profitable for the bakery in Alicante to mass produce croissants and ship them around 1,500 miles to the UK, but this is environmentally highly destructive. If we compared the energy that went into the two croissants, the one from Alicante would only make financial sense if the full cost of energy was not included.

Transport fuelled by oil contributes to a wide range of environmental hazards – local air pollution, international acid deposition and global warming, as well as depleting a non-renewable resource. So does it *really* make sense to transport identical goods around the world in the name of free trade? The European Commission's Taskforce on the Environment has calculated that there will be a 30–50 per cent increase in trans-frontier lorry traffic from 1993 with the trade liberalization following the opening of EC borders in the single market.[4] In the middle European countries, public opposition to the growth of traffic has risen. Austria reported an increase in through traffic between 1975 and 1990 of 1,000,000 tonnes a year. One narrow Alpine valley, the Inn Valley/Brenner pass, takes 75 per cent of the total. Roads now carry the majority of transport, compared to 15 years ago when less polluting rail took 70 per cent.[5]

Consumers are paying for this. One Danish study of the price per kilo paid by consumers for flour found that the farmer got 21 per cent, the flour mill 11 per cent and 46 per cent was spent on packaging, transport and retailing.[6] Of the money the consumer pays for bottled water: the water is only 8 per cent, the bottle 24 per cent, advertising, shipping and retailing 50 per cent, tax 13 per cent, and manufacturer's profit only 5 per cent.[7]

Raw material extraction

The gearing of entire economies to increasing raw material exports for international trade also has its environmental impact at the point of extraction or production, especially in developing countries. Tropical timber is perhaps the best publicized case. Although the massive deforestation of the last decade has a range of causes, including clearing land for agriculture and grazing, mining, fuelwood gathering and trees felled for domestic use, the timber trade represents a significant proportion, about 50 per cent of the total production of industrial hardwood in tropical countries.[8] The effect of timber trading on deforestation is larger than the mere numbers of trees cut down for export, since roads built for commercial logging bring in their wake farmers, miners and those seeking fuelwood.

In 1991, this tropical timber industry was worth $6 billion, but it is beginning to decline as forests are decimated in one country after another to provide for the needs of Europe, Japan and North America. Thailand and the Philippines, which were once exporters, are now net importers; Nigeria's exports have slumped over the last decade and several other countries will soon be in the same position. At its most extreme, Sarawak, which along with Sabah provides more than 90 per cent of Japan's tropical imports, is predicted by environmentalists to have no trees left for felling in five years time. This would be both an environmental disaster and a human tragedy, since it would destroy the homeland of the local Penan people, who are aggressively fighting this trend.[9]

The fate of timber in international trade is repeated with other commodities sold by the South. Developing countries exploit resources such as food, fish, minerals and energy for export mostly to repay debts, with often dire adverse environmental effects. Unfortunately when trying to halt the ill-effects of such trade, developing countries can be blocked by the free trade system. Indonesia, for example, banned the export, though not the felling, of raw logs and rattan from its rainforests in 1985. It justified this ban on environmental grounds, but the EC referred this to the GATT surveillance body as the forerunner to a formal challenge to try to overcome the ban.

Indonesia's view was that by carrying out more processing it received greater profit and therefore has more incentive to protect a natural resource giving a high economic return. The EC's view was that Indonesia is restricting the supply of raw materials to allow it to take over more of the manufacture of 'value added products', such as furniture previously made in Europe and Japan. This contravenes Article 1 of GATT which says that foreign and domestic industries must be treated equally.

Other countries such as Ghana, the Philipines, Thailand, Uganda and even the USA have restricted the export of raw logs in some circumstances. The USA imposed restrictions on unprocessed log exports from the forests in the Pacific Northwest, as part of a strategy to reduce logging to protect the habitat of the northern spotted owl, and to secure supplies for the local industry, and thus maintain local employment levels. As we reported in Chapter 5, Japan immediately complained that this infringed GATT.

Fisheries management schemes have also been challenged. GATT ruled that Canada's export restrictions on unprocessed herring and salmon as part of its West Coast fisheries conservation and management scheme was not allowable. The restrictions were to enable local fishermen, many of them native Americans, to continue to earn a living while limiting fishing. GATT argued that the measure was not allowable since it was designed to protect Canadian processors and employment and that therefore the primary goal of the policy was not protecting fish.[10]

GATT regulations restrict the sovereign rights of countries to exercise control over their natural resources via export controls. The same constraints apply to import controls. GATT could stop attempts by some tropical timber importers to take trade initiatives to promote sustainable management of tropical forests. The Dutch Government, for example, has approved a unilateral import ban on unsustainably logged timber, from the 1st January 1995. Other European countries are considering similar measures. The European Parliament has adopted the 'Muntingh Proposal', which if implemented would provide incentives for sustainably logged timber imports to all EC member states by 1995, and disincentives for unsustainable production by 2000. But unofficial reports have indicated that a preliminary evaluation by the Dutch Ministry of Economic Affairs concluded that the proposed ban is incompatible with GATT and could therefore be challenged under the GATT.[11]

Industrial production and waste disposal

The environmental effects of industrial production for exports include intensive energy use with its depletion of non-renewable resources and effects on climate change, air and water pollution and toxic chemical production and waste disposal. These problems occur predominately in the developed countries, Eastern Europe and the NICs of the South. There is even a trade in the end products of industrialization – toxic waste. Greenpeace research shows that at least ten million tonnes of wastes of all types have been exported over the last few years and over half of these have gone to developing countries or Eastern Europe, where regulations and enforcement tend to be laxer.[12]

Is trade always bad for the environment?

Of course adverse environmental effects occur with the production of most primary and industrial goods, whether they be traded internationally, regionally or locally. However, present international trade rules and those of regional trading blocs encourage more environmental degradation by maximizing trade. They hinder national, regional and international measures to protect the environment by calling them 'barriers to trade'.

By expanding markets, trade almost inevitably increases the adverse effects of extraction, production and disposal. Companies are increasingly mobile and able to move where resources are abundant and where environmental and labour laws are less stringent, thus improving their competitiveness, but generally worsening conditions.

On the other hand, trade can help spread technologies to help protect the environment. Trade in pollution control technologies is increasing, particularly in countries where environmental laws are strengthened. Renewable energy industries are also increasingly focused on international markets. Trade can also cause companies to emulate the environmental innovations of their international competitors. US car companies, for instance, had to improve their fuel efficiency in order to compete with Japanese car imports. Even rules governing international trade can be beneficial if they have the right priorities. For example, rules to stop Northern agricultural overproduction being dumped in the South would benefit both the environment and the economies of the South.

GATT and international environmental agreements

Trading away the ozone

We have already mentioned in Chapter 5, GATT's threats to international agreements for protecting the environment, such as the Montreal Protocol to reduce and eventually halt the emissions of ozone-depleting substances such as CFCs. The Montreal Protocol is the only existing agreement using trade instruments to protect the global commons. It contains no restrictions on trade between signatory countries, provided they keep within the agreed limits of production and consumption of controlled substances. Signatories are progressively to ban products containing these substances and possibly products produced with these substances.

The import of controlled substances from non-signatories is banned, and the export to non-signatories of controlled substances is also to be banned and the export to non-signatories of technology for producing or using controlled substances is 'discouraged'. The rationale for these trade measures was to encourage states to participate by eliminating any competitive advantage that they might gain if they were not subject to the Protocol restrictions. These measures are likely to breach the free trade rules of the GATT.

In response to these concerns, GATT argues that not one complaint has been lodged to it.[13] However should a country which is a non-signatory to the Montreal Protocol, but a contracting party to GATT, choose to do so, it could challenge the Montreal Protocol. This is because it breaches GATT principles prohibiting trade restrictions which discriminate between GATT members. Trade in controlled substances is permitted between signatories of the Montreal Protocol, but not with non-signatories.[14] Such environmental concerns were reinforced by the 1991 ruling of the GATT Dispute Panel, which sustained Mexico's challenge to the US import embargo of non 'dolphin safe' tuna.[15]

The tuna dolphin decision

Since 1972, the USA has had a Marine Mammal Protection Act (MMPA) designed to protect dolphins from the worst excesses of tuna fishing in the East Pacific where dolphins and tuna often swim together. Despite the

MMPA, over seven million dolphins have been killed by fishing, so in 1988 amendments to the MMPA set conditions on the importation into the USA of tuna caught by the encirclement method. Under these amendments, countries exporting tuna to the USA, such as Mexico, were allowed to kill 1.25 times the US dolphin kill, but the rate was exceeded by Mexico, Venezuela and Vanuatu and the USA embargoed imports of their yellow-fin tuna. Mexico brought its case against the USA to GATT in February 1991 and it was decided in its favour in August 1991. The ruling by the three man panel, which met behind closed doors, gave new interpretations of GATT Articles 20(b), on conservation of natural resources, and 20(g), on the protection of human, plant and animal health, which have been seen by a wide range of US environmental, conservation and animal protection organizations as a direct threat to their efforts to promote simultaneously sustainable trade and conservation.[16]

The panel interpreted GATT rules 'very restrictively' and this has implications for the environment far beyond the specific dispute.[17] It decided that GATT prevents countries from taking trade measures to protect the environment or natural resources beyond their national boundaries.[18] The implications of this for international environmental treaties or conventions are disastrous. It 'unequivocally' rendered illegal trade measures applied by individual nations to conserve wildlife and ecosystems beyond their national boundaries, including the high seas and all other global commons. This judgement removed the only compliance mechanism – economic sanctions – available to protect these habitats and natural resources and could therefore threaten the Convention on the International Trade in Endangered Species (CITES) and any climate convention.

The CITES lists more than 100 species in which trade is banned, except in limited cases. It allows the use of trade sanctions to penalize non-signatories or even reluctant signatories and could therefore be legitimately challenged under GATT.[19] Similar problems could arise with other negotiations in progress such as those for a convention to limit carbon dioxide emmissions. This convention could make use of trade restrictions, but has much less political support than that enjoyed by the Montreal Protocol and is even more likely to be challenged under GATT.

Import restrictions based on production methods were also barred, thus as far as GATT is concerned, environmental impacts associated with the production methods used are irrelevant. Thus GATT could be used to challenge trade measures which discriminate between, for example, sustainably or unsustainably produced tropical timber, or similar manufactured goods from pollution-controlled and highly polluting industries.[20]

Although the panel ruling has yet to be passed by the GATT Council, its decisions unofficially enter the jurisprudence of the GATT, even before its adoption. Certainly, if adopted, subsequent rulings never contradict an established panel ruling, so that this interpretation of GATT rules will constitute a precedent. Furthermore, in January 1992 a US Court ruled in favour of a ban on tuna imports from countries such as France, Italy and Spain which buy their fish from Mexico, Venezuela and Vanuatu. This prompted the EC to push the GATT Council to adopt the dispute panel decision at its February meeting. The move failed due to US opposition. The EC has taken it up again with GATT and the dispute panel began to consider the case in April 1993.[21]

Europe's response

A report from the European Commission has strongly questioned the ability of EC environmental legislation adequately to protect the environment in the face of adverse trends in past and future consumption patterns.[22] These include a projected 20 per cent increase in carbon dioxide emissions by 2010 unless growth rates change, a 63 per cent increase in fertilizer use between 1970 and 1988, a 13 per cent increase in municipal waste between 1986 and 1991, and a 35 per cent increase in the Community's average water withdrawal rate between 1970 and 1985.

The review records some progress in reducing sulphur dioxide emmissions, suspended particulates, lead and CFCs, but notes that serious concerns are emerging over 'greenhouse gases' such as carbon dioxide, nitrous oxides and air quality deterioration related to road traffic. It recognizes too that the quality of water is 'under threat' and that there is growing eutrophication (the enrichment of water by run-offs from fertilizers) of both fresh and seawater. Intensive agriculture is causing extensive deterioration of soils, and habitat destruction is accelerating. The report also says that the 'Community's enormous waste stream is far from being under control'. All in all, it gives no grounds for complacency, yet the EC is often thought to have a relatively benign effect on the environment. A recent US review of trade's effect on the environment stated that the EC:

> 'now has hundreds of common minimum standards on products and production alike that member countries are in general free to exceed if they wish. These have helped improve environmental conditions across the continent, while making it difficult for any member to derive unfair competitive advantage through lax environmental law'.[23]

For the UK environment movement, the EC has been a valuable lever to combat the UK government's deregulating tendencies but to a country with a good environmental record like Denmark, the EC's role looks very different – EC regulations have weakened their existing or proposed domestic environmental laws and have thwarted attempts at rigorous labelling of solvents and paints. The maintenance of prohibition of a substantial range of pesticides is also threatened by the EC Directive on Pesticides.[24] Environmental concerns were a factor in Denmark's first vote to reject the Maastricht Treaty in 1992 and the case of reusable bottles illustrates why.

Denmark's reusable bottles

In 1981 Denmark passed a law requiring all beer and soft drinks to be sold in refillable bottles; to succeed it required limiting the number of different bottle sizes and shapes of both domestic and imported bottles. The latter had to be dropped following a 1988 European Court of Justice ruling against it, following complaints from foreign bottlers that this was a disguised restraint on trade, and thus in breach of EC law. The EC judgment ruled that the 1981 Danish law was a barrier to trade.

The Court did state, however, that while foreign bottlers were disadvantaged by other aspects of the law such as a ban on the selling of beer and soft drinks in cans, the environmental benefits of most aspects of the law outweighed the constraints on trade. Some saw this as a landmark decision that strengthened environmental law over the dictates of free trade.[25] But the judgment, although bowing in the direction of Denmark's right to act on its environmental concerns, constrained the reuse of bottles, and favoured recycling.

Recycling is not as good as reuse, from an environmental point of view, as it tends to require more energy. Friends of the Earth now campaigns firmly for reusable containers, and a review by Simon Fairlie, co-editor of *The Ecologist*, concluded that when waste for recycling is itself globally traded, recycling is becoming another form of commodity trading. In 1991, for example, 200 million pounds of US plastic waste was exported to 20 Third World countries, where cheap labour manually sorts through the waste. In Indonesia, one estimate is that 40 per cent of such 'recycling' material ends up in landfill sites.[26] Big business is deeply opposed to reusable bottles, as their economies of scale would be threatened. Fairlie concludes that: 'the conflict between refillable and recyclable containers is in essence a conflict between local distribution systems and centralized international ones.'[27]

At stake, he argues, is a choice between making products to be thrown away or to be durable. Cars are now being marketed on their recycling capacities, which is pandering to consumer guilt about contributing to waste and doing little to tackle the source of the problems. In cultures where containers are expensive and therefore valued, comprehensive reuse systems are still in place. However, Hungary's deposit bottle scheme collapsed in a few weeks after a Western company opened a disposable carton factory partly financed by the World Bank.[28] A double blow for the environment!

Waste dumping

A more positive decision from the European Court of Justice casts doubt on waste being considered an ordinary 'good', ie a commodity that can be traded without restriction. The EC asked for a ruling on this following pressure from Dutch waste exporters, who were protesting against the ban on hazardous waste imports passed in 1987 in the Belgian region of Wallonia, in response to public opposition to foreign imports.[29]

In 1992, the Court gave an ambiguous ruling prohibiting blanket bans on hazardous waste imports under existing EC law, yet allowing for restrictions on specific shipments. The Court ruled that waste is not an ordinary good and should be disposed of as near its source as possible.[30] The subsequent passing of a new EC regulation allowing member states to close their borders to waste from other EC countries has further distinguished between a waste and a 'good'. This distinction means waste is not subject to the usual free trade imperative of EC laws. In an effort to make clear that this was not the thin end of an environmental wedge into free trade, the EC Environment Commissioner Karel Van Miert warned: 'We are prepared to accept this, but in no circumstances should it be regarded as setting a precedent.'[31]

Sweden versus the EC

In 1992, the European Commission warned the Swedish government that its draft regulation on ozone-depleting substances was contrary to the trade arrangements between them.[32] Sweden is part of the EEA, the joint EC–EFTA free trade agreement, whose 1992 founding treaty has a chapter pledging signatories 'to preserve, protect and improve the quality of the environment.'[33] Sweden wants to introduce a ban on the imports of products containing or produced with CFCs, HCFCs and other ozone destroyers. The European Commission thought Sweden's measures are too stringent, going further than EC regulations and creating barriers to trade between the EC and Sweden, contrary to the provisions of the EEA.[34] [35]

Thus, despite the need to take urgent steps to halt the destruction of the ozone layer, the Commission objected to the progressive Swedish proposal, primarily because it sets out a different approach to the phase-out of ozone-depleting substances than EC law. The Commission fails to recognize the benefits that would result if the Swedish law achieved a more accelerated development of non ozone-depleting products and production processes and, even worse, obviously considers that the trade impact overrides the environmental rationale. In the light of this, it is ironic that in its comments on the application of Sweden to join the EC, the Commission stated that:

> 'The accession of Sweden [to the EC], with its sound and long-term environmental policy, would not only add to the quality of environmental standards, but would also promote a comprehensive approach aiming at an overall integration of environmental considerations in all relevant policy areas.'[35]

The 1989 Canada–USA Free Trade Agreement

The environmental effects of deregulated trade have been made clear as a result of experience under the Canada–USA Free Trade Agreement (FTA), the prototype for NAFTA, which was implemented on January 1 1989. The Canadian Government did respond to questions about the deal's prospective environmental impacts by asserting:

> 'The free trade agreement is a commercial accord between the world's two largest trading partners. It is not an environmental agreement. The environment was not, therefore, a subject for negotiations nor are environmental matters included in the text of the Agreement.'[36]

Before the agreement came into force, the impact of free trade was uncertain and the Canadian and US Governments were able to smooth over environmental concerns about the trade deal's impacts. Four years of experience with this precedent-setting free trade agreement reveals just how false those denials were.[37]

In export controls, the FTA goes much further than present GATT proposals and removes virtually every sovereign prerogative to control resource exports. The effects are particularly apparent in the energy resource sector where export licences have been granted for two of the largest energy projects in Canadian history: a $10 billion natural gas extraction plan for the Mackenzie Delta in the Canadian Arctic, which will allow up to 90 per cent of the gas to be exported to the USA for 20 years; and the $50 billion James Bay hydro-electric development in Northern Quebec, which will reshape a territory the size of France. Both developments will have enormous environmental effects. Moreover in a feature unique to the FTA, government subsidies for oil and gas mega-projects are explicitly immune to trade challenge or countervailing duties.

Thus, not only will these energy mega-projects predominantly serve US markets, but they will into the bargain be heavily subsidized by Canadian taxpayers. On the other hand, subsidies and other programmes to encourage energy efficiency and conservation are given no immunity from trade challenge.

Since the FTA, there has been a massive increase in proposals for large scale logging and pulp operations in Canada, often to serve US markets (although the biggest proposal is Japanese). The Canadian pulp and paper industry wants the Canadian government to challenge as a trade impediment the US recycling laws that require the use of recycled fibre in newsprint. British Columbia had to abandon reforestation programmes when it was challenged by the US forestry industry as an unfair subsidy, and hence contrary to free trade. More recently, the US Department of Commerce has imposed a countervailing duty against Canadian lumber exports on the grounds that Canada's log export restrictions represent a subsidy to Canadian producers.

The prohibition against resource export control applies equally to all Canadian resources, and many Canadian environmentalists foresee large scale water diversion as a strategic goal of free traders. The impacts of the FTA have also been felt in the fisheries sector. In the first dispute to proceed under the FTA, the USA was able to successfully challenge a fisheries conservation programme for salmon and herring fishstocks off Canada's West Coast.[38]

Both the FTA and GATT have been used by the Canadian government to protect the Quebec asbestos mining industry. It has challenged the plans by the USA's Environmental Protection Agency (EPA) to phase out the production, import and use of asbestos over seven years. The US Court of Appeal upheld the Canadian challenge on the grounds that the EPA had rejected alternatives less burdensome to industry and had failed to observe correct procedures. In explaining the challenge, the Province of Quebec explained its desire to block a precedent-setting regulatory standard that might be followed by other countries, and particularly those in the developing world, where many asbestos industries have migrated.

Both governments use the trade liberalizing FTA to attack regulations of the other, which are against its own (or its companies) interests. For example, the FTA is being used by Canada to oppose US controls on the trade in hazardous waste; and by the US Non Ferrous Metals Producer Committee to oppose various Canadian workplace safety and emission reduction programmes.[39]

Finally, the successor to the FTA, the NAFTA, which includes Mexico, hardly promises a better environmental approach. Environmentalists see NAFTA giving opportunities to dirty industries to relocate into Mexico, a process which has already begun. In the early 1980s, Mexico, like many

Third World countries, began to remove trade barriers in an effort to attract export manufacturers to set up within its borders. Approximately 1800 factories with half a million workers now operate in this 'Maquiladora zone', virtually unhindered by the weak environmental and labour regulations. For ordinary people, as Susan George of the Transnational Institute states: 'crowded and unsanitary living conditions, social degradation and rampant environmental destruction have combined to make the Maquiladora zone a reasonable facsimile of hell on earth.'[40]

In Ciudad Juarez, on the Texas border, more than 300 companies have opened up to take advantages of low wages and duty-free exports to the USA, but 400,000 people live in neighbourhoods without sufficient housing, running water, sewerage, pavements or electricity. An open canal carries 55 million gallons of raw sewage for 17 miles alongside the Rio Grande, polluting water wells and the river itself.[41] Concern about laxer environmental standards in Mexico has led to growing opposition in the US Congress. Congress warned President Bush in July 1992 not to use NAFTA to lower US protection laws for the environment, safety standards or employment regulations.[42] Over half the Congress voted to limit the NAFTA. President Clinton now faces the challenge of what to do.

In the next chapter, we go on to look in more detail at the effects of free trade on work and the resultant competition for jobs. Increasing competition for jobs means more cost cutting, which decreases environmental protection and affects the chances of environmental costs being internalized in prices (see Chapter 8) and leads to pressure against standards (see Chapter 9). In Chapter 8, some of the effects of debt for Third World countries are also covered; these too often have adverse environmental implications.

7. On Work

The old notion of full employment appears increasingly obsolete. In the early 1990s, the EC had 16 million unemployed people, 10 per cent of the 'would-be' workforce. Ten million new jobs will be needed by the year 2000 just to cut the rate to 7 per cent, according to the European Commission.[1] A further 25 million new jobs will be needed by 2010 just to cope with the 15 per cent growth in the EC's labour force. Where are these jobs to come from? The loss of jobs has a destructive effect even on developed national economies as fewer wage-earners try to provide more and more social security and pensions for the unemployed and the elderly; it also increases the inequality within societies, the long term unemployed both growing in numbers and being at the bottom of the social structure.

If the problem of generating employment is daunting for developed countries, it is much more so for developing economies where the family provides the only social security. Most people live their lives in chronic insecurity, and in agrarian societies, entitlement to land gives probably the only security. Land rights allow the land user to grow, both for family use and for sale.[2] There is, of course, a distinction between paid and unpaid work. According to Marilyn French, the novelist and author of a major review of the state of women world-wide, farm women in India and Africa are probably the most overworked people on earth, working 10 to 15 hours a day. In Burkina Faso, women do all the household work and *still* spend 82 per cent more time on farm work than men.[3] A study for the UN Conference on Women in 1980 calculated that women do between two thirds and three quarters of all the work in the world and produce 45 per cent of all the food, but gain only 10 per cent of the world's income and own at the most 1 per cent of land.[4] Even worse off than women in the developing world are the estimated 200 million children working in near or actual slavery conditions.[5]

There is obviously much to be done before world employment can be said to be in a satisfactory state. But in the 1990s recession there is an almost total absence of any debate about structural unemployment which doesn't first pay homage to the market and the need to outdo other countries or companies in 'efficiency' or competitiveness. Efficiency means replacing people by machines, and competitiveness means tough marketing, pricing policy and financial management, and resiting plants and obstructing labour and environmental legislation. Politicians seem frightened of being radical, or of questioning the free market, despite the obvious need.

Employment is a thorny issue, with politicians clearly unable to deliver full employment. Unemployment carries heavy social costs. In the UK, since the recession began to bite in 1990, one quarter of the working population has experienced a period of unemployment, according to a special *Financial Times* survey. Almost half the unemployed in Britain today are home owners, with all the accompanying worries of meeting mortgage and debt payments.[6]

As well as increasing unemployment, there has been a corresponding downward pressure on wages of the employed. Between 1978 and 1988 in the USA, for instance, 7.5 million new male jobs were created but, in 1988, 18.4 million males had jobs with wages below 1978 levels. The number of women's jobs, however, rose and their median wage rose from 43 per cent of male's in 1978 to 54 per cent in 1988. But real wages were down over the decade for a staggering two thirds of US workers, male and female. Between 1973 and 1990, real hourly wages for non-supervisory workers, about two thirds of the US workforce, declined by 12 per cent and real weekly wages fell by 18 per cent. As a result there has been a sharp rise in social inequality in the USA.[7] With the effects of some new technologies – such as robots, electronic data and communications technology, statistical process control systems and Computer Aided Design (CAD) – still to come, we think the decline in wages for billions of people will continue. There is no magic wand for politicians to wave and the nature of work in post-industrial society will have to be rethought.

New working practices

In the last few years, managers have come to realize that their problems will not be solved simply by curbing trade unions. They have looked elsewhere for ideas – at the most successful economies, in particular Japan. New management techniques include Total Quality Management (TQM), Team Working, Just in Time, Flexibility, Quality Circles, Kaizen Groups, and Caring Management. TQM is where the employer presents the increased quality of a product or service as something which assists the business, the worker and the customer. This, and approaches such as Quality Circles and Kaizen Groups, where management and workers work co-operatively, are intended to show that industrial practices have got over their class confrontational period.

These techniques are often called 'Japanese Working Methods' and in any description of them, there is usually a reference to how good Japanese labour relations are. This is doubly misleading. Firstly, the glorification of Japanese working practices assumes there is a need to increase output per worker in the first place. Secondly, it is based on a myth of what Japanese work is all about – that there exists a labour relations system that genuinely benefits workers and management alike, that by some sort of mystical process Japan has dodged the problems of Western companies. When Westerners talk of Japanese management they usually mean as practised in the large corporations. Japan's economy is in fact highly stratified, with the well-known giant TNCs feeding off a huge small and family firm sector. The cohesive nature of Japanese society hides the tensions.

More jobs for more people?

The world's population was 5.3 billion in 1990. By 2025, the UN estimates this will increase 61 per cent to 8.5 billion;[8] the population of more developed regions will increase 12.5 per cent from 1.2 billion to 1.35 billion, and the population of less developed regions is expected to increase 74.8 per cent from 4.09 billion to 7.15 billion in 2025.[9] Today, the world receives another population equivalent to the UK's every six months. The global population is expected to double from today's to ten billion by 2050, but this is based upon an *optimistic* set of assumptions, where more resources are put to meeting this new population's needs, and the pessimistic assumption anticipates a population of 12.5 billion.[10]

According to Paul Harrison, chief researcher for the UN Population Fund's 1990 and 1992 *The State of World Population* and author of *The Third Revolution*, a study of population and environment, a world of 11.5 billion people would need roughly an extra 12.6 million square kilometres of land for farms, towns and roads – equivalent to almost a third of today's world forest area, and double the world's protected areas.[11] At an Action Aid seminar to discuss the future, Harrison said: 'Population, consumption and technology are the only factors which impinge directly on the environment. They are never found separately. They only act together.'[12] Some countries with high standards of living can sustain a high population at present, whereas others with a sparse population cannot. The Netherlands, for instance, has 1044 people per square mile, whereas Sudan has only 27 per square mile.[13] Although part of this discrepancy is to do with climate and fertility, a crucial factor is the Dutch farmer's ability to purchase resources such as timber and oil from all over the world.

Solutions to any problems involving population should address problems of consumption and technology at the same time. It is no good, for instance, arguing, as car manufacturers have, that more cars will be acceptable as long as they are more efficient in energy use, or are recyclable. In the West, petrol consumption per car fell by 26 per cent in the period 1973–1988. Consumption per kilometer fell even further, by 29 per cent, but these gains were reversed by a rise in car population by 58 per cent, which meant that overall petrol consumption went up by 17 per cent, despite two giant oil price rises in that period.[14] According to Worldwatch Institute, except in a few countries with rising incomes, the growth in the world's car fleet – 450 million cars in 1990 – has been more due to human population growth than to increasing rates of car ownership.[15]

Whatever the causes and impact of population growth, more people need more, and more stable, work, but this pressure is coinciding with enormous technical change in which people are no longer required in large numbers to produce things. Already, as we have noted and will see later, there is a downward pressure on wages in the heartlands of the superblocs.

Technology replacing people

Robots can now do complex manufacturing and service tasks. From bank teller machines to car assembly plants, automation has both removed jobs and increased manufacturing output potential. Robots can be useful aids in minimizing drudgery – if only they were used to reduce working hours rather than the number of jobs. Old skills – often at the cutting edge in their day – are becoming obsolete.

Large scale production can now be flexible enough to allow short runs of products. This 'flexible specialization' is the very antithesis of Henry Ford's mass production where the customer could choose any colour of car as long as it was black. Now customers can choose what colour their car is, but the diversity which post-Fordist production technology enables is only superficial. The consumer may get an apparent choice, but from a declining number of companies, producing an inappropriate technology for mass transportation. Car components are restricted because the mass scale of such production demands security of raw materials from which to make apparently different products.[16] A radical rethink of the role of technology in replacing people with machines is long overdue.[17] We have to get back to basics and ask: what sort of work, for whom, providing what, do we want?

Expectations that new hi-tech manufacturing opportunities will create significant new employment should be taken with a pinch of salt; they ignore the advances in robotics, as well as the shift to lower paid, less skilled workers. In the past, discussion centred on the size and scale of factories, with thinkers such as Fritz Schumacher, founder of the Intermediate Technology Development Group and architect of the 'Small is Beautiful' school, arguing that society would have to embrace smaller scale production or face a continuing rise in structural unemployment.[18] Technology also had to be appropriate, he argued, or else it contributes to debt and neo-colonialism. For example, Schumacher told of visiting a textile mill in Africa and asking the manager why it was so automated:

> '"Because", he said, "African labour, unused to industrial work, would make mistakes, whereas automated machinery does not make mistakes. The quality standards demanded today", he explained, "are such that my product must be perfect to be able to find a market." He summed up his policy by saying: "Surely my task is to eliminate the human factor."'[19]

Worse than this anti-human sentiment, said Schumacher, was that all the equipment, management, trained staff and raw ingredients had to be imported. This, he said, was economic folly, underpinned by trade. We believe a more humane, small scale approach to employment could be a vital contribution to a more diverse regional economy, but it cannot provide all the jobs that are needed. Nothing less than a dramatic reduction in the working week has a hope of spreading the work out among the population.[20]

Wage disparities

One of the arguments in defense of TNCs is that they can be better employers and can use their muscle to raise wages and conditions, even among their subsidiaries above the level of local rivals. This can be true. By the 1990s, a different global wage pattern has emerged. Far from having global wage settlements, TNCs have localized negotiations at plant level, but made decisions about maximum pay at head office miles away, or even countries away.

Wages can be compared in two main ways – what it costs employers, and what workers can buy from their wages. According to the US Department of Labor, international comparisons of labour costs show enormous differences, even among labour forces within the three superblocs. Taking the USA's labour cost as 100, other developed economies' labour costs range from 148 in Norway to 12 in Mexico (see Table 6). But there is a big disparity still between the wages of the rich superbloc countries and the poorer NICs and developing countries.

Britain's labour costs in 1992 remained near the foot of the European league table, 12th out of 16 EC and EFTA states. However, UK wages' purchasing power, taking account of the exchange rate to determine the worker's power to buy, is better (see Table 7). The Purchasing Power Standard (PPS) has been calculated from hourly earnings for both manual and non-manual workers in a number of European countries in 1990, and the table shows how varied earning power can be, even within one superbloc, Europe.

Table 6 *Labour costs in developed countries*

Country	Labour cost *(USA equals 100)*
Norway	148
Germany	146
Sweden	142
Switzerland	141
Finland	141
Belgium	128
Netherlands	123
Italy	111
Canada	108
France	103
USA	100
Australia	88
Japan	86
UK	84
Ireland	80
Spain	79
Portugal	25
Hong Kong	22
Brazil	18
Mexico	12

Note: Figures are based on compensation costs that include pay for time worked, other direct pay, employer expenditure for legally required insurance and contractual and benefit plans, and for some labour taxes. Figures are based on percentages of US costs of 100 per cent.
Source: US Bureau of Labor Statistics.[21]

The difference in position of the UK wages calculated in these different ways is due to the non-wage costs (national insurance, social security, etc) being much lower in the UK than the rest of Europe. Individual workers in the UK have a similar potential to buy as workers in the Netherlands, Luxembourg, Denmark and Germany, according to the PPS, but the social wage is much lower, ie as the level of these services is lower, the deductions from the pay packet are lower, hence their relative disposable income is higher.

Within these generalizations about countries, enormous differences exist between different workers. Many women are on part-time work that may look good on a per hour basis, but does not add up to a decent weekly wage. The gap between the weekly incomes of the richest ten per cent in the UK and the poorest ten per cent has grown in the 1980s; from ten to one in the late 1960s and 1970s to 18 to one (nearly double) in 1985. Wages for the top ten per cent of male full-time workers gained 35 per cent between 1979 and 1991, whereas for the bottom tenth they went up only 5 per cent. In the same time, the taxes for the poorest fifth went up by 6 per cent of their income.[22]

Table 7 *The Purchasing Power Standard (PPS) for manual and non-manual workers, selected European countries, 1990*

Country	Manual	Non-Manual	
		Retail	*Wholesale distribution*
UK	10.48	10.48	14.9
Portugal	3.80	4.05	5.6
Netherlands	10.62	—	—
Luxembourg	10.65	—	—
Ireland	9.19	—	—
France	7.39	—	—
Spain	8.41	7.71	7.97
Greece	6.4	—	—
Germany	10.74	9.68	12.40
Denmark	11.89	—	—
Belgium	9.89	8.84	13.1

— Not available
Source: Eurostat[23]

Jobs, FTAs and TNCs

Free trade agreements (FTAs) mean TNCs can more easily relocate work to cheaper wage zones, although proximity to markets can be as important in deciding where to locate a factory as wage levels or labour force skills. Canadian labour leaders estimate that more than a quarter of a million Canadian jobs have been lost in the last two years due to the FTA between Canada and the USA.[24] NAFTA, as signed by President Bush in 1992 but to be ratified by President Clinton, has been projected to cost between 290,000 and 490,000 US jobs.[25] The ESI, based in Washington DC, has calculated that NAFTA will stimulate foreign investment in Mexico, and provide an overall gain for the USA in both jobs and overall trade balance between 1994 and 1998, but be a net loser for both by the year 2002.[26] Echoing our themes, the ESI stated:

> 'the NAFTA is not so much about free trade as it is about investment – who gets it and what kind of production (high value-added or low value-added, export-oriented or domestic-oriented) it engenders. Hence the detailed 2,000 page text.'[27]

The USA can expect a growth in export of computers and telecommunications, but a rise in imports of cars from huge, state-of-the-art plants in Mexico. On these calculations, if investment to Mexico was only 10 per cent higher than anticipated, the USA's trade deficit would increase by a huge $14 billion. No wonder many economic and employment strategists throughout North America are nervous. The political stakes of this trade are high, with jobs particularly sensitive. One US trade unionist has commented:

> 'Mexico's single comparative advantage is the poverty of its citizens and their willingness to work for subsistence wages . . . No matter how productive, US workers cannot compete with labour costs of less than $1.00 an hour.'[28]

Although Mexico may gain some jobs in manufacturing, there could be massive disruption in other sectors as a result of NAFTA. More than 500,000 people could leave the land if Mexico opens its borders to US feed grains alone,[29] and 700,000 people may lose their jobs in the corn (maize) industry.

The free marketeers argue that relocation is good, an aid to global efficiency. The reality is that the company benefits and workers everywhere lose security. At the most extreme, free trade means that employers can flourish where life literally comes cheap, like the carpet companies in Asia which rely entirely on indentured, low or no waged labour. A fruit farmer in both the UK and Brazil, stood up at the National Farmers Union 1993 AGM in London and said:

> 'Free trade and a level playing field are illusions. If I told you the details of social and environmental policies in Brazil I would make you weep. Suffice to say they consist mainly of bullets, bulldozers and boxes of matches. Farmers in the UK can never hope to compete with that and I don't advise them to try.'[30]

An argument used to sell the advantages of regional trade blocs is that they protect jobs within the region. In practice, TNCs have already internationalized to such an extent that they can play the advantages of either the global scene or the region. The well-known US sports shoe manufacturer, Nike, is one recorded example of how a company can play the field to its own advantage and profit.

The Nike example

Between 1982 and 1989, 65,300 US footwear jobs were lost or went abroad. An analysis of Nike found that it had closed its last US factory in Maine in the 1980s and established most of its new factories in South Korea. Following strikes over wages and union rights, the company had shifted production and made contracts with several dozen factories around the world, including six in Indonesia.

An Indonesian shoe worker's pay rate is US $1.03 per day, well below the US shoe industry average of $6.94 per hour. This wage is less than the Indonesian government's figure for minimum physical need. We can see the advantage to the US parent company of lowering its costs of production, despite the added cost of transport back to the USA. A recent International Labour Organisation (ILO) survey found that 88 per cent of Indonesian women working at this rate of pay were malnourished. Most workers in this factory were women. The labour costs to manufacture a pair of Nike's that sell for $80 in the USA, according to one estimate, is approximately 12 US cents.[31]

Bidding for work

One of the features of the modern free trade package is the removal of national restrictions on the export of capital. For example, following the 1979 UK election of the Conservative Government, restrictions were quickly lifted, with devasting effect. From 1979–89, the net amount of money going out of the UK compared to that coming in was £70 billion: that is equivalent to one year's investment by all of UK private industry and three or four times that for manufacturing alone (which invests about £20 billion). By the early 1990s, the situation was potentially nearly twice as bad with a net £1 billion flowing out of the UK every month.

The free trader's defense is that the money will go to where investors can make best use of it. In fact, big capital tends to be concentrated in the 'core' world of the superblocs. To try to attract some of this investment, national and local governments in both developed and developing countries have been forced to adopt ever more desperate measures, bidding and counter-bidding against each other to win jobs and factories. In the UK, the national economic policy now is to offer itself to TNCs on the world and European markets as a cheap wage, deregulated environment with relatively pliant workforces. Other countries vie with it. As Robin Cohen, a researcher into the phenomenon concludes:

> 'A number of governments in the Third World passed laws restricting the organisation and bargaining powers of unions. They provided freedom from planning and environment controls, poor and therefore cheap health and safety standards, permission to repatriate profits without restriction, tax holidays and in some cases like Singapore, a powerful paternal state, which appeared to guarantee political stability.'[32]

Export processing zones

These conditions are often created and concentrated in particular areas called Export Processing Zones (EPZs). These grew significantly in the 1980s, with around 260 EPZs in 67 countries, employing 1.3 million workers – mostly young women (85 per cent in Malaysia). While EPZs' aim is to promote exports, they do not necessarily use raw materials or parts from the host country. It is the labour the companies want – cheap with no restrictions on money, administration or geography. Usually there are no trade restraints; regulations are simplified and often incentives added too. Trade unions find it difficult to organize in EPZs. As the International Confederation of Free Trades Unions (ICFTU) says:

> 'Frequently high wire fences around production facilities, extensive security presence and the firing of Union sympathizers serves as a clear message to EPZ's workers that Unions should be kept out.'[33]

It could be argued that such practices are exceptional, but these zones are the cutting edge of free trade. More familiar territory is, perhaps, the kind of factory closures and country-hopping that hit domestic headlines. They happen all round the world. In the UK, in the depressed winter of 1992–93, for example, public attention was grabbed by the closure of the US TNC Hoover plant in France and the company's transfer of orders to an expanded plant in the UK, though with an overall cut in jobs and working conditions. Another example was the lock-out at the Timex plant in Dundee, Scotland, another TNC plant, where management 'offered' workers a pay freeze and a ten per cent cut in fringe benefits, such as the company's contribution to the pension funds. Such events are likely to be ever more common features of national and neighbouring economies, if trade is further liberalized. Deregulation of wages and conditions, and of health and safety laws, gives employers the freedom to be tougher, ultimately to move altogether, if markets allow, as we saw for sports shoes. The quality of life of whole communities and millions of people are the hidden down-side of this ceaseless exertion of power. Jobs, however, are not the only feature of modern life structured by trade. In the next chapter, we look further at the way free trade causes money to flow around the world, trailing debt in its wake.

8.

On Money Flows and Social Costs

Despite gradual trade liberalisation modern economies are still plagued by cycles of overproduction and cut-throat competition, known as business cycles, or 'boom and bust'. These lead to lower prices in the short term and market concentration in the long term. An essential part of the free trade package is the need to deregulate the flow of money to allow it to seek maximum reward. This is a source of great tension in North–South relations, as the North is capital-rich and the South capital-starved, so, as we will see later, the people of poorer countries tend to lose out, even if their governments have borrowed money ostensibly to improve living standards.

Poorer countries, as the World Bank has pointed out, tend to suffer from poor sanitation and water quality, whereas richer countries – being more industrialized and urbanized – generate more waste and pollution.[1] However, richer countries also are under pressure to decrease some pollution, which is why one notes a decrease in some more noticeable pollutants, such as sulphur dioxide, as the income level of countries rise, yet an increase in other less obvious pollutants, such as carbon dioxide. The reduction in pollution can come from three sources: the introduction of environmental controls or the relocation of factories to areas with lower environmental standards; or the closure of factories.[2]

Economic maps, even in rich areas of the world, have been redrawn over recent decades as money flowed in and out. In Western Europe a golden triangle of affluence and economic activity has emerged from London to Milan to Frankfurt. In newly liberated Eastern Europe, only Hungary and the Czech Republic are showing any sign of receiving significant entrepreneurial cash flows from the West, while Germany's economy is hard pressed paying for the costs of reunification. In the USA, the Midwest rust belt – the northeastern industrial heartlands – has declined, while the sunrise states – based upon new technologies such as electronics, in the West and Southwest – have grown. In the developing world, two classes of country exist – the raw material suppliers (most developing countries) and the newly emerging industrial countries (NICs), mainly in Asia. Countries in sub-Saharan Africa are fast being consigned to a permanent peripheral status, starved of money and generally lacking resources that the affluent North wants.

The UN has calculated that inward investment – investment coming into countries from across borders – within the world's three most powerful regions, the USA, Europe and Japan, which it calls 'the Triad', tripled between 1980 and 1988 from $142 billion to $410 billion and accounted for one third of world-wide inward investment. It added: '. . . in terms of trade, interactions *within* the Triad have outpaced both interactions in the rest of the world, and interactions between the Triad and the rest of the world, indicating a faster rate of integration within the Triad than between the Triad and the rest of the world.'[3] This movement of money adds to global inequality.

Debt and structural adjustment programmes

The flow of debt monitored by the World Bank shows a rising trend: external finance for developing countries' debt was $115.2 billion in 1991 and was estimated to reach $134.3 billion in 1992.[4] The World Bank admits that the poorest countries have not benefited from this cash flow. Most Third World countries had borrowed heavily in the 1970s, on World Bank advice, as it now admits.[5] It also expresses concern that middle income countries could be caught in a double bind – hooked on foreign investments, but unsure if they would be sustained. The total foreign debt of the 116 countries reviewed by the World Bank rose by over 6 per cent to $1700 billion. But, claimed the Bank, growing indebtedness by developing countries was not a cause for concern as long as it went into economic development and to stimulate exports. Foreign direct capital investment – for business, rather than debt servicing – was $24 billion in 1990, $34 billion in 1991 and $38 billion in 1992.

However, the economic situation for many developing countries is desperate. Inextricably linked into the global economy, yet caught in the grip of a long term decline in their terms of trade, indebtedness is a major factor contributing to poverty and environmental destruction in many of them. They cannot get out of the debt cycle because, under the trade system, prices for their commodities are declining in real terms. According to UK Overseas Development Institute data, commodity prices declined in real terms consistently from 1870 until World War II, when they rose sharply to an all-time high. Since 1950, however, they have declined to a point as low as they were in the 1930s.[6] So developing countries are trapped. Meanwhile, manufactured goods prices have risen eight-fold over the last 100 years.[7]

World markets lock Third World countries into an artificial division of labour: they provide commodities that others profit from, while they have to produce more to stand still – which is why indebtness rose so alarmingly over recent years, as Third World governments tried to buy their way out of their vicious circles.[8] Sub-Saharan Africa's debt in 1989 was nearly four times its GDP, whereas Latin America's was nearly three times its GDP.[9] As John Madeley, author of *Trade and the Poor* has said:

> 'Whatever the reasons, the theory of comparative advantage has not led to a flow of venture capital that would equalize wages and living standards between countries. But it has also failed to raise living standards in the South for deeply entrenched historical reasons.'[10]

Blame for debt is flung in all directions – on callous bankers, corrupt politicians, indigent populations – but the net result was that in the 1980s many developing countries in Africa and Latin America were bankrupt. World bodies such as the IMF were called in and would only lend them more money if the country implemented rigorous controls over public spending. To do this, the World Bank set up many so-called Structural Adjustment Programmes (SAPs). According to Susan George, these programmes can be summed up in four words: *earn more, spend less*. The economy is restructured towards investment and exports. The currency is devalued to boost exports and pay off more of the debt. The promise is that suffering in the short term will put economies into better shape in the long term.

Faced with the downward trend in the value of their commodity exports, government officials and politicians frequently fixed the rules to maintain or enhance their own lifestyles, but the debt turned into punishment for ordinary people as currencies were devalued, earnings fell and social programmes, such as education and health, were cut. Ben Jackson, Campaigns Officer for the World Development Movement, a UK development NGO founded by Oxfam and Christian Aid, has catalogued the suffering of the world's poor in this global tragedy. In Venezuela, for instance, a $35 billion debt had to be serviced by annual payments of $3 billion.[11] As a result, in 1989, the people in Caracas rioted for three days, leaving 250 people dead. Zambia rioted in 1990. In 1993, Kenya caused bankers' hearts to miss a beat when it refused to pay its debts. Hardly a paragon of economic or moral virtue, the Kenyan government spoke for many in the developing world when it said: enough was enough. The treadmill is so fast, it is only sane to step off. To what alternative, we return in Chapter 12.

The export treadmill

In the 1980s for much of the Third World, the pressure of debt repayment meant that more and more exports had to be produced and sold, as their value declined. Susan George points out that:

> 'While such advice might be valid if it were given to only a few countries at once, dozens of debtors are now attempting to earn more by exporting whatever they have at hand; particularly natural resources including minerals, tropical crops, timber, meat and fish . . . The "export-led growth" model, on which the Fund and the World Bank insist, is a purely extractive one involving more the "mining" than the management – much less the conservation – of resources.'[12]

One study found that nearly $75 billion out of the debt total of $179 billion accumulated by Latin America between 1980 and 1988 – ie 42 per cent of the total – was the result of deteriorating terms of trade.[13] In total, the developing world owes approximately $1,300 billion to the governments and banks of the industrialized financial institutions. Debt repayments by developing countries are three times what they receive in aid.[14] Paying back the debt accounts for a third of the foreign exchange earned by African and Latin American exports.[15] Worse, few of the projects undertaken to earn foreign currency are sustainable. Susan George illustrates this with the example of cash-cropping:

> 'Soils are exhausted to grow cash crops. Senegal, for instance, borrowed heavily to install refining capacity for a million tonnes of groundnuts. But its soils are so depleted by groundnut production that today it can produce nowhere near that amount. Still, the cost of the industrial plant must be reimbursed – through exports of groundnuts.'[16]

Michael Barratt Brown adds that one of the worst effects of the groundnut scheme in Senegal was damage to the extended family farming system.[17] Sub-Saharan Africa has also suffered the strictures of SAPs. A review by Fantu Cheru of the American University, Washington DC, makes stark reading:

> 'Virtually all indices of economic development registered stagnation. During 1960–80, per capita income in 19 of the 39 countries in the region grew by less than 1 per cent a year. During 1970–80, only eight countries achieved an increase in agricultural production per person.'[18]

No wonder there is increasing cynicism about the free market in the South. Humberto Campodonico, a professor at the University of Lima and representative of the Peruvian NGO, Desco, speaks for many in arguing that free markets and trade liberalization do not work because of income inequality: 'People come to the market with the income they have. But since many people in Latin America have very little income, they are left out if the free market reigns.'[19] The debt problems are compounding inequality and environmental degradation – a connection the World Bank tries to argue is not causal.[20]

Inequality and environmental degradation

In Africa as a whole, in the early 1980s, the richest 20 per cent of the population had an income four times that of the poorest 40 per cent and 3.8 million hectares of forests and woodlands disappear every year, with 4 per cent of closed forest going each year in West Africa alone. A colonial legacy of commodity dependence from the 19th century has been compounded in this century by land tenure problems, incompetent government, and export-led attempts to pay off debt. The result for the people can be near disastrous. In Botswana, for instance, barely 5 per cent of food requirements are produced internally, and the emphasis on beef exports is environmentally awful and socially inequitable:

> 'In 1989, there was 2.5 million cattle, 1.8 million goats and 290,000 sheep. About 110 ranchers together own as many cattle as 29,000 small farmers. In the early 1980s, the World Bank poured in an estimated $10 million into cattle projects in Botswana, disregarding the country's environmental reality. Beef processing accounts for 80 per cent of agricultural output in Botswana and over 95 per cent of production is exported . . . This emphasis on beef export has accelerated the rate of land degradation and has increased stratification among Batswana.'[21]

According to the UN, the income of the wealthiest 20 per cent of Botswana's people is 24 times that of the poorest 20 per cent,[22] a ratio only exceeded by Brazil's! A culture which was based on cattle for the majority has been turned into a source of power and profit for a few.

According to Fred Pearce, thousands of miles of strong, seven foot high fences have been erected to keep ranched cattle in, and wild animals out of ranches, to meet EC health concerns about imports of Botswana beef becoming a route for foot and mouth disease into Europe.[23] A 1992 scientific mission to review the conflict between wildlife and the cattle trade concluded that the wildlife loses. Despite protected areas for wildlife, the fenced-off areas for cattle ranching 'block off the necessary migration routes of the wildlife from the Kalahari to the Okavango delta.' Trade needs are continuing to be promoted. A proposed 80 km Northern Buffalo Fence will, says Pearce, cordon off the northern borders of the Okavango swamp and: 'give cattle safe, disease-free access to the last commercially unexploited dry grasslands in the far north of the country – an area that the scientific mission proposes should become part of an international wildlife reserve.'[24]

Such conflicts between trade, ecology, and equity in order to generate export earnings may seem far away from the dining rooms of Europe, but it is here that the problem is being fuelled – by a trade in beef, and most ironically, by demands for free-range, healthy beef. What starts with export-led attempts to pay off debt often inexorably leads to other policies being introduced which might generate cash but at the expense of social justice and environmental probity. Having reviewed the impact of SAPs on Sub-Saharan African countries' peoples and ecology, Fantu Cheru concludes that a radical change of economic direction is needed – one which includes land reform, easing debt burdens, making government more accountable, addressing the problems of women farmers, easing fuelwood shortages and diversification of the economy. This last proposal is echoed by Peter Madden of Christian Aid in his review of the Third World commodity crisis:

> '. . . producers can move sideways into producing a wider range of products for domestic markets and try for greater regional or local trade. Ultimately, for any country, some kind of manufacturing base is desirable.'[25]

But such a change of direction is unlikely, the rule appears to be, the poorest receive the least. According to the *World Development Report 1992*, developing countries received $32 billion in inflows of capital in 1990; which was a drop of a quarter since 1980 – from 25 per cent of world total to 18 per cent. The capital flow is skewed against the poorest. Africa received only $2.2 billion, 7 per cent of total investment flows to developing countries; Asia attracted 61 per cent, and Latin America 32 per cent; the least developed countries received less than 1 per cent.[26] To add insult to injury, banks in the North are now turning to their customers to bale them out for their incompetant lending policies in the 1970s and 1980s by huge increases in bank charges; this, in addition to governments already providing massive tax concessions to the banks to subsidize their loans or write off their bad debts.

Reforming global institutions

These examples underline the urgency of the task of reforming global institutions. While the public might have contradictory feelings about bodies such as the IMF or World Bank, they generally expect good works from the world's official aid institutions and national aid programmes. Graham Hancock, formerly East Africa correspondent of *The Economist* and co-editor of *New Internationalist* magazine, in his devastating indictment of the world's official (as distinct from the voluntary sector) aid institutions draws pessimistic conclusions about the feasibility of reforms.[27] Hancock argues that so much money is involved – $60 billion a year – and that accountability is so low, that the only answer to the systematic corruption is to *close* the international aid institutions. Neither more aid, nor redirected aid faces the extent of the problem. He argues that:

> '. . . official development assistance is neither necessary nor sufficient for "development": the poor thrive without it in some countries; in

> others, where it is plentifully available, they suffer the most abject miseries. Such suffering, furthermore, . . . often occurs not *in spite* of aid but *because* of it.'[28]

But within the aid institutions, the lifestyle for office holders is so comfortable and interesting – there are almost never any sackings, and pay scales are generous – that there is no internal pressure for change, despite years of external pressure. It is ironic that officials of these global institutions seem almost untouchable. A task force on the World Bank's lending policy concluded that the number of projects with major problems rose from 11 per cent in 1981 to 20 per cent in 1991; projects with an unsatisfactory conclusion rose from 15 per cent to 38 per cent; and cancellations rose by 50 per cent in just the last three years.[29] With a track record like that, one would have thought the officials would get a dose of the medicine they have meted out to others to such brutal effect – cuts in pay, sackings, and loss in quality of life. It appears that there is one rule for the advisers and one for the recipients of advice, which belies all the free trade talk about level playing fields.

We now turn to another problem area in the free trade package, the issue of whether prices set by market forces accurately reflect the full environmental (and social) costs of production. Environmental economists have argued that free traders at best collude and at worst actively promote environmental degradation by allowing cheapness to reign.[30]

Misleading prices

The free trade approach to pricing is short-sighted and misleading: the future is discounted and efficiency is viewed too narrowly. Environmental economists assert that conventional mechanisms for setting market prices do not reflect the full environmental and resource costs of a traded product, ie those costs involved in its extraction, production, transportation, use and recycling or disposal.[31] Society is usually left to bear these external costs. Free traders argue that the price has to be what the market can bear. Environmentalists are concerned about prices which squeeze out environmental protection or undervalue long term and hidden costs such as health hazards from pollution caused by transport, for example. The consumer may be getting a bargain, but is this costing the earth?

In the long term, we believe that all costs will have to be internalized, with a strict application of the 'polluter pays' principle at every stage of a product's life cycle (see Chapter 13). To calculate such costs can be extremely difficult, but the process of incorporating some costs ought to be started. The insurance industry has been the first to begin this process, forced to raise premiums and sometimes withdraw cover by the huge costs of the impact of climate change on insurance claims after disasters.

Pricing climate change

Climate change and the destruction of the ozone layer are causing and will cause more and more ill health from changes in food, skin cancers, etc.[32] The *British Medical Journal* introduced a review of the health implications of climatic change with the words: 'Every age has its catastrophe theory'.[33] It was not joking. Each year, 17 million hectares of tropical forest are being destroyed – an area the size of Austria – and this, plus emissions of fossil fuel waste is creating the greenhouse effect, which will seriously affect food production. The effects of climate change are interlinked and potentially catastrophic. Sea levels will rise, which will reduce the amount of low level farmland. A rise in sea level of only one metre will put at risk 3 per cent of the world's land. This sounds small, but accounts for one third of the world's crop-growing land and the homes of one billion people.

Catastrophic windstorms may well occur with greater frequency and intensity with potentially serious consequences for the insurance industry. The recent record is already portentous. Between 1967 and 1987, there were no windstorms anywhere which caused insurers losses of more than one billion dollars. Since 1987, there have been no less than 11 such storms, wreaking damage totalling over $50 billion to the world's worried insurance companies.[34]

Other sectors will be threatened by the predicted 20 per cent increase in winter rain and 5–10 per cent reduction in summer rain. This would turn the USA's grain belt into a desert, according to the Intergovernmental Panel on Climate Change.[35] A two degree centigrade rise in temperature could mean a decline in wheat yields in Europe and the USA of between 3 and 17 per cent. Already in recent years, yields have fallen due to drought. Crops are also damaged by excess ultraviolet light. The market alone cannot cope adequately with these costs. The challenge is starker still: a choice between policies for survival, and continued profligate use of fossil fuels and wasteful consumption. Another case of the environment paying for human failure to account for damage is the well-known issue of the need to phase out ozone-damaging CFCs and HCFCs. Some of the barriers which the free trade approach throws up to the halting of the use of such ozone depleters have already been discussed in Chapter 6.

Some still claim that the solution to such problems is best dealt with by consumer information about greener products. Such information will lead to people choosing green products in preference to others, and that by this process of consumer-led choice the market will adapt. We are sceptical about whether it can be left to individuals to compensate for the failings of governments and trade, although a recent alternative fridge provides a heartening example of the role of such consumer choice. Greenpeace in Germany developed a CFC-free refrigerator called the Greenfreeze with a company in the former East Germany, which, thanks to marketing by Greenpeace, has sold 150,000 since it was launched in 1992.[36] For this example to be repeated on a sufficiently large scale it would also require national and global bodies such as the IMF or World Bank to encourage such innovation.

Conventionally, fridges have been commonplace and cheap in the North. But they work by using ozone-damaging CFCs, which are released when a fridge is broken up at the end of its life. This environmental cost does not feature in the original price. This realization does not mean, however, that all fridges should be banned or be withheld from poorer societies which have never had them. Nor does the inadequacy of past prices mean that in future it should be left to the altruism of ecologically aware consumers to solve the problem by buying ecologically correct machines.

Our point is that how the humble fridge has been designed, built, priced and sold is a symbol of a wider problem in pricing policy. Technological alternatives often do exist, but are either more expensive or not invested in. Better costing of the environmental effects of resource use, if combined with strict regulation, would direct investment and research and development into less damaging products.

Free riders

There is little point one country going it alone on any such environmental improvement, unless it has the option of protecting itself against unfair competition from others that do not. But GATT regulations prevent GATT contracting parties from discriminating between 'like products on the basis of their method of production'. Import tariffs or subsidized exports, whatever their reason, are therefore viewed as impediments to free trade, rather than aids for environmental protection. The resulting threat to competitiveness is then used by companies to oppose cost increases due to environmental pricing. This argument was used in 1992 to stop the EC from unilaterally introducing a carbon/energy tax as a way of cutting carbon dioxide levels.[37] Also efforts to control 'free riders', ie any industries which by dint of lax environmental standards in their host region avoid incorporating environmental costs, are potentially hindered by such GATT regulations.

The example of steel

The sort of threat posed by these ecological free riders is illustrated by the problems facing European steel companies; similar problems exist in

North America. Already in 1993 there was an estimated 40 million tonnes annual overproduction in the EC alone. In addition, new methods of mass producing steel are coming on stream and there is a slump in manufacturing. Yet European steel companies face competition not only from exports from the hi-tech and lower labour costs of the NICs, but also from the low labour costs and lax environmental standards of Eastern Europe and by cheaper supplies of steel from Brazilian pig iron smelters. The latter's costs are low through the use of charcoal as a fuel. This charcoal production leads to large scale deforestation. Despite this, 13 similar smelters are planned or under construction.[38] At the time of going to press, the Ravenscraig steel plant, Scotland's sole surviving mill, which had been closed down by its privatized owner British Steel, was being considered for purchase by PT Gunawan Dianjaya, an Indonesian steel company. This company wanted to relocate the Ravenscraig equipment to the largest mill in South East Asia, in Indonesia, and, with the benefit of its cheaper labour, anticipated being able to export some of its production back to Europe.[39]

Although resiting plants such as Ravenscraig is always a theoretical possibility under free trade, the prospects of many of the developing countries, where free riders find it convenient to base their companies, being able to afford the investments needed to meet higher environmental standards is generally poor. Developing country economies are already under severe strain and much of the necessary new technology which features in modern production is concentrated in the North. So the South may receive the occasional resited plant, and be used systematically for its cheap labour, but the control, the hi-tech design, the research and development and the capital will all be firmly based in the North. Far from breaking the culture of underdevelopment, this will probably accelerate it. The affluent of the South may be enthusiastic about the benefits of free trade, but for the mass – both the world's 3.3 billion ecological middle class and the 1.1 billion poor – the search for 'efficiency' will yield little.

Costing welfare

Another difficulty for the free trade package's approach to pricing is illustrated by the cost of welfare in developed countries. As unemployment goes up, so does the cost of welfare, but the numbers of those in work who earn enough to pay for the welfare of others falls. In the UK, social security expenditure was 26.6 per cent of government expenditure in 1990–91. This rose to 28.7 per cent in 1991–92, and to 29.5 per cent in 1992–93.[40] With unemployment at around 3 million in March 1993, costs will be higher again in 1993–94. Meanwhile the tax base – the number of people paying taxes which pay for welfare – is dropping. The government either has to raise taxes and U-turn on a central feature of the free trade package, or cut welfare.

The number of people reliant on welfare had risen in the trade liberalizing 1980s. The number of UK families receiving Supplementary Benefit or Income Support rose from 2.9 million in 1979 to 4.1 million in 1989; the individuals involved rose from 4.6 million to 7 million.[41] The number of people with incomes below 50 per cent of average rose from 6.4 million (10.6 per cent) in 1979 to 11.8 million (22 per cent) in 1989. The House of Commons Social Security Committee deemed 22 per cent of all families with dependent children to be in poverty in 1989. These rising welfare costs and the rising numbers involved show how the present economic system is spreading inequality.

In the USA, the public outcry over the cost of health care insurance led to Hillary Clinton's policy search for how to reduce the high costs of private insurance. Health care is now 13.5 per cent of US GDP, over twice the proportion of UK GDP spent on health care. Ironically, the UK's National Health Service (NHS) is now being restructured on market lines – inspired by US health economists! The administrative overheads of the US privately-based health care system are more than double the *full* cost of running the UK NHS.[42] Meanwhile, the UK government is attempting to persuade people that the cost of the NHS must be brought under control. Markets in health provision and services are being introduced, with whole new bureaucracies being set up to buy and sell health care. Similar market reforms have been brought into UK social security and there is talk of the need for fundamental reform. For reform, read cuts. The social security budget, which pays for those put out of work by the effects of free trade's economic restructuring, now threatens the capacity of the UK government to meet its own borrowing targets and it will be the poorest and most defenceless who will inevitably suffer disproportionately.

By contrast, in the midst of World War II, when Sir William Beveridge built his plan for the modern UK welfare state around the notion of social insurance, he did so to tackle what he called the five Giants: Want, Ignorance, Squalor, Idleness and Disease.[43] The crisis of war was an opportunity for social planners to prepare for better things. Everyone knew what he meant by the 'Giants'. Even if people had not experienced them, they saw and knew the indignity of these. Beveridge did not apologise for his vision. How different from today.

Costing food

Food is another classic case where failure to internalize full environmental and social costs has been damaging.[44] On every continent, the policies which serve interests of traders are threatening the capacity of local farmers to feed their populations. The numbers of people leaving or being driven from the land is huge. Recent figures put the world's rural population at an estimated 2.9 billion people out of a total 5.3 billion.[45] If that rural population was to be reduced to the levels of, say Canada or Australia, 1.9 billion people would leave the land for towns and cities, with consequent enormous changes in land tenure and ecological stability.[46]

The way food has been costed and the drive for efficiency has led to enormous reductions in the numbers employed on the land in the industrialized world. At the turn of the century, 38 per cent of the US population worked on the land, now it is 3 per cent. The size of farms has increased markedly. The US Office of Technology Assessment (OTA) estimates that the 50,000 largest US farms will produce 75 per cent of all US food by the year 2000.[47] In the UK, between 1980 and 1990, almost 20,000 full-time farmers and 50,000 farmworkers lost their jobs, the total dropping from 366,034 full- and part-time agricultural jobs in 1980 to 293,053 in 1990, a fall of 20 per cent.[48] Across Europe, a similar picture is emerging.

Free traders will argue that the loss of jobs and heritage is the cost of cheap food and the advantage is that the proportion of a household budget expended on food has dropped. The average UK household in 1990 spent around 13 per cent of its income on food, a third of the proportion spent 40 years ago. There are hidden costs to this approach, including: the nitrate pollution of water from fertiliser run-off; pesticide residues; the loss of wildlife and habitat; the massive increase in transport costs and damage through roads and pollution; and the £10 worth of packaging each UK family buys each week (90 per cent of which is thrown away after a single use).[49] These are the overt results and hidden environmental costs of agricultural intensification, which are excluded from the costs of the so-called cheap food, and ushered in by market forces.

Affluent consumers and Northern countries can shop from the world's bread basket, but they have to trade for the pleasure. The UK has come to rely increasingly on imported foods. Even in conventional terms the folly of this policy is apparent. It creates unnecessary economic strains and more goods have to be exported to set against the cost of imported food. Concern is rising about the UK food trade gap. Here is a country blessed with ample water, a soft climate, and yet its food import bill is immense, £6.3 billion more in 1991 than its food exports.[50] The UK Government's response to this trade gap has been to encourage more exports, not to stop imports of what could perfectly simply and effectively be grown here. In 1992, the UK food industry responded; exports grew by 13 per cent, but imports grew by 8 per cent. So while UK companies exported their poultry products for example, others imported French birds. Such trade is almost as ludicrous as bottles of water jetting across the Atlantic from Europe.

Experience, particularly in time of war, suggests that food security is not just an issue of balancing trade accounts. Nation states such as the USA in the 1980s and the UK in Victorian times can and do run horrendous balance of trade deficits – but most states, even rich ones, are nervous about food dependency. One of the unwritten responsibilities of state machines is to ensure reasonable supplies of food. Arguments start, however, over what is an acceptable price for such food. It may often be a choice between who benefits from cheap food versus self-produced food.

By the late 19th century, UK policy was dominated by manufacturers and traders who favoured *cheap food*. Food imports really only became a significant proportion of domestic consumption when transport became easier and costs fell, eg for meat when refrigeration became possible in the late nineteenth century.[51] The repeal of the Corn Laws in the mid nineteenth century ended the protection of the home grown cereal markets and made more distant trade possible, but did not encourage it directly. The UK food policy became an appendage to its trade policy rather than geared to meet the needs of its people. The UK manufactured goods for export and fed its workers on colonially-derived food at lower cost than protected home agriculture or European sources could produce. So, the classical free trade argument on food is to buy food on the world market, rather than to subsidize or ensure that there is security of home supply. Cheap food enables employers to hire cheap labour.

From the South's perspective, a cheap food policy does not have a positive ring. The so-called world price of grains, for example, is actually the price set by subsidized exports from the over-producing Northern blocs. Developing countries' agriculture cannot actually compete with these artificially low prices, dependent as the latter are on energy intensive methods and polluting inputs and, often, state subsidies. The imports of such food to the South undermines the production of local food staples. Another threat comes from the demands of the world's aid and trade system (plus the imperative of debt repayment), such that Southern countries gear their economies around exporting food. Lands which could produce staple crops are put down to cash crops for export. The shape of agriculture is quickly geared to others' needs. If subsidized agriculture systems such as the Common Agricultural Policy, with its massive surpluses produced by intensive farming, bring one well-documented set of environmental and social problems, free trade brings another.

Globally, the figures on the failure to meet food needs are sobering. According to the UN Children's Fund (UNICEF), one in five persons in the developing world suffers from chronic hunger – 800 million people in Africa, Asia and Latin America. Over 2 billion people subsist on diets deficient in the vitamins and minerals essential for normal growth and development, and for preventing premature death and such disabilities as blindness and mental retardation.[52] The great irony is that there is more than enough food to go around. It's what UNICEF calls the 'paradox of plenty'.[53]

Farm subsidies

The talks in the GATT Uruguay Round have been dominated by a battle between the US, the EC and, to a lesser extent, the group of exporters known as the Cairns Group (Australia, New Zealand, Brazil, Argentina and others). The aim of the Uruguay Round has been to reduce subsidies, the argument has been over what is a subsidy. Each group has accused the other of subsidizing their farms more than their competitors. Australia has poured out a series of reports accusing Europe of undermining its efforts to practise unsubsidized free trade.[54] The USA has in turn accused Canada and Australia of subsidizing their farmers more than itself.[55] And the OECD every year accuses all of them![56]

The truth is that most countries subsidize their farmers, but they do it in different ways and for different reasons. And why not? Does the state have a responsibility to ensure that its citizens are fed? Surely the experience of wars,[57] trade wars[58] and economic recessions[59] all justify a nation in ensuring that a good quality diet is reliably available for its citizens? Alas, the subsidies are often for different purposes in the free trade battle. David Morris of the Institute for Self-Reliance in Washington DC, USA, illustrates what subsidies are often for with the case of Brazil:

> 'Brazilian per capita production of basic foodstuffs (rice, black beans, manioc and potatoes) fell 13 per cent from 1977 to 1984. Per capita output of exportable foodstuffs (soybean, oranges, cotton, peanuts and tobacco) jumped 15 per cent. Today some 50 per cent of Brazil suffers malnutrition. Yet one leading Brazilian agronomist still calls export promotion "a matter of national survival". In the global village, a nation survives by starving its people.'[60]

In the next chapter we look further at how free traders use regulations and standards in their interest.

9. On Regulations and Standards

To free traders regulations are another word for protectionism. A business seminar reviewing 'the menace of environmentalism' after the Earth Summit in 1992 was concerned that environmental regulations would be covert protectionist devices.[1] Deregulating trade always carries the threat that environmental and health protection standards will move to the lowest common denominator of a trading block. Deregulation encourages competition and a hunt for the lowest wage and standards. As industrialist and US Presidential candidate, Ross Perot, said about NAFTA:

> 'If I can build a factory in Mexico, pay my labour a dollar an hour, hire a 25 year old workforce, have little or no health-care [costs], little or no retirement [costs], have no pollution or environmental controls, then . . . trying to compete with me, you cannot even get into the ring with those numbers.'[2]

Under deregulation, barriers to trade are dismantled and prices fall, allowing a rise in trade and consumption. This is sometimes seen as enough to justify the claim of greater efficiency and wealth for all. However, where the market is flawed, as it is in externalizing so many critical costs, it will actually lead to *less* efficiency. Any increase in consumption will bring with it pollution and waste, in the form of external costs which fall upon society. This is the phenomenon known as 'ecological dumping', where the cost of pollution or waste to the environment is excluded from conventional accounting and financial practices.

Reducing standards

Privatization of state water authorities in 1989 in the UK exposed previously hidden costs and may threaten standards. For years, environmentalists and consumer groups had criticized UK authorities for not meeting tougher European water contamination standards.[3] After privatization, the industry was faced with what three years on had turned into a bill of £29 billion. Scotland's bill is estimated at 1992 prices to be an additional £4–5 billion.[4] Despite this, the new private water companies were in 1992 among the most profitable sectors of the UK economy, mostly due to substantial price increases. Now that it has shareholders' interests to protect, the industry has begun to argue that public expectations of high water safety standards – for contaminants such as pesticide residues and nitrates from fertiliser run-offs[5] – should be toned down. European standards, it says, are unnecessarily high.

After a decade of being forced onto the defensive over water contamination by groups such as Friends of the Earth (FOE),[6] and being forced to redouble efforts to clean up their act, the privatized water companies are now facing the awful truth that the cost of the clean-up will be huge. They will have to introduce expensive filtration plants to take out the residues, and will have to stop farmers polluting in the first place. Faced with these bills which would erode profits, it is not surprising the companies are fuelling the debate about whether tough standards are necessary. Whether they will get away with this public relations initiative remains to be seen; much depends on how vigilant both public and environmental NGOs are. As we will see later in this chapter, companies may one moment argue for tough standards (to squeeze smaller companies' costs) and the next moment for weaker ones. Only the public and the environment have a consistent interest to maintain and improve standards, as they carry the true long term costs. Whatever happens in the case of UK water, the conflict between corporate profits and protecting environmental and human health will continue, with the issue of standards at its centre.

Food standards

Even powerful countries can be forced to accept low standards. Germany's centuries-old pure beer laws, the *Reinheitsgebot*, under which beer could only be made from malt, hops and barley, with no additives or sugar, has been overturned and any EC-produced beer may be sold in Germany. Similarly, as we saw in Chapter 6, the Danes had to give up the chance of tough regulations to encourage reusable bottles. Under the GATT, there will be a global harmonization of standards to the international level. In almost every case this will mean less control by governments, a threat to standards, and more opportunity for TNCs to do what they like.

In the rush to meet the self-imposed EC deadline of removing barriers to internal trade by the end of 1992, harmonization of standards has often reduced them even, as happened with some food standards, below the lowest common denominator. When lists of permitted additives were harmonized, all countries adopted an expanded list. Germany, which previously only permitted the use of 150 additives with an 'E' approval number and Greece which used to permit only 120, will now both have to permit 412. Even the UK with the largest initial 'E' list of over 300 will rise to the 412 total.[7] Consumers had been urging a reduction in additive use but industry won an expansion. Regulations can also reduce diversity. For example, faced with new EC regulations on seeds, the Director of the UK Brogdale Horticultural Trust, which has 2,300 varieties of apples, says only 20 or 30 will be worth registering because of the cost of paying a registration fee. This means it will be illegal to sell the others.[8] In the negotiation of EC-wide standards, multinational food manufacturer interests have taken precedence over consumer and public protection interests.

GATT also has a potentially huge influence on food standards. 'Sanitary and phytosanitary measures,' the extraordinary phrase GATT uses to mean animal and plant, ie food, standards, come under a special chapter of the GATT 1991 draft. Though food standards may be set by governments, for international trade, they will be subject to disputes settlement procedures in which the GATT will rely on, or be 'influenced' by in GATT's words, the standards set by a little known UN body, the Codex Alimentarius Commission. Some food safety standards may even turn out to be 'technical barriers to trade', and so could be overturned by the GATT, as we will explain below.[9]

Technical barriers to trade

Changing standards can be used to squeeze the competition. Richer companies can afford to invest in new technologies to enable higher standards to be met, but companies will also source products to lower standards if they can get away with it. The transition to the EC's single market has already threatened product quality by linking it to a notion of 'good manufacturing practice' (GMP). This, as Dr Erik Millstone of the University of Sussex's Science Policy Research Unit indicates, merely rubber-stamps standards which manufacturers choose but consumers would rather were tougher. The EC has now replaced the notion of GMP with an equally opaque phrase *Quantum Satis* – meaning a level of use which is supposedly sufficient.[10] The sections of the GATT on Technical Barriers to Trade (TBT) could, as we have already mentioned, threaten existing standards.

The preamble to the current GATT draft on TBT, for instance, states the 'desire': 'to ensure that technical regulations and standards . . . do not create unnecessary barriers to international trade.' It goes on in Article 2.2 to say:

> 'Parties shall ensure that technical regulations are not prepared, adopted or applied with a view to or with the effect of creating unnecessary obstacles to international trade. For this purpose, technical regulations shall not be more trade-restrictive than necessary to fulfill a legitimate

objective, taking account of the risks non-fulfillment would take . . .'

The EC's standards-setting machinery, for example, is liaising closely on harmonizing its standards with world bodies such as the International Standards Organization (ISO). In theory, there will be a seemless web of agreement between the UK, the British Standards Institute (BSI–controller of the 'kitemark'), the EC and the ISO. Whoever is given responsibility for setting standards and judging when they are 'legitimate' rather than spurious – this would have to be in consultation with the ISO – will carry considerable power in the new free trade order. Food standards are a case in point.

The Codex Alimentarius Commission

Codex, as the Commission is known, will become the focus of world food standards under present GATT proposals. It was set up in 1963 as, 'a result of a widely perceived need to facilitate the world trade in foods . . . Internationally accepted standards were seen as the means.'[11] Trade interests were written in from the start. It is an intergovernmental body, run jointly by the FAO and the World Health Organization (WHO). Over 130 member nations work together to establish standards on subjects, such as pesticide residues, additives, veterinary drug residues and labelling, and on specific commodities, such as cereals, fish products, meat, tropical fruit and vegetables. In practice, only 105 nations participated from 1989 to 1991.

Decisions on standards made by the working parties are subject to the approval of the full Commission which meets every two years. At present, member nations may use Codex standards as guidelines, especially when negotiating the complexities of the international food trade. Yet some countries have already begun to adopt Codex standards as a result of the GATT approach. Nations are neither obliged nor pressured to alter nationally established regulations to those established by Codex. But when and if the Final Act is ratified, GATT contracting parties will be obliged to set standards in line with those established by Codex on as wide a basis as possible. Any national food standards set more strictly than those could be challenged as a violation of GATT if they were applied to imports, and the offending country would have to prove the scientific legitimacy of its higher standard.

Multinational or trading companies are likely to argue that international standards should take precedence over national standards. Many NGOs fear that this will lead to a downward pressure on standards, just when for health and environmental reasons they should be strengthened. For example, a country might prohibit the sale of food containing certain pesticide residues for public health or environmental reasons, but if internationally determined lower limits, established by Codex, for the pesticide were available, another country could challenge the ban as an unfair barrier to trade. If the offending country then failed to justify the scientific legitimacy of its higher standard (and Codex will be the body expected to provide the scientific guidance), it would have two choices. It could apply its standard to home-produced goods only and use lower ones for imports or pay some sort of compensation to the country that had lost opportunity to trade, or keep its standard applied to both domestic and imported items and face trade-related retaliation in many sectors of its economy. The new GATT will allow 'cross-retaliations' of this type. In short, Codex is about to be an extremely important world body.

A recent study for the UK National Food Alliance (NFA) and a coalition of 30 NGOs around the world reviewed an entire two year cycle of Codex meetings and identified the national and business affiliations of the participants – a total of 2578 people – by contacting companies and embassies and governments world-wide.[12] The study found that during the last full session (session 19) of 1989–91, which included 16 committees as well as meetings of the full Commission:

- 105 countries participated and 140 of the largest multinational food and agrochemical companies.
- The vast majority (81 per cent) of non-governmental participants or national delegations represented industry.
- Twenty six representatives from public interest groups compared to 660 industry representatives participated on Codex committees.
- Nestle, the largest food company in the world, sent 38 representatives in total to Codex committee meetings, more than most countries.
- Most representation came from rich, Northern countries: 60 per cent came from Europe and North America despite these regions accounting for only 15 per cent of world population. Poor countries of the South were dramatically underrepresented – only 7 per cent from Africa and 10 per cent from Latin America.
- There were 381 participants at two meetings of the committee on standards for food additives and contaminants; 41 per cent representated TNCs or industry federations, including 73 representatives from some of the largest food and agrochemical companies in the world.
- Of the 374 participants at two meetings of the committee on pesticide residue levels, 127 (33 per cent) came from agrochemical and food corporations – 44 from the world's top 20 agrochemical companies; only 80 participants represented the interests of developing countries.
- The USA sent more representatives to Codex than any other country (49 per cent of them representing industry) and almost twice as many as the entire continent of Africa.

This pattern of participation in Codex Alimentarius procedures is deeply disturbing. Professor Philip James, Chair of the WHO committee that produced the 1990 report on diet and health, has said of Codex:

> 'Nutrition development would literally be stopped in its tracks. Codex is dominated by the food industry. In terms of labelling foods, it believes in labelling the toxins in the kinds of gobblydygoop only a chemist would understand.'[13]

The NFA commissioned a study on the workings of Codex's advisory committee on additives, the WHO–FAO Joint Expert Committee on Food Additives (JECFA). This included the following startling observation made to Dr Erik Millstone by a senior toxicologist at the US Food and Drug Administration (FDA), that: 'if he were to conduct himself as some members of JECFA routinely do, he would by now be in jail'[14] – meaning that the conduct was neither ethical nor legal in the view of a civil servant. Dr Melanie Miller, then of Greenpeace International and formerly with the UK's Consumers Association, exposed what went on in the JECFA approval process for a new sweetener: two scientists, members of JECFA, had been paid as consultants by the manufacturer of the sweetener, and, 'worked hard in JECFA meetings to persuade the committee to accept the weakest possible standards, despite concerns about immune system effects, and a lack of studies on some specific aspects of safety.'[15]

Codex's participation is biased toward the interests of industry. However, following pressure from consumer NGOs, Codex has begun to encourage member nations to hold meetings in their own countries with both industry and public interest groups. This has started in Denmark, the Netherlands and the UK, but there is a danger that unless the international meetings are radically reformed, these national meetings could be token democracy, leaving the real work unchanged at international level. Nevertheless, openness and effective pressure can affect things, as the following example shows.

The hormone vote

Since the 1980s, the USA and EC have been at loggerheads over hormones. The EC banned these for use in cattle in the mid 1980s following consumer health concerns. Beef imports from the USA, where hormone growth promoters are widely used, were subsequently banned. The USA saw this as an unnecessary health regulation and retaliated with a tariff on almost $100 million worth of EC food imports.[16]Pharmaceutical companies and beef traders on both sides of the Atlantic are desperate to end the EC hormone ban. At stake here is whether factory farmed, feedlot beef is to undercut less intensive production and whether consumer protection is to take priority over cheapness of production. No consumers on either side of the Atlantic were or are calling for hormone-fed beef.

In 1991, a Codex meeting discussed a US proposal to approve the use of hormones in beef-rearing, as scientifically acceptable. This would have overturned the EC's ban. Dr Melanie Miller attended this Codex meeting, representing the International Organisation of Consumers Unions (IOCU) and was able to prepare a briefing paper on the spot. By arguing that consumers see no need for extra hormones to rear beef and are worried about abuses and being human guinea pigs, IOCU was able to encourage countries which normally fall in line with the USA to reject the US proposal in a vote of 27 to 13.[17] The Codex vote did not go down well with Dr Lester Crawford of the FDA. He argued that the European ban on hormone use and residues in meat was unjustified and unscientific. The 1991 vote, however, had a sting in the tail. Another discussion was scheduled for 1993![18]

The vote was a welcome acknowledgment that consumer wishes should be a factor in setting food standards. Consumers have good grounds for concern. In July 1991, the UK Ministry of Agriculture, Fisheries and Food (MAFF) had to introduce tougher controls on drug residues in meat[19] just as the first case of residues of the illegal growth promoter Clenbuterol, known as 'Angel dust', in meat for sale in the UK was announced.[20] If producers are under pressure to reduce costs and compete on cross-border markets, any speed-up in production looks tantalising, which is why rigorous standards and enforcement are essential, though not loved by free traders as they add to costs.

The trade in live farm animals

The effect of the EC single market on UK animal welfare standards also illustrates how removal of barriers to trade can threaten standards. It also allows regulations to be used to help concentrate markets, for example, by helping close small abattoirs, thus forcing animals to be transported longer distances for slaughter. This means more transport and worse conditions for the animals.

Britain has longstanding laws to limit how far live animals may be transported before they are slaughtered.[21] In October 1991, after pressure from NGOs, the European Commission allowed the UK to keep its rules banning export of horses for slaughter.[22] However, the Royal Society for the Prevention of Cruelty to Animals found that UK rules which demand export animals have a ten hour rest near a port prior to embarcation, with food, water and an inspection by a vet, were being broken.[23] The UK law that animals must be fed and watered every 12 hours was replaced in 1992 by an EC rule requiring this only every 24 hours. The ironic thing about the live export trade is that most of the animals will be slaughtered on or soon after arrival at their destination. The European Parliament and the UK

Farm Animal Welfare Council has suggested that the EC should encourage slaughter as close to the farm where animals are reared as possible.[24] But many small, local abattoirs in the UK are closing down because they cannot afford to invest to meet EC meat hygiene standards. The UK Minister of Agriculture, when EC President in 1992, pledged Britain to pressure fellow EC members to improve welfare standards, while denying financial support to small abattoirs at home. Indeed, in 1993, it transpired that MAFF had drafted the new abattoir regulations more stringently than the EC had required. As a result, 80 per cent of UK abattoirs were deemed unfit, allowing more trade to go to the 20 per cent of large establishments, which already had a large share of the market in slaughtering animals. Smaller, local abattoirs would have stopped longer journeys than necessary, improved animal welfare, and cut down the chance of bacterial cross-infection spreading through the huge numbers of carcases which pass through giant plants.[25]

Concerned by their experience of standards being lowered in the trade, UK animal welfare NGOs lobbied hard to have appended to the Maastricht Treaty a declaration on animal welfare. The UK government did this, and the original draft declaration included a reference to animals as 'sentient beings'. But this reference was strongly opposed by the Spanish and French governments and the final declaration was therefore much weaker.[26] How that commitment will be interpreted is still another matter.

Stricter regulation to suit the powerful?

Powerful forces do not always want lower standards. Large corporations may sometimes unite with others within a sector to argue for higher standards to cut out medium and small firms. Every country has companies who made their name by raising the calibre and quality of the products. The free trade argument in favour of letting industry set its own standards may look attractive in a boom period, but in a slump higher standards look costly to company financiers. The advantages for companies of fewer or lower regulations under the free trade system are that regulations cost. They are a challenge to management; they put companies in regulated economies at a disadvantage compared to less regulated producers and processes. It was using these sorts of arguments, that the UK Prime Minister launched yet another deregulation initiative in February 1993.

The UK Minister of Agriculture enthusiastically backed the initiative,[27] after meeting food industry representatives and a barrage of right-wing criticisms about 'unnecessary' hygiene regulations which they felt contradicted the government's commitment to roll back the 'nanny state'. With food poisoning figures still going up, and being found by the

Industrial Society, which monitors industrial relations, to be in the top three reasons for absenteeism from work,[28] this was a strange time to relax hygiene control. The Department of Health also relaxed controls on temperatures at which chilled foods had to be kept, which were criticized by some as already inadequate, saying that the food industry found the previous controls 'too prescriptive' and enforcement officers found them 'unduly complex and difficult to enforce' – a clear statement of free trade ideology coming before public need.[29]

Standard setting does and should have a positive role. Planning laws, housing standards, common electrical-goods standards, product liability laws if goods do not meet set safety or performance criteria, all testify to their importance. The downside of standards is that larger companies may use them to squeeze smaller competitors or to push for fewer, lower controls. An example of the former is now emerging in the agrochemicals sector, where the higher costs of meeting environmental criteria is now being argued for by the big companies as a means to gain competitive edge. According to James Otter, General Manager of ICI Agrochemicals in the Nordic countries:

> 'Therefore in marked contrast to the past, the large corporations wishing to continue to do research should favour tougher, new environmental standards. The regulators, who were considered by some industry observers to constrain the activities of the business in the 1960s – 1980s, now provide the barriers to entry from generic producers as well as the force to maintain the incentive for research for yet further technical innovations.'[30]

These examples have shown how the public needs to be vigilant about standards. It is important always to find out who is pushing for standards either to go up or to go down, and to what ends industry and government will entertain standards being pushed up or down. The lesson behind the story of rising standards is that public pressure must be kept up – look how UK food hygiene standards are being undermined only three years after a period of food scandals, which forced a reluctant government to introduce a new Food Safety Act 1990. Sometimes public pressure can ally with industry interests, but the public – and certainly public interest groups – should be wary about being used by any powerful industry to squeeze its competitors, and thus decrease long term economic diversity.

For the last 500 years or so, the powerful have exploited trade to their advantage. Many of the world powers now extolling the virtues of free trade expanded their own economies and industrialized behind tariff barriers and then, in the colonial period, stopped others doing likewise. In the last century, the UK sent in gunboats to China to force open the Chinese economy, resulting in the so-called Opium Wars, all to benefit UK tea and commodity traders.[31] More recently, the World Bank, which today is one of the fiercest advocates of free trade and tight fiscal management in Africa, in the 1970s was encouraging African governments to invest in indiginous agricultural industries and to develop cash-cropping behind tariff barriers.

In the North, the old protectionism is still rampant. Both the UK and USA, vociferous countries in promoting the joys of free trade, have protected their textile industries which have delayed, with government support, the ending of the MFA set up two decades ago as a 'temporary' agreement. The list of protected sectors is long and includes the French computer industry, the Italian typewriter industry, and the European high definition TV industry.[32] The fundamental question is who sets the standards, and to what ends. Free trade agreements can clearly help the means and ends of the powerful, and not necessarily the interests of the average citizen.

10.

On Citizens and Democracy

Free trade shifts the power over economies and the quality of life further away from ordinary people. The subversion of democracy is nothing new, nor the exclusive property of free trade. In this chapter, we draw attention to the false promise of free trade, so often promoted as the economic theory that best introduces and ensures human liberty. In the name of free trade, deregulation can quietly disempower citizens. The potential for people to become full citizens of their countries and of the world is being eroded by a process in which a narrower ethic of consumerism – you are what you consume – triumphs. Free trade's ersatz global influence undermines the capacity of people to exert more control over their everyday lives. A centuries-old tension between cultural convergence and diversity is entering a new, critical phase.

Increasingly aware of this, throughout the world, popular pressure is having to fight to maintain, or restore, or improve democratic rights. But the present wave of trade liberalization is a qualitative set-back for the long march for democracy. If decisions about your life and environment – in its broadest sense – are taken by far-off people and bodies, it is almost impossible to affect those decisions directly. People are forced to confront the results of those distant decisions, rather than participate in them directly. It is easier to get to a local council or committee meeting, than to one the other side of the world. And once committees go global, they are quickly shrouded in gobbledygook, rules and regulations and cushioned or guarded by officials.

Free trade, promoting competition and claiming comparative advantage, cuts down the number of workers and the number of places where work occurs. As a result, local economies are sacrificed and soon suffer from a downward spiral of declining infrastructure, low morale and the blight of unemployment. Governments (both local and national) are relatively powerless against this widely accepted economic logic. Throughout the 1980s, if ever the UK government did acknowledge this local haemorrhage, its answers were limited and paltry. Local authorities competed for the favours of TNCs. One image promoted in the 1980s was 'the Park' – business parks, industrial parks, shoppings malls, heritage parks, theme parks, and garden exhibitions.

With the best will in the world, such developments are no substitute for a diverse local economy. A garden festival may mean an environmental clean-up of former industrial ground, as happened in Liverpool, Glasgow, the Potteries and South Wales, but it can rarely provide long term local economic answers. Local economic policy is required, but the scale of what has been lost and what has to be created is enormous. Local jobs are lost through the working of the market, and all people are offered, if they are lucky, is Enterprise Zones or EPZs, an excuse, as we saw in Chapter 7, for the state funding a few private companies. As people become aware of this process, and that essentially they are on their own, because the 'new' government style is supposedly 'non-interventionist', they are beginning to have to think of alternatives for local economic regeneration. In the South Wales valleys – devastated by the loss of mines and steel jobs – that process is beginning, linking the search for secure employment with the need to protect the environment.[1]

New bureaucracies

Mrs Thatcher's Conservative government was elected in 1979 with a commitment to reduce the power and influence of Quasi Autonomous Non Governmental Organisations (QUANGOs), bodies like health and water authorities which regulate and carry out administrative tasks on behalf of and funded by central government, but are technically semi-autonomous. In 1978–9 such bodies employed 1.2 million UK citizens and spent £14 billion annually.[2] Fourteen years later, after massive privatization, the number of QUANGOs had fallen from 1846 to 564, but any savings to the taxpayer were illusory.

The new QUANGOs, such as the National Rivers Authority or Training and Enterprise Councils and the remaining old ones such as the Medical Research Council spent £40 billion a year, three times the 1978–9 figure and 20 per cent more in real terms. These new QUANGOs have been made less accountable. Their boards are political or career appointees, subject to fewer or no democratic controls. Baroness Jean Denton, junior Minister of Trade and Industry and a former member of the Board of Directors of the UK's last home-owned car company, Rover, now gradually merging with Honda of Japan, is responsible for 804 public appointments to QUANGOs. As a result of this new patronage or 'matronage', the loss of local control – over water, health, education, police, and schools – was one of the central features of life in the deregulating 1980s.

Consumer or citizen?

A key element of the social vision propounded by free traders is that of *the consumer*, rather than the citizen. Though the *word* citizen may be used (as in the UK Citizen's Charter), the reality is still *consumer*. The difference is critical. The consumer choses between products on the shelf, designed, built and profited from by others; the consumer is an end-user. In contrast, the citizen is actively involved in all stages of a process, directly or by representation.[3] The word consumer indicates at worst a passive role and at best someone who can only act on the market through their purchasing power.

Tourism is a form of consumption which illustrates how culture has been turned into a traded commodity. During 1992, 500 million people travelled around the world for pleasure, generating $2 trillion and providing 130 million jobs. Tourism is overtaking oil and arms sales as the largest generator of income and employment, but it can also be the cause of social injustice and environmental degradation. Pollution around the Mediterranean is well known. European capitals are being worn away, and there is soil erosion and litter on Alpine and Himalayan slopes. Local communities are threatened all over the world; a 'heritage' culture emerges, selling the past, and too often damaging the future. The Chair of the International Federation of Tour Operations in 1990 said:

> 'We have to rethink our approach, not simply in pursuit of economic objectives but ecological and sociological ones as well. We have to find a sustainable balance. If we don't our successors will never forgive us.'[4]

Cultural diversity is a sensitive issue. There is little point in romanticizing a fictional, glorious, cultural past, but equally it is foolish to ignore the tremendous cultural power being heralded by the global reach of televisual media. As the electronic revolution continues, international channels for radio and TV multiply. At first sight, choice for the consumer has increased, but control over them has diminished. The global media market is controlled by a small number of international companies, and presents relatively few images to its viewers. 'Dallas-ification', where US fantasy entertainment becomes the global vision, can foster new consumer demands and undermine traditional cultures so fast that people have little time to reflect on what is happening and then, if they regret it or wish to recover important features of their original culture and lifestyle, it is too late.[5] Helena Norberg-Hodge's study of Ladakh, Northern India is a classic study of this process.[6]

Consumers in and against the market

Anyone familiar with the daily work of consumer organizations knows that most of their effort is spent on arguing with the market-place. Consumers rarely know the significance or implications of goods they are offered by retailers, not because they are stupid or unthoughtful, but because information is withheld from them. The act of consumption is an exchange of cash for goods or services and the implications may be long term or far away. One reason we favour a shortening of trade routes is to make this structured ignorance – not the fault of consumers, as we will see for the issue of labelling information – harder for traders to capitalize upon.

Trade detaches production from consumption. Both producers and consumers find it difficult to see or empathize with the other end of the chain. In winter, UK diners can now savour the delights of fresh green summer vegetables grown across the world, without knowing the seedy underside of this trading connection – malnutrition. We may like to drink real orange juice, some of it coming from Brazil, without knowing that plantations of oranges are being planted to quench this thirst, which throw small farmers off the land. Brazil has a high infant mortality rate: 57 deaths per 1000 live births in 1990 compared to 8 in the UK.[7] At present, there is little way of knowing or caring about the ecological and social cost of consuming what is produced far away. Deregulating global trade makes consumer awareness even harder. This is a problem for the consumer movement, but a problem now being debated.

Consumerism's three waves

In the post war period, there have been three discernible phases and styles of consumerism. By 'consumerism' we mean consumer movements dedicated to arguing for the consumers' interest. The GATT has brought a discussion within consumerism to a head.

In the first consumer movement, the focus was on value-for-money, information and labelling. Is this food or fridge or washing machine better value for money than that? Can the purchaser get legal redress or the money back if things go wrong? The first wave of consumerism has been brilliantly and justly successful particularly in more affluent countries. It captured consumers' minds and refined the post-war boom but it is a model predicated upon wealth and a role for the consumer as a refiner within the market mechanism.

The second wave of consumerism is most closely associated with the tough, investigative, anti-corporatist consumer work of Ralph Nader. His seminal book *Unsafe at any speed*[8] exposed how a multinational car company had continued to produce and market an unsafe car, after estimating that insurance claims on accidents due to poor design and dangerous siting of its petrol tank would be a cheaper option than redesigning the car.

The wider thesis was that large corporations could not be trusted to look after ordinary consumers' interest. It follows that the task of the consumer group – more often described as a public interest group, a key change of emphasis – was to champion the individual: 'us' versus 'them'. The logic is simple but realistic. If we are citizens, and they (the companies) want us to consume (for why else do they try to mould our consumer consciousness?),[9] the task of consumerism is to encourage people to see themselves as active citizens, not just passive purchasers.

The third wave is what has emerged in the 1980s, as a marriage of environmentalism and citizenship. Food has been one of its major expressions and grounds for development. This wave is sometimes called the new consumer movement. It has taken distinct but related forms: one ethical, the other ecological.

In general, the ecological consumer asks about a product's quality. What is its impact, not just on the purchaser's pocket but on health, the environment, distant parts of the world? The ecological consumer recognises the limits of individual solutions to global problems. 'Sure, I can do my bit, but there is a limit to what I can do'. Heavily influenced by both the new public health and the environmental movements, this third wave questions the technological fetishism of post war growth. It raises the question of need. Why is this process or product needed? Who says so? On what grounds?

The ethical wing of this new wave consumerism is asked to buy appropriately, to invest ethically. Price is not the only or even main criterion of successful purchasing. Investment research and ethical investment funds have sprouted in all Western countries: the Council of Economic Priorities in the USA, the Ethical Investment Research Service in the UK.

All over the First World, Third World oriented and solidarity movements have set up trading wings – to support production, to cut distribution chains, to help indigenous production, to by-pass boycotts. In the USA and Europe magazines and guides to ethical consumerism have been published.[10] Dissatisfaction with the initially narrow consumerist position on trade has grown, particularly among environmental and development NGOs. What is at stake is not just whether there are goods but how they are produced, by whom and for whom? And not just what decisions are made, but how they are made, which is why the lessons learned from attempts to get better labels on goods is so pertinent to the trade debate.

The restriction of information

The European single market promised industry greater efficiency by deregulating or harmonizing national standards, and consumers cheaper products and more information through improved labels.[11] This latter has not happened. Information, the theory goes, makes the market work more efficiently by helping consumers make informed choices. In practice, the history of the struggle by public health and consumer advocates to get full nutrition labelling in the UK and throughout the EC suggests there are strong forces wishing to withold information rather than release it.

Consumers are waiting for better nutritional information 19 years after the UK Committee on Medical Aspects of Food Policy (COMA) first recommended it. The neat boxes of 'Nutritional Information' on the side of many UK food products are strongly criticized by public health NGOs for being only voluntary and often misleading. For instance, companies disguise a high sugar content by listing nutrients under three sugar headings. Only after years of campaigning has the EC decided labels will have to be to standard formats from October 1993. Unfortunately, there will be more than one format and, according to the Coronary Prevention Group's research for the UK government, they are formats least intelligible to and least favoured by consumers.[12] In any case, these labels are purely voluntary.

This reluctance by European industry and the EC to divulge information is not restricted to nutrition. In the new area of labelling of genetically engineered products, the EC is being similarly industry-friendly and consumer-indifferent. The EC's draft Novel Foods Regulation is obtusely worded, but is being taken to mean that the Scientific Committee on Food may request that certain genetically engineered foods be labelled as such, but there is no mandatory requirement.[13] Paradoxically, in an EC regulation on organic foods, a statement was inserted by the Commission at the last minute to the effect that genetically engineered foods may also be deemed organic.[14] This undermines the capacity of consumers to use the 'organic' symbol as a guarantee that it is *not* genetically engineered and undermines the integrity of organic foods.

Since the early 1980s, food additives in Europe have had an 'E' number to indicate that the EC approves their use.[15] At least the 'E' system set the principle that consumers have the right to know what is put into their food, even if in infinitessimal amounts. Yet, when NGOs across Europe campaigned for this principle to be extended to a 'P' label system telling consumers if foods have been produced with the help of pesticides,[16] the food and agrichemical industries and the UK government argued that if consumers are concerned about avoiding pesticides, they should eat organic products.[17] The EC has consistently favoured industry and, if not withholding all information from consumers, has given industry the benefit of any doubt.

Consumer labelling often tells only part of the story – that which helps marketing. The environmental movement, particularly in Europe, has pressed for green labels, but there is some scepticism about the value of such labelling. Unfortunately, environmental labelling is hard to produce, in part because there would be too much information on it.[18] Another problem is whether the label should convey information about the product only, or the process which lies behind its manufacture. The issue raised for consumers may not just be the product itself but the adverse environmental effect of its production – often thousands of miles away. Therefore, to put responsibility upon the individual consumer in the free trade system to know and, through their choice miraculously to overcome both lack of information and controls on far-off effects, is ridiculous.

People's lives are made, not just by *products* but by social *processes*. This is an important distinction at the heart of our case for the New Protectionism – the difference between being a consumer linked to the world by a cash relationship, and a citizen who acts in and on the world. In theory, citizens should have a hand in shaping the world by helping frame policies and laws which enable them as private actors to operate constructively. The free market model of the consumer is more passive, leaving the framing of the world's business to trade and the market mechanism. As we have seen, neither are up to the job on their own.

Free choice?

Free trade is supposed to be synonymous with free choice. Everyone likes to think they choose. In practice, everyone chooses within limits set by income, culture, aspirations, family, etc. They are also bombarded with messages not just to consume, but to consume in particular ways, through particular products, buying certain brands of anything from cigarettes to banks. Writing of the 1980s when British banks were deregulated, former adman Martin Davidson wrote: 'Deregulation and competition have entailed . . . an orgy of advertising and consumer solicitation.'[19] Banks which had previously been just banks, were marketed as companies with carefully contrived connotations: UK banks became listening banks, action banks, thoroughbred banks, 'yes' banks. It would be laughable if we had not just experienced it. The key to this transition is branding, and brands are crucial in global markets:

> 'Brands are products with something extra. All brands are products, but not all products are brands, and the difference is advertising. That extra is called *added value* . . . These added values were the object of 50s conspiracy theory, 60s satire and 70s semiology. In the 80s they became all-powerful, an esperanto of desire and relevance, the language of the tribe.'[20]

When TNCs go shopping for companies, the brand can be as important as the manufacturing facilities. A 1990 survey for the world's most powerful brands concluded that top was Coca-Cola, then Sony, Mercedes–Benz,

Kodak, Disney, Nestle, Toyota, McDonald's, IBM and Pepsi-Cola.[21]

If branding is very important to global markets, so is getting brands into brains at the earliest opportunity. Television is the main medium for targeting the young; an estimated 90 per cent of advertising is aimed at under 20 age groups. As a result, 85 per cent of children have been found to ask parents to buy them something seen on TV, the 'pester-power' factor.[22] With the vast majority of the annual £558 million spent on UK TV advertising for food and drinks being for products generally regarded as sugary and fatty, it is no wonder that children's consumption of convenience and snack foods has risen while their consumption of fresh fruit and vegetables has dropped by up to a third.[23]

Auditors in the UK can now ascribe a financial value to a company's brand(s) and include their worth as an asset in company accounts. What does this say about modern life? That we are what we consume? Bigger brands make for bigger company profits with little assessment of any social effect. Even attempts to use advertising for socially more equitable ends are fraught – only the biggest charities can afford to advertise.

In conclusion, we have suggested that the free trade system brings with it an important and under-explored distinction, between consumers and citizens. We are not arguing for a mythic, past world where no-one consumed; it is inevitable that humans consume. What is at stake is what *sort* of consumption, how extensive it is, its impact on the environment and social equity, how many goods are consumed, how long goods last and what effects the decision-makers have over the processes which make the goods. Just when society has the potential to enfranchise its people into citizens, it offers them an inferior package – the chance to be consumers, if they can afford to be.

In Part Four, we move on to what could and should be done to protect the future. We sketch out an agenda for the way the New Protectionism could begin to tackle the problems of free trade, but we start with a current movement that falls somewhere between the two – the alternative trading movement, which offers a rich seam of thought and experience on the practicalities of trading against the interests of the powerful.

PART FOUR

Protecting the Future

'Protectionism is . . . viewed as the only alternative to "free trade". Such stereotyping is unwarranted. However, we would be willing to accept the label of "protectionist" if it were understood that what we want to protect are: efficient national policies of cost internalisation; health, insurance and safety standards; and a reasonable minimum standard of living for citizens. Historically these benefits have come from national policies, not from global economic integration. Protecting these hard-won social gains from blind standards – lowering competition in the global market is what we are interested in – not the protection of some inefficient entrepreneur who wants to grow mangoes in Sweden.'[1]

Herman Daly and Robert Goodland

11. Trading Alternatives

Piecemeal efforts or bolt-on additions to existing economic policies are not enough to foster more appropriate use of the earth's resources. Nor can it be left to consumers on their own to turn whole economies round to a more appropriate form. Laws need to change; aspirations be redirected; and policies co-ordinated. The cycle of more international trade, which threatens the environment, social justice and sustainable employment, has to be broken. So what prevents it? There are a number of reasons: vested interests, a narrow vision of economics (which externalizes environmental and human costs, for example), and also, unfortunately, a dearth of radical thinking about alternative visions for trade. It is some of these that we explore in this chapter, looking at the goals of the practical alternatives currently on offer.

In the past when trade became an issue – for instance in the mid to late 19th century UK – critics suggested the case for *fair trade* rather than free trade, so the distinction between free and fair trade is not new. In 1903, the British politician, Chamberlain, gave a speech on tariffs called 'Free trade versus fair trade.' Since the repeal of the Corn Laws in the 1840s, there had been a plethora of subtly different positions, dividing mainly between those who wished to encourage home production and those who said it was better to harvest from the world.

In the imperial-colonial period, free traders won the argument for feeding Britain from external agricultural production, with the convincing reason that, not only was it cheaper to produce food abroad, but it meant that there was an 'exchange' since the colonies would buy (or be persuaded to buy) UK manufactured goods. Thus, India would produce the cotton, but Lancashire mills would weave it and sell it back to the Indians (forcibly). This sometimes brutal 'exchange' troubled liberal, progressive and leading working class thinkers greatly. The Fabian Society was split at the turn of the century over the issue, and in something of a classic compromise, settled half-way between backing tariffs and free trade, to George Bernard Shaw's irritation.[1]

Shaw described himself as, 'a Protectionist right down to my boots'. Influenced by thinkers such as William Morris, he argued a fiercely anti-imperialist line. He was, like us, against free trade as an excuse for 'sweated labour', both at home and abroad, and he thought state 'interference' was necessary. But he argued for state action 'to guide and assist our exporters abroad', proposing in his Fabian Tract, *Fabianism and the Empire*, that shipping should be free for trade within the Empire. In modern terms, this means that the cost of transport was externalized, being paid for out of the public purse – not unlike the present US and EC subsidized export dumping!

Fair Trading: pointing the way?

Since the 1970s several alternative approaches to trade have emerged, based upon a rejection of the old paradigm of free trade *versus* protectionism. Michael Barratt Brown, chair of TWIN Trading, has characterized alternative trading as being 'in and against the market', operating within market systems but being opposed to their usual effects.[2] In Europe, there has been an active Fair Trade movement bringing goods from developing countries to European markets for over 25 years. The sector is growing rapidly, with an estimated worldwide turnover of $200 million. Oxfam shops in the UK now sell fair-traded coffee and tea, and a new Fair Trade Mark, with accompanying logo and monitoring scheme, is to be launched in 1993, promoted by Oxfam, Christian Aid, New Consumer, CAFOD, Traidcraft and the World Development Movement.[3] This new mark will endorse certain products, such as coffee or textiles, which give the primary producer a fair return. In North America, an estimated 10 million people are active consumers in the 'solidarity' market for products. Alternative Trading Organisations (ATOs) such as Oxfam and TWIN Trading fund and help organize producers and NGOs in the Third World.

The basic aim of ATOs is to help producers – conventionally fleeced by the trade system – to receive more for their goods and labour. This is done by adding value at source, rather than just selling raw commodities from which others in the North take the lion's share of the value. ATOs are helping put together complex multilateral deals for a collection of countries, North and South, that have goods to sell and product needs, but not all of which match bilaterally. Alternative trading efforts have been supported by Third World support groups. One recent assessment listed 24 NGOs in the UK alone associated with or practising alternative trading.[4] Fair trading has been described by Mandy Jetter of *New Consumer* as:

> '. . . paying a price which reflects the costs of production and quality of the product plus a reasonable margin for investment, development and production uncertainties. Evidence is sought that where the producers are waged labourers, a fair rate of pay and good working conditions are provided. Where producers are self-employed, for example smallholders,

> the organisation which represents them clearly operates for their for their benefit. The trading relationship also involves ensuring that financial credit is available and that quality, continuity and mutual support are maintained.'[5]

In the Netherlands, an ethical and fair trade coffee brand, Max Havelaar (named in honour of a 19th century Dutch author who exposed the horrors of the coffee trade)[6] now has 2 per cent of the market and in October 1991 became the official supplier of coffee to the European Parliament.[7]

Fair trade schemes are always voluntary arrangements between the marketers and the consumers, usually with development NGOs acting as intermediaries and supporters. They work within the market system, leaving it to consumers to choose to pay a premium for such goods. Almost inevitably, fair-traded goods will be a small sector in the market. Seen optimistically, ATOs could be prototypes of a fairer system of trade, distributing profits more equitably and ethically than the conventional market. On the other hand, fair trade could also represent a threat to the environment.

The dangers of success

Environment and development NGOs have been discussing potential conflicts. Often these conflicts are due to poor mutual understanding, for example the pressure to destroy local environments often arises from the urgent need for land or income,[8] and once this is understood it can be tackled. A more thorny problem, however, is posed by the theoretical possibility of an extraordinary expansion of fair trade – if the barons of today's commodity trade disappeared and ATOs became huge concerns. In our view, ATOs need to accept paradoxical goals: In the short term they do all they can, but in the long term they should ideally work for less global and long distance trade and more local trade.

We want all trade to be fair and to make the final price of all products reflect the full cost of production to both producers and the environment. This would require wholesale reform of the international trading system, but there are things which can be confronted quickly and immediately. High on the list of development agencies is inappropriate aid and long overdue reforms of the regulations of commodity markets which currently merely benefit the world's powerful in both North and South.[9]

Michael Barratt Brown's theoretical example on multilateral ATO barter deals makes the point (see Table 8). The ATO's job is to put together the composite deal to everyone's satisfaction. By doing so, small and powerless interests in both North and South can all benefit. None of the countries in the Table can find another county with which it can do a bilateral deal, simply exchanging 'wants' and 'needs', because there is no other country which has on offer what the original country wants and which needs what it has to offer. Yet, in theory, everyone has something to sell that someone else wants. The challenge is to put together a composite deal to work to all their mutual advantages. All honour to ATOs for forging such deals, but there should be a note of caution. Today, it may make sense for the North to trade its fishing tackle to India and buy coffee beans from Nicaragua, but in the long term it would be ecologically better to have Indian fishing tackle production to supply the local market without having to ship bicycles to Nicaragua. Ideally, the New Protectionist goal would be for both to satisfy their needs locally. Perhaps it is skills and technical developments, not goods which should be shared, but we shall return to this in the next chapter.

Table 8 *An example of multilateral deals*

Country	Offers	Wants (or will take)
India 'A'	Bicycles	Woodworking tools
India 'B'	Jute bags	Fishing tackle
Nicaragua	Coffee beans	Bicycles
Argentina	Corned beef	Jute bags
UK	Woodworking tools	Corned beef
Netherlands	Fishing tackle	Coffee beans

Source: Barratt Brown, 1993[10]

Going bananas

The development lobby argues that Northern protectionism should be dismantled to increase Southern access to markets. In practice, the South needs protectionism itself, partly to allow it time to develop, and partly to alter the gross inequalities of terms of trade. But many of the conventional preferential access treaties, such as the EC's Lomé Convention, benefit big traders more than small producers. Under the Lomé Convention, former European colonies in Africa, the Caribbean and the Pacific have guaranteed access for their goods into the EC. The current round of GATT trade talks, threatens such preferential access agreements. In 1992–3 TNCs were lined up on both sides in a battle over access to the EC for bananas – both for and against the EC preferential access treaty for ex-colonial producers.

Within Europe there are two banana regimes. Bananas from former colonies such as the Dominican Republic, which come from mostly family farm producers who have small plantations on steep terrain, are protected by the Lomé Convention. The rest – known as the dollar banana regime – come from large banana holdings in Central America. Dollar bananas are cheaper, critics say, because of the poor working conditions of the labourers and the intensity of production. The GATT pressure to liberalize markets have brought the two systems into conflict. The World Bank is already critical of the EC's proposals to defend its existing Lomé Convention-based banana regime.

The EC in 1993 resisted pressure to open up the Community completely to dollar bananas – to the fury of Germany, where bananas have been cheap and consumption the highest in Europe, being supplied by dollar banana countries. The EC's argument was that to abandon Lomé producers would only generate 'immense monopoly profits for importers'.[11] In fact, TNCs sit on either side of this argument, but the Lomé TNCs, such as Geest and Fyffe's, are smaller than the dollar ones. Will former colonial powers continue to stand by their commitments or will they in the future put low cost first? Choosing small scale production before price *must* be the answer. For Dominican farmers, knowing that they would be crushed by dollar banana plantations with superior economies of scale, the moral choice is hardly an academic exercise. Their choice is bananas, drugs or poverty.[12]

The preferential access option argues for exceptions to the rule. It is a first line of defence for small farmers in ex colonies, but in the medium term the economic viability of such farmers must be based more on the diversity of the local economy, rather than on total dependence on one or two cash crops. Globally, the banana market is highly concentrated, consisting of three dominant TNCs, whose operations are centred in Latin America, see Table 9. With such power, there can be little long term

Table 9 *Sales of the big three banana companies*

TNC	**Percentage of trade with:**		
	USA	**Europe**	**Japan**
Chichita	29	43	22
Dole	29	13	21
Del Monte	17	10	21

Source: Watson, 1992[13]

security in preferential access agreements under the present system, as the market will inevitably favour cheaper supplies. Nevertheless, the battle over bananas has been symbolically important and so far the EC has to some extent maintained its support for Lomé producers, although there is tremendous pressure from outside the EC, via the GATT, and inside, led by German consumers' huge appetite for cheap bananas.

One aspect to the argument over banana supplies (and to fair trade practice) which receives too little public attention is the ecological implications of the different systems, ie small or large holdings. Which producer is more ecological? Development agencies are already concerned at intensive farming practices targeted at the export trade. Oxfam, for instance, has taken a leading role in exposing the use of pesticides in the Third World.[14] In the large scale banana plantations, found predominantly in Latin America, there is a huge use of such pesticides.[15] This is a problem hidden from consumers' view, in part by the absence of labelling. Every year in Chile around four million kilos of pesticides, three kilos per person, are routinely dumped on the 220,000 hectares of land that are devoted to fruit production for export. Many of these chemicals are highly toxic, among them are nine of the 12 most toxic pesticides in the world.[16]

Although there is always likely to be a market for bananas, and for exotic fruits impossible to grow in cooler climates, in the North, the choice of suppliers should be dictated by not only whether the farmers concerned get a reasonable price for producing in an environmentally sustainable manner, but *also* whether the trade helps in the transition process towards a more diverse regional economy.

Local initiatives

The environment movement, which has burgeoned in the North since the 1960s, has generated many experiments in alternatives, ranging from environmental audits to local initiatives on recycling waste. In Germany and the Netherlands, progressive local authorities have tried to develop the local economy in a greener direction. This has not happened in the UK to the same extent, perhaps due to central government's unparalleled hostility to local government and pruning both its powers and budgets. In some countries, communities have taken green initiatives without help from government.

In the community-supported agriculture movement, people in towns club together and create a formal link with growers or farmers.[17] Consumers co-operate to buy into a share of production costs and develop a close link with the land. Such initiatives have developed in the USA with enormous success.[18] The first group started in 1985 and it is predicted that there will be 5000 groups by the year 2000, a marvellous start, but, if we are honest, hardly scratching the surface of what needs to be done.

Often, when looking at alternative options, people in the NGO movement refer to the consumer co-operative (or Seikatsu Club) movement in Japan. This is a large scale movement involving approximately 20 per cent of the population, and has grown to be a huge retailing chain with considerable influence on the conventional market in terms of food quality and environmental practices. The co-partnerships, or 'teikei', represent smaller scale, more intimate partnerships between consumers and producers – between 10 and 25 thousand farms are probably involved.[19] It bears a strong resemblence to the UK's co-operative movement in its original 19th century form.[20]

Such consumer arrangements are usually motivated by two concerns. The first is the desire to bypass existing distributors and shops and get better value for money. The second is to provide consumers with high quality food from a trusted and known source, and so avoid contamination. Such motives are not limited to the ecological or Seikatsu Club type movements. In Glasgow, a network of 40 food co-operatives has helped people in a number of working class districts to fill the retailing vacuum created by the retail chains pulling out.[21] We think that more such reactions will occur in both poor and more affluent areas, as retail sectors concentrate. The trend is for mainstream retailers to get the shopper to travel further and further to make their purchases. Essentially, modern large supermarkets are symbols of the retailers' success – consumers now go to the warehouse. This means they travel further, use cars more, and subsidize retail profits by adding to home transport bills. All this in the name of 'convenience'.

Another interesting development occurred in Britain in the 1980s, which saw a flowering of local authority economic development units trying to create jobs and to compensate for the destruction caused by the Thatcherite market place. But, by the 1990s, local authorities had been left with little choice but to enter an unseemly competition to beg for favours such as being awarded 'assisted area' status or Urban Aid Grants. Unfortunately, the competition to woo incoming TNCs is not a solution to underlying economic crisis and decline, and is no compensation for the dismantling of around a fifth of UK manufacturing during the early years of the first Thatcher government, or for the relative decline that is likely to continue through the nineties. So, the chance for local authority economic development units to experiment with the radical changes needed has been put 'on ice'. The promise and much expertise are still there, but the political climate of the 1990s means that national attention is now directed not just to the new regional realities of the trading blocs, but the global economy being forced in under the GATT.

Are these experiments enough?

These experiments are testiments to the grassroots concern that current economic policies are not working, and that what is needed is a different direction. However, unless such initiatives move from being marginal to being mainstream, the overall effect of trade in damaging the environment and increasing inequity will remain unchallenged. These small alternatives are like valiant canoes paddling against the current flow of history. What we need is a change of direction in the stream. None of these alternatives is yet sufficiently politically powerful to challenge the current economic structure. And their efforts may be partially counteracted by deregulation under the new GATT. A more appropriate economic framework is needed, which is why we need the New Protectionism and outline its agenda in the next chapter. It is also why, in the face of the accelerated globalisation of economics, there will have to be better coordination between all sectors of societies which recognise the enormous impact this process will have. Alliances need to be cross-sectoral and to use all possible networks – NGOs, local authorities, businesses, citizens' groups professional associations, trade unions. Their constituencies of interest and their members will be hit hardest by what is unfolding or being planned for them, and they are much closer to the people than national or international bodies. The alternatives we have pointed to in this and other chapters are stirrings. It remains to be seen how and when the stew comes to the boil.

12. The New Protectionism

We have seen how free trade can discriminate against and hurt the *environment*; how the *economy* of many countries is being damaged by structural unemployment, debt and deregulation; and how *equity* throughout the world – within and between societies – is decreasing. We have also seen in the previous chapter how alternative trading is beginning to tackle some of the issues, but against daunting odds. The extent of the change that is needed cannot be left to the whims of affluent 'green consumers', as Frances Cairncross, Environment Editor of *The Economist*, has indicated.[1] Business needs to be given a framework in which to work, yet free trade, which many – particularly big – businesses favour for its deregulation, fails to meet our wider criteria. What is needed is to tackle all the three 'E's' simultaneously.

Meeting the three 'Es' for all

A sane approach to trade would protect citizens and their environment, so the goal of the New Protectionism has to be to redirect the world economy to meet the three 'E's' by:

- making regions (both within countries and groups of countries), not the globe, the focus of economic activity;
- reducing unsustainable and unnecessary global trade;
- increasing local and regional self-reliance, as much as possible;
- making environmental protection a priority;
- making the improvement of the processes of production and the minimization of their harmful effects as important as improving the products themselves, and adjusting processes, controls and products to meet environmental, economic and equity criteria;
- understanding the links between production and consumption;
- maximizing local and regional diversity, from culture to flora and fauna;
- reducing inequalities both between and within economies;
- improving local democracy and control over economic decision making, especially over TNCs and world bodies;
- enabling *all* people to meet their basic needs for decent food, clean air and water, housing, health and employment;

- fostering social mechanisms whether by community or state which allow better welfare, and a more sensible and even pace of life;
- toughening up standards, and helping those who currently do not meet standards to do so.

Our main purpose in this book is to argue for a rejection of the current perspective on international trade and to argue for a more local and regional approach to economic activity. The debate about the failure of current policies, based on an ever faster treadmill of international competition has begun, but the debate about solutions has a lot of catching up to do. It is not as though the free traders are on firm ground. Their experimentation with the world's future is in some respects a breath-taking confidence trick. Having seen through that process, other guiding principles and goals for economic activity are urgently needed. If present global development means power accruing to the powerful, we are mindful equally of how oppressive inward-looking local societies can be, too. It was with great relief many, especially women, escaped their traditional social fetters. Forcing people into social straitjackets is the last thing we have the right to propose, nor would we want to. What is needed, as David Morris implied in the statement we quoted at the end of Chapter 8, is a relook at what could be meant by self-reliance.

Self-reliance – a new regionalism

In the 1980s, many high profile appeals were made for emergency aid to the South but, by the end of the decade, cynics were talking of 'donor fatigue' as recession seemed to curtail altruism. If the 1980s message was 'Aid', the 1990s message appears to be 'Trade, not Aid'. We say the ideal for the 21st century should be 'Aid and Trade only for self-reliance'.

Self-reliance should be a goal for localities within countries (where it applies) and regions of countries, allowing them to meet the maximum possible number of needs and services from within their boundaries. If economies were to work for self-reliance, they would be considerably less dependent on international trade and its ruthless competition for growth. The challenge is to reorientate economies away from being export-led when production and employment really should be geared to meeting local needs. Sometimes, trade-oriented economic activity is shamefully wasteful and exploitative, as in the arms trade or in some Asian carpet production, where consumers buying a luxury product are in ignorance of the pitiful, child labour conditions and slave wages.[2] On other occasions, it is not just labour, but ecologically sensitive local resources which are distorted or damaged for external trade.

In Kerala, India, for example, the fisherfolk are under pressure to sell food they previously ate. In practice, this translates into a stark choice: export or eat. Their waters have been overfished as a result of a combination of factors: modern trawlers, subsidies, abandoning of traditional methods and a rise in numbers of fisherfolk. Common space has been damaged by encouraging the fisherfolk to increase production.[3] A member of the UK NGO, Farmers' Third World Network, visited the Anjengo Fisherman's Society in Kerala and reported:

> 'In the past, fish was eaten with the local staple tapioca. Consumption of fish protein made them more resistant to diseases. Now all cuttle fish and prawns, for example, go for export – the prices are better. The cost of their craft and gear has increased, so they can not afford to miss out on the higher prices. Fishing families eat less fish and malnutrition occurs.'[4]

The President of the Fisherman's Society said: 'Those who don't need it get more fish; those who need it don't get it.' This is morally unacceptable.

In our vision of the future, trade will still occur, but the issue becomes *what sort of trade, how far, and for what.* Economic activity in our New Protectionist future would still have some negative environmental effects, but two factors could ensure that such effects would be minimized. The first would be that entire economies would not be geared to maximizing production for exports at the cheapest, most competitive price, with the resulting tendency to minimize environmental protection. The second factor is that since the effects of an increasing percentage of extraction and production will be experienced locally, as international trade is decreased with the transition to more regional self-reliance, then the pressure from local people to clean up will increase. Any adverse environmental effects will be experienced locally, which will increase the chance of strong support for environmental controls more than if the production process was taking place thousands of miles away. An 'out of sight, out of mind' business mentality will be replaced by 'why dirty our own backyard?'.

We also want to see new rules of international trade to foster such environmental improvements, since they will be set up to help secure one of the cornerstones of the New Protectionism – the encouragement of economic activity which protects the environment. At present, international trade rules and those of regional trading blocks encourage more environmental degradation by maximizing trade, and seriously hinder effective national, regional and international measures to protect the environment by calling them 'barriers to trade'. Their main emphasis is on deregulation of trade, as a principle; ours is to ensure that trade does not lead to pollution, lower standards and greater inequality. Some trade agreements do have important clauses on the need to protect the environment – the EC's Single European Act's article 100a, for instance, assures that the Commission will take a high level of protection of public health, environment and consumers. Yet articles 73 and 74 of the treaty founding the EEA give just 11 lines out of 784 pages to protection of the environment.[5]

The successes of this new economic system need to be measured by something more relevant than GNP and GDP. This out-of-date system of measuring total economic activity was never designed to relate to welfare – it is flawed, misleading and totally inadequate. Work is already underway on more realistic indicators which would indicate the quality of life in other than purely financial terms.[6] Indicators such as infant mortality, life expectancy, the gap between richest and poorest fifths in a society, literacy, security of employment, air pollution, soil loss, ozone layer depletion and greenhouse gas production tell us much more about a society. The rate of increase or decrease in the gap between rich and poor, less waste of raw materials and a decrease in pollution and waste can also be relatively easy to show.

For self-reliance to take hold, a number of practical steps will need to be worked out and the practicalities detailed. The framework suggested by Daly and Cobb in their excellent book, *For the Common Good*, is a useful starting point. It looks at measures to strengthen regional and local economies, improve conditions for the poor and to protect the environment.

Balancing Trade

Current trends and encouragement to increase international trade should be reversed. We look to less trade, and for whatever trade there is to be balanced as far as possible; a start would be limiting imports to a rough equality with expected exports. There is little equity in economies haemorrhaging through a negative balance of trade, nor in being in a hefty surplus with others, which indicates, at worst, exploitation and, at best, others being out of work. The basic aim is only to import what materials are not available, or whichever goods and services it is not possible to provide. Every effort should be made to meet requirements from local sources first, then nationally, then regionally, and only after that internationally. Like John Maynard Keynes, we favour localizing production but encouraging culture and ideas to flow widely. He wrote, from a national perspective:

> 'I sympathise, therefore, with those who would minimize, rather than with those who would maximize, economic entanglement between nations. Ideas, knowledge, art, hospitality, travel – these are things which should of their nature be international. But let goods be homespun whenever it is reasonably and conveniently possible; and, above all, let finance be primarily national.'[7]

We understand the thrust of what Keynes meant, but the principle should be that it is not just *what* is done that matters, but *how* it is done and *to whom.* To that end, national governments should introduce import and export restrictions to protect the environment. These restrictions should incorporate strong standards on health, safety, environmental impact and consumer education, not just labelling. Export restrictions should comply with sustainable and ethical criteria. These could include:

- restricting the export of scarce national resources where they are not managed sustainably;
- stopping the export of pesticides or other products which are banned in the exporting country;
- restricting the aggressive marketing of unnecessary goods, such as cigarettes or some drugs;
- halting government-subsidized dumping of food surpluses onto world markets.

Import restrictions would be based on similar principles. Tariff barriers would protect domestic industry where competing countries failed to comply with such principles. These tariffs would not be placed on goods per se, but on the environmental impact of goods. They would become 'ecotaxes' or taxes on energy, waste, toxins, and so on. It would be the responsibility of the country opposing the tariff to prove its dismantling would not undermine sustainability. Regional and international agreements would guarantee that standards of environmental protection are constantly improved. Tough regulations should be enforced and standards should act as non-tariff barriers to poor quality imports. Members of the region would be encouraged to raise their standards to create a 'floor' in contrast to free trade which, as we saw in Chapter 9, tends to create 'ceilings' above which no company or country has an incentive to rise – except when business is happy to use tougher standards to squeeze its competition. The accepted environmental standards of trading regions, should become the floor that no member could go below.

We want to see an economy in which some industries wither and others grow. For example, we would like reusable packaging and bottling industries to grow, and throw-away packaging industries to be reduced. Similarly, we would like to see industries which foster public and mass transport systems grow, and those which service individualized systems which pollute, such as the car, to end their domination of the manufacturing sector. The skills currently locked up in socially and environmentally undesirable industries should and could be better deployed. The transitions to such a state will require adequate planning and funding. Ever-rising environmental standards, built in to the economic framework, will act as a substitute incentive for industry not to rest on its laurels and to fossilize – the great fear of industries under the old protectionism. Within regions and localities, there would still be the pressure of competition, locally rather than internationally. Innovation and skills would be developed to meet more local and ecological ends, rather than the international market-place.

Introducing tariffs and guiding capital

Tariffs would protect endangered industries from further erosion and allow them to recover lost ground. They would also encourage new enterprise in areas where a country has become dependent on imports. Once industries are assured of a secure future, provided they can compete successfully with local rivals and are profitable, local capital should flow to them. Balancing trade through tariffs should lead to the maximum feasible level of self-reliance. It will also need policies to prevent consolidation of economic power in a few hands. This could be achieved by limiting the number of mergers and take-overs, and increasing the number of smaller businesses and manufacturers.

New trade rules

New trade rules will be particularly necessary for reducing inequality and for coping with environmental problems, such as the limitation of cross-boundary pollution. The purpose of trade agreements will no longer be to eliminate barriers to trade but to ensure that economic activity provides maximum protection for the environment and people. Agreements such as the GATT, which we would want to become a General Agreement for Sustainable Trade (GAST), and all regional trading blocks should have a three-stage focus: towards sustainability as the goal; member countries being encouraged to improve their standards constantly beyond the norm, while being adequately protected; and towards harmonized levels of environmental protection as the floor below which no region or country can go.

Community-based decisions and enterprise

One of the key goals of the New Protectionism is to raise the standard and quality of living of those currently pushed to the periphery by free trade. Emotions about trade's impact on conditions and livelihoods can run high – as we saw in 1993 with French fishermen blockading ports and burning imported Russian and British fish. Trade carries such effects wherever it goes. As President Franklin Roosevelt said: 'Goods produced under conditions which do not meet a rudimentary standard of decency should be regarded as contraband and not allowed to pollute the channels of international commerce.'[8]

If the goal is to have a diverse economy, the impetus, the ideas and the implementation will have to transfer over time from the global or regional level to the local and community level of decision making and resource control. This is a reversal of the free traders' globalization project, which enables them to globe-hop and free-ride. The EC's Maastricht Treaty principle of subsidiarity, if greened, could be a useful precedent.[9] Giving more power to local levels, which have seen previous responsibilities eroded, and to create new levels, where previously there were none, is a major long term goal for the New Protectionism. For communities – towns, villages – to survive, let alone prosper, diversity is essential. A report written for the EC in 1990 estimated that, on current trends, 100,000 small towns and villages in Europe will cease to function within the next ten years.[10]

In the periphery of Europe, communities are having to dig deep into their collective energies and ask: what do they want? Their response may take the form of setting up a local shop, vacated as multiple retailers pull out because a store is 'too small' or 'uneconomic'; or it may take the form of a local dialogue about the future of the locality – as has begun in parts of Scotland or the South Wales valleys, devastated by the collapse of 19th century industries and mines and the rise of larger firms. In the UK, local enterprise has often been the only resistance to the effect of the government's assault on jobs in the 1980s. A review by the New Economics Foundation of London in 1992 paid ample tribute to the lessons learned by community enterprise initiatives.[11] But these experiences need to be part of a co-ordinated national strategy, rather than a patchwork of relatively few, under-supported and unrecognized pilots. Ironically, in Britain, there is more support for this kind of community enterprise from the EC than there is from national government. The goal of self-reliant enterprise should be good quality work, improving, not blighting, lives and environmental conditions.

A European Environmental Community

Few words are more torpor-inducing, even in EC-speak, than the term subsidiarity. The way this word is interpreted, however, could hold the key to whether Europe's environmental policies improve or worsen. At present, there is a strong possibility that it will be used to water down future and existing environmental legislation. Subsidiarity means that action should be taken at EC level *only* where it would be more appropriate and effective than action at a national or local level. The concept was hastily dragged out of obscurity to counter the growing public Euro-scepticism following the

Danes rejection of the Maastricht Treaty, the narrow French vote, and continued UK confusion.

Although subsidiarity appears to increase the potential for national control in an EC context, it can be misused. For instance, under the guise of limiting excessive EC meddling, Tory UK ministers have already sought to eliminate environmental legislation they did not like. Foreign Secretary, Douglas Hurd MP, complained of interference in the UK's road building programme and Sir Leon Brittan, the former Tory minister and now an EC Commissioner, urged 'repatriating' laws such as the drinking and bathing water directive whose high standards have embarrassed the UK government. The 1992 Edinburgh EC Summit compiled a list of directives deemed to fail the subsidiarity test, which fortunately did not include many of the measures that the UK would have liked under its national discretion. Existing EC environmental policy is expected to remain virtually unscathed, and rolling back directives (laws) that are now domestic UK legislation would be too difficult and unpopular and would anyway be blocked by the European Parliament.

The more likely effect of the emphasis on subsidiarity is that some future EC environmental policy will never get off the ground. A jittery Commission halved the number of environmental proposals for 1993 compared with 1992 and some policies, like the requirement of governments to produce coastal management plans, are reportedly likely to be abandoned. David Wilkinson of the London-based Institute for European Environmental Policy predicted that proposed EC legislation could increasingly take the form of framework laws with member states allowed maximum flexibility in the details. He also feels that less intrusive forms of policy, like depending on environmental informa-tion for consumers to encourage tighter standards, may become common.[12]

European policy-makers ought not to consider the impact of progressive environmental policies a drain on their economies. Apart from significant health, social and wildlife benefits, there are also very real economic arguments in favour of establishing high environmental standards, since they result in more efficient use of energy and materials.

Just as we favour the EC becoming a European Environmental Community, so we want to see the Clinton administration in the USA move beyond its first phase of encouraging investment in skills and environmental protection in order to out-compete the EC and Japan and to win global markets. US Vice President Al Gore has pointed out in his book *Earth in the Balance*,[13] that industries which are able to develop the most environmentally-friendly technologies and processes will increasingly be the most competitive internationally. If Europe does not set challenging environmental standards, other nations will. The EC may then find itself not only with an irreversibly degraded environment, but having to import costly clean-up technologies.

Eventually, the driving force of improved environmental conditions should be, *not* international competitiveness, but regional trade rules which lead to local economic diversity while protecting the environment. Such 'green' subsidiarity should therefore not be a threat, but an opportunity. It would ensure that decision making was taken at a level which would ensure the maximum environmental protection and economic diversity. According to the conventional definition of subsidiarity, decisions currently taken at the regional EC level should be handed down to the national level. While welcoming the return to the more local level, in the case of the UK, this would mean tougher EC environmental protection standards could be weakened by being handed over to the deregulating UK government. So a green subsidiarity principle balances localness of decision making with the need to protect the environment. It should become the mechanism whereby EC policy increases not only Europe's environmental security but also its economic one. In short, it is the key first step to a *new* EEC – the European Environmental Community.

Protecting the improvements

In the move to the New Protectionism, existing trade agreements such as the GATT or EEA or NAFTA or APEC should be scrutinized and, where appropriate, renegotiated to guarantee that standards of environmental protection are constantly improved, economic activity diversified and local economies strengthened. In practical terms, the agricultural, industrial and service sectors in a country are likely to incur additional costs for the environmental improvements and would oppose such improvements unless they are adequately compensated for raising standards, and protected from outside competitors not having to incur such costs. There are two ways of doing this. The country's taxpayers could provide the sector or industry concerned with grants, tax breaks, etc, but this has two disadvantages: firstly it makes the residents of the country introducing the environmental measure pay, and secondly it provides no inducement for other countries to match the higher standard. The other way of supporting higher standards is tariffs, which we favour. Tariffs have the additional advantage of potentially encouraging other supplier countries to improve their standards in order to be able to export successfully. Some of the tariff revenue could also be used to help finance poorer countries who would otherwise not be able to afford the necessary environmental improvements.

Self-reliance in practice

Countries and regions should provide as much of their own food, goods and services as possible. If internal economies could no longer flourish by being dependent on growth through more international trade, stronger internal buying power would have to be generated. In the Third World, this would mean transforming social needs into effective demand, and in the North it would mean turning the provision of regional economic security and environmental sustainability into jobs, and hence effective demand. Ideally, in the long term, we favour societies producing more locally, but rather like turning round a supertanker in mid-ocean, this will take some time. And for the Third World, dependent on selling goods, to cut off such trade overnight would be both callous and cause severe employment problems, even if it was possible. In the medium term, we would like to aim for a situation where First World countries reduce the export of goods and services, while the Third World and former communist countries get direct cash support and debt relief to help them move from a dependency on exports whose value is constantly declining towards policies providing for sustainable regional economies. We say more about how to pay for this in the next chapter. In the Third World, spreading income more evenly would require, amongst other changes, extensive land reform, progressive taxation policies and guarantees of workers rights.

Most Third World countries remain predominantly agricultural societies, hence the starting point for internal demand-led development must be farming. Agrarian reform is the major means of distributing wealth and income and thereby of increasing the effective purchasing power of the rural population; then small farmers, as their income increases, would buy more locally produced goods and services. Industrialization, in the medium term, should be based on maximizing industrial linkages with agriculture – agricultural inputs, processing farm products and basic consumer goods – and use of least polluting technologies.

In the North, the emphasis would also be on regions and countries providing the maximum amount of their own food, goods and services. As with the Third World, what cannot be produced locally is produced nationally, and then regionally. This would require the rethinking of basic economic priorities of regional organizations such as NAFTA or the EC and the fledgling ASEAN or Mercosur. For certain economic sectors, this would actually mean lowering demand and diversification into new markets.[14] The car industry is an obvious candidate for transformation. The future health of an economy or even its manufacturing base should no longer be linked to car sales or car production. Daly and Cobb ambitiously recommend a ten-year turn round of the world economy towards a restructuring that ensures maximum regional and national self-sufficiency in food and industrial goods, to be produced with minimal environmental degradation.[15]

Once this is in place, countries' national economies will be – or have the basis for becoming – more diverse, more decentralized and, perhaps most importantly, more under their own control. Part of our concern is to encourage the transition from consumer societies to citizenship societies, as we explored in Chapter 10. Then societies will be in a position to decide how much trade they need to indulge in. Free trade will no longer dictate the shape and emphasis of local economies and countries can choose when they want to trade. They would also have the protective barriers to allow the creation of industries which international trade had previously prevented because they were non-competitive.

Textiles are a case in point, where a medium term New Protectionist goal would be, for example, for India to produce shirts for the Asian market, and Europe to have a textile industry of its own, with cotton, say from the Mediterannean or North Africa, ie via shorter trade routes, involving less transport. A priority would also be to develop agricultural systems for growing cotton without pesticides – cotton production is a heavy user of agrichemicals with devastating environmental impact.[16] Both continents should aim for economic diversity, rather than trying, from unequal starting points, for global markets. North Africa, too, should develop its own textile industry.

Potential problems to be overcome

Getting multilateral agreements can take years or decades, as the lengthy Uruguay Round and the Tokyo Round before it suggest. In the meantime, a country introducing legislation to improve the environment is likely to have to protect its domestic agriculture or industry from products from countries without such legislation. A ratchetting up effect is needed, not down as the GATT is likely to introduce. Such trade policies by one or a number of countries can be a step along the road towards an environmentally satisfactory multilateral agreement. Even if such an agreement is signed, trade sanctions should remain an effective way of ensuring that it is upheld. International exhortations, alone, have a very poor record of success.

Neither fortress nor global economies

Under the old protectionism, some countries have followed an import substitution model, where national industries are protected and the state helps and guides investment with the private sector. After an initial phase of building up industry, they – in theory – switch to exports and compete in world markets. This model has been partly responsible for the emergence of such trumpeted economies as Brazil and South Korea, but with appalling social inequalities and at considerable environmental cost. Brazil, for instance, has the worst rich–poor gap in the world. The top 20 per cent of earners in Brazil earn 62.6 per cent of national income, while the bottom 20 per cent earn 2.4 per cent.[17]

In theory, another option to the free trade route is to stop trading and build a fortress economy. The former Eastern blocs, such as the USSR and the Comecon countries, went down this route, with many oppressive social and disastrous environmental results. The strategy resulted in economic stagnation and loss of both productivity and innovation. The repressive nature of those political regimes and the corruption of their economic systems should not blind us to the potential of an area as large and rich as the former Soviet Union to become largely self-sufficient in terms of resources, food and manufactured goods.

Our vision of regional or local self-reliance is not one of *laager* type fortress economies. Rather, it is for local trade with an emphasis on reducing distance wherever possible. Localities, countries, regions . . . whatever unit of economic activity is to be taken, we would like a change of trading priorities between them, with diversification of local production the goal, and only after that the satisfaction of needs through external trade. In the long term, moving to maximum regional self-reliance is a move into a new economic practice, and will need detailed analysis of the mechanisms to make it work. No one country or region can go it alone; coalitions must be built, and the case patiently put before the public. The history of free trade has been one of bitter disputes, trade wars and military intervention. The New Protectionism requires negotiation and difficult decisions.

Helping poorer countries

Resistance to unilateral trade blocks, particularly when introduced by the wealthy countries against those countries that do not or cannot afford to internalize environmental costs to the same degree, has and will occur. Internalizing cost is not cheap. It has been estimated that developing countries exporting to the OECD countries in 1980 would have incurred pollution control costs of at least $5.5 billion if they had been required to match US standards.[18] Although unilateral steps are vital for increased global environmental protection, so too are mechanisms to help poorer countries pursue the same ends. Tariffs on the imports of goods that do not meet national environmental standards could be recycled for investment to improve the environmental levels in the poor countries concerned.[19] On a multilateral level, commodity agreements could incorporate an Environmental Fund for the same purpose, jointly administered by the parties to the agreement.[20]

Poorer countries dependent on primary exports could impose an environmental export tariff on their goods, to be used for domestic environmental programmes. Importers should require such a tariff to ensure market access, so that a country that adopted such measures was not undercut by nations without such an environmental approach.[21] In the transition phase towards New Protectionism, resource flows from the richer countries to the poorer countries will be vital to enable poorer countries to improve their environmental practices. Two factors are likely to make such resource flows likely. One is the increasing realization that what is done in one area of the globe affects all. Thus, if poorer countries continue producing and using ozone-depleting substances and increasing their output of greenhouse gases, then we are all affected. It is to everyone's mutual self-interest for richer countries to fund some of the transitional costs away from such practices, as it is to help finance the Third World's self-reliance. The second factor is that Third World countries are likely to become more vociferous in so-called 'greenmail', making the joining of international environmental agreements or the changing of domestic activities dependent on an adequate cash compensation.

Institutions for transforming trade

Trade is currently regulated (and being deregulated) at all levels and the institutions involved are of paramount importance to any new vision for trade. Trade cannot be treated in isolation – current political structures will probably require considerable change too. New institutions will be needed, such as environmental and fair trade commissions, with the power to take action on trade regulations, and an International Monopolies and Mergers Commission, with trust and cartel-breaking powers. Such bodies would probably be most appropriate operating both regionally and globally.

The range of *theoretically* publically accountable bodies which presently affect trade is extensive: the UN bodies such as UNCTAD and UNCED, the GATT, the IMF, the World Bank, and the OECD. But too few citizens understand what they are, how they work and how they affect lives – a state which requires urgent rectification by NGOs. The bodies such as the IMF and World Bank, deriving from the 1944 Bretton Woods agreement, need not just revising or making more open,[22] but changing into a New Protectionist equivalent of Bretton Woods to plan for the 21st century. The regional bodies and trade agreements, with accompanying secretariats, as we discussed in Chapter 4, all need revision. Meanwhile, as part of the new world order, new institutions are being mooted which could accrue substantial power. The MTO has been discussed in Chapter 5. The Global Environmental Fund (GEF), discussed at the UNCED in July 1992, is sponsored by the World Bank, UNDP and United Nations

Environment Programme (UNEP). However, two thirds of the projects are proposed and administered by the World Bank. Given the latter's track record it is not surprising that many NGOs are already deeply sceptical about it. Generally, these institutions need challenging and changing in two key respects: their basic aims and how they operate. The global NGO alliance built up in recent years around the GATT process should take up this challenge by helping educate both public and politicians.

The democratization and accountability of institutions like the IMF, World Bank and the GATT is a particularly pressing problem. Public interest groups who watch global institutions get so exasperated with them that it is difficult to know whether to recommend substantial reform or complete replacement. We have considerable sympathy with Graham Hancock's case for abolishing existing official aid bodies (see Chapter 9), but aid, as we have argued here, is needed. The arrogance with which these bodies have carried out socially unethical and environmentally destructive policies makes it difficult to trust them again. On the other hand, they exist now, and will continue to do so in the near future.[23] In the end, most critics advocate reform, while reserving the right to contemplate abolition. Even the global institutions themselves are becoming sensitive to the rising level of criticisms from NGOs, though they are unlikely to contemplate anything more than cosmetic reforms. At all costs, NGOs, from as wide a spectrum as possible, should be encouraged to target these global institutions in their campaigns, public education and policies.

The New Protectionist agenda

The challenge of the New Protectionism is formidable, but exciting; ideas need to be developed, policies made specific, and new issues explored. We now summarize ten key elements of the New Protectionist Agenda before, in the next chapter, discussing how to pay for it.

1. *Economic policy – away from the global towards the regional and local*
   Instead of organizing the world's economy to become ever more internationally competitive, we want the reverse: economies to develop locally and regionally, emphasizing local production to meet local need, and encouraging co-operation rather than competition.

2. *Building and supporting communities*
   The destruction of local economies, as jobs depart under the pressure of international competition, undermines the capacity of local communities to look after their populations. We want to see this process reversed, with the goal being to increase the number of people having control over their lives and work. A diverse local economy will require

the encouragement of a network of community initiatives, which could be the source of new employment, resource allocation and support for those in need.

3. *Aid and trade for self-reliance, fostered by an exchange of appropriate technology and skills*

   The new imperialism that the South needs the North's skills, goods or services needs to be replaced with a more co-operative approach. We want to see less physical transfer of goods around the world. To protect the future, there needs to be a free and equal exchange of skills and technical knowledge to produce goods and services in localities, but not an increase in international trade. A two-way exchange, North and South, East (meaning the former Communist countries) and North, East and South, which is not capital-intensive, is needed.

4. *Sharing out the work*

   If technology continues to displace human labour, while, at the same time, population figures continue to rise, then sharing the benefits and burdens of technology more equitably is essential. In hi-tech economies, the working week should be considerably shortened over the next 20 years, while new priorities for rebuilding communities are developed. Everywhere, but especially in developing countries, the need to improve the quality of life of the world's poor, particularly to lighten the burden of women, is a major goal. Investment and research in technology and infrastructure should go in that direction, unlike current World Bank projects which tend to be capital-intensive large scale and hi-tech, when they should be much more appropriate to local needs and resources.

5. *Raising environmental and public protection standards*

   Standards need to be ratchetted up, not down. International standards bodies such as Codex and the ISO should be made more open, more democratic and their standards should be 'floors' rather than ceilings on national standards.

6. *Controlling TNCs*

   There should be an international enquiry into the role and power of TNCs. We want to see an international Monopolies and Mergers (or Anti-Trust) Commission established to break up cartels and TNCs, and to set up and enforce a new international legal framework for both analysing TNCs and providing social and environmental criteria for policy on size of companies. This should build on the experience of the recently dismembered UN Centre on Transnational Corporations, and other independent research. Governments of countries where a TNC operates should work together to decide how to break it into smaller units.

7. *Evening out the money flows*
   Third World debt should eventually be written off, via a process which encourages increased regional economic diversity. Write-offs should be dependent upon setting up effective mechanisms for greatly reducing the gap between rich and poor within countries, as well as between countries. The slogan should be 'Aid and trade for self-reliance'.

8. *Dismantling or reforming world finance and trade bodies*
   Fifty years on, there needs to be a re-evaluation of the goals of the institutions set up in the wake of the Bretton Woods agreement in World War II. Bodies such as the World Bank and IMF should be radically overhauled so that instead of maximizing economic growth their remit becomes one of encouraging local and regional economies where the environment is adequately protected, there is shared employment and more equality within and between countries. GATT should become GAST – the General Agreement for Sustainable Trade – and the rationale behind trade rules should also be to improve environmental standards, diversify local economies and reduce gross inequalities. All other trade agreements (eg EEA, NAFTA, Andean Pact, etc) should be renegotiated, following environmental audits, to similar ends.

9. *Curtailing superbloc power to allow local and regional trade*
   The superblocs need to be made less powerful and the embryonic southern blocs given more room to develop. Any economic security and environmental improvements secured by the superblocs should not be at the expense of the developing world's ability to form their own regional and environmentally secure blocs. To that end, we want more Southern trade blocs to be set up with financial help from rich blocs, such as the reformed European Environmental Community and new North American Sustainable Trade Agreement (NASTA), which should supercede NAFTA. We also support the right of countries to remain independent from formal trading blocs.

10. *Changing consumption patterns*
    For local and regional trade to be ecologically sound, the consumption patterns of the world's rich consumers – what they buy and how they live – will have to change. Green consumerism, which leaves such changes to the whims of market-place choice is not enough. Consumption patterns – and what is available to consume – have to change to avoid damaging the world's resource base. Overconsumption by the wealthy in the North, will have to decline, encouraged by wealth and pollution taxes. The goal is quality consumption, stressing durability and good design to meet real needs. Better services, such as ecologically more appropriate housing, transport and social services, should improve the quality of life for everyone.[24]

13. Paying for the Transition

The New Protectionism requires a fundamental change in the way international markets are organized and will require enormous amounts of money to pay for the reorientation of regional economies. The world is actually not short of money; the problem is its misallocation and who controls it. Substantial resources could be provided by a significant cut in global arms expenditure, for example. The scale of the resources allocated to defence is huge, with a high proportion going not on people but weapons; government defence expenditure as a percentage of total government spending, according to the World Bank, accounts for 22 per cent in the USA, 12 per cent in the UK, 11 per cent in the Philippines and 8 per cent in Kenya, for example.[1] For the poorer countries, debt relief should be granted in proportion to the amount of resources allocated for the fostering of regional economies, the reduction of inequalities – particularly in land ownership, and protection of the environment.

During the process of curbing the powers of TNCs and redirecting international capital flows to build up regional economies, an international transfer tax on foreign exchange transactions should be considered. This was first proposed by the American economist James Tobin in the 1970s. Only a fraction, perhaps only 10 per cent of the £900 billion exchanged each day on the worlds currency markets are now used for facilitating trade. The rest is traded for risk management or profit.[2] In 1992, in what might be a tentative first step towards controls, the then US Treasury Secretary, Nicholas Brady, called for an examination of global capital flow, a proposal seen as a move towards a greater degree of government control of currency markets after a decade of financial deregulation.

Another enormous source of revenue could come from taxing economic activities resulting in excess resource use and pollution. This will have the twin benefit of raising money to help fund the transition towards the New Protectionism and altering the way society meets its needs to protect the environment. The case for transfering to a more organic agriculture, for depending increasingly on renewable energy and energy efficiency, for cleaner and more efficient production, and for less wasteful consumption and disposal patterns is already obvious. What is missing is the political will to pay for them, which is why the glorification of free trade and the acceptance of its anti-tax philosophy has to stop.

An idea of the scale of revenues that governments could raise from taxing the undesirable to encourage the desirable is illustrated by the estimates from the Washington-based World Resources Institute (WRI) of the revenues that could be generated in the USA. These include taxes on carbon dioxide releasing fuels, pay-by-the-bag charges for solid waste collection, and road tolls pegged to congestion. These alone would generate annually $100 to $150 billion in federal, local and state revenues. Furthermore, WRI calculate that the economy would 'reap dividends of $50 to $80 billion per year, in the form of reduced environmental damage and greater economic productivity as a result.' The WRI also analysed a wide range of other environmental charges (see Table 10), which could generate over $40 billion in revenues per year.[3] Similar comprehensive exercises to that conducted by the WRI need to be done in all countries.

Table 10 *Revenues from potential environmental charges / taxes in the USA*

Kind of charge/tax	Likely revenue (*$ billions*)
General tax on carbon dioxide releasing fuels	36.0
Pay-by-the-bag solid waste collection charges	1.65–4.67
Road tolls in line with congestion	48–98
Charge on toxic releases	20–30
Fee on vehicle hydrocarbon emissions in regions not meeting air quality standards	0.5
Water effluent fee	2.4
Recreation fees in national forests	5.0
Tax on other ozone-depleting substances	0.5
Charge on pesticide and fertilizer use	1.0
Reducing depletion allowance for fuel and non-fuel mineral extraction	1.2
Increasing royalties for hardrock mining on public lands	0.6
Full-cost pricing of Bureau of Reclamation water	0.5
Full-cost pricing of Forest Service timber	0.4
Total	117.75–180.77

Notes: the $50 billion variation on road tolls depends on whether that sum is spent on highway construction

Source: WRI, Nov 1992[3]

Resource Taxes

Most serious environmental threats arise from the economy's failure to value and account for environmental damage. Because those causing the harm do not pay the full costs, other parts of society and the planet have had to bear them, eg pollution from cars. By taxing products and activities which pollute, deplete or otherwise degrade the environment, governments can cause some environmental costs to be taken into account in commercial or private decisions. Each individual producer or consumer then decides how to adjust to the higher costs. Such taxes are what economists call 'corrective taxes'. They actually improve the functioning of the market by making prices reflect an activity's true cost. And if the undesirable act (eg using a scarce or polluting resource) costs more, there will be an incentive to reduce the amount of undesirable acts that happen.

The other advantage of resource taxes is that they can provide enormous amounts of revenue quite quickly, particularly an energy tax. However such a tax need not be dramatic in the first stage, but its continued increase can provide both growing revenue and the signal to society that the sooner it changes its behaviour the better. One suggestion from Professor von Weizsacker of Essen University is the introduction of what he calls 'Ecological Tax Reform', whereby taxes would involve a steady price increase of some 5 per cent annually over some 30 to 40 years for fossil fuels and nuclear energy, as well as for other 'problematic natural resources . . . to provide strong and enduring incentives to invest in new technologies geared to reducing significantly the energy and raw material inputs per given unit of output'.[4]

Regulations can still play their part. Indeed to change behaviour rather then just raising money also requires, for example, efficiency standards, subsidies, public education campaigns etc. But the advantage of taxes over just regulations is that they can prompt the development of technology and processes which may go far beyond standards set by any regulations. Regulations often soon become too weak, and require enormous political effort to upgrade.

Energy taxes

An energy tax would have other benefits. The increased financial costs of transportation and the lessening of dependence on imported energy, with the shift to local renewable energy sources and energy efficiency, would speed up the trend for regional self-reliance. Most governments raise the bulk of their revenue by taxing income, profits and the value added to goods and services. While convenient to collect and often serving a crucial redistributive purpose, they can amplify existing distortions in the economy by discouraging work, savings and investment. Taxing resource use, such as energy, on the other hand, is a way of changing behaviour – taxing 'the bad' so that less energy is used and pollution is decreased. Part of the revenue generated can then be used to ensure that taxes on 'the good', such as labour and investment, are not increased and are even decreased.

The USA

The method proposed by President Clinton for the US energy tax is to tax energy at source, ie at its point of entry into the economy, and in relation to its calorific value. Such an energy tax would be passed on by energy producers to their customers, by them to their customers, and so on right through every stage of economic activity to final consumers of goods and services. It would thus have a potentially conserving effect on all economic activity. It would also be progressive. Those who use more, pay more than those who use less; we consider how to overcome the problems energy taxes cause poor consumers below. President Clinton's relatively modest energy taxes are estimated to raise net revenues of $22.3 billion annually in 1997.[5]

Another proposal is a carbon tax levied on coal at the mine or dock, on oil at the wellhead or dock, and on natural gas at the wellhead or dock. A US Congessional Budget Office report in 1990 estimated that $36 billion a year could result from phasing in a carbon tax over five years. Emissions of carbon dioxide would be stabilized at the 1990 level by the year 2000. Internationally, an extra tax of $10 per ton of carbon emitted in industrial countries (excluding Eastern Europe and the Soviet Union) would initially generate $25 billion per year for a global fund. But collecting such taxes nationally is very much easier and requires less agreement than such a worldwide approach.[7]

Europe

The proposed EC carbon/energy tax, at present stalled by concerns about its effect on competitiveness with the US and Japan, is supported by Belgium, Denmark, France, Germany, Italy and the Netherlands. The less wealthy EC countries are worried that such a harmonized tax would jeopardize their growth, while the Netherlands is concerned that the tax might be too low.

To obtain further reductions in carbon dioxide emissions after 2000, more fundamental changes in lifestyle and the increased use of non-fossil energy will be necessary. This will require some of the tax revenue to be recycled to subsidize the required changes in energy use.[8] Carbon taxes do already exist in Finland, the Netherlands (since 1990) and Sweden (since 1991). None of these are high enough to induce major changes in energy use. In the UK it has been estimated that the price of petrol would have to rise to between £2.50 and £3.00 per gallon for private consumption to fall just 10–15 per cent.[9]

Making taxes more acceptable

High energy taxes on their own would not be politically feasible unless some of the tax revenue was spent on ways to lessen their adverse effects. One of the major objections to these energy taxes is that they will cause prices to rise and be inflationary. The most effective way to counter this is to use some of the funds for cuts in income, payroll and corporation tax, or for guarantees for the period of the energy tax of no increase in such taxes. Reducing other taxes on spending, such as Value Added Tax (VAT), will also dampen any inflationary effect. Also, if governments announce well in advance plans for real energy prices to rise and stay up, investors will bring forward investments to reduce energy bills. This process can be further helped by some of the energy tax funds being used for subsidies for adapting to more energy efficient behaviour, and also to assist in the provision of less polluting substitutes, such as improved public transport or research and development into new technologies.

To protect the poor, whose energy bills are highest relative to their incomes, some revenue from energy taxes can be steered into welfare benefits or into a flat-rate energy allowance, ie a certain amount of energy is obtainable at a guaranteed low rate. Also, with overall taxes lower or not increasing, it might be more politically palatable to raise proportionately taxes on the rich and lower those on the poor. The increased emphasis on local energy sources and efficiency, resulting from effective energy taxes, would help reduce the national deficit problems of countries. It is always the poor who bear the brunt of the normal strategies used to 'correct' economies; they suffer disproportionately from higher interest rates, value added taxes and cuts in social infrastructure and services, let alone from the draconian packages in Structural Adjustment Programmes.

Industry in general may argue that a high energy tax will make them less competitive. But the real effects of an energy tax will be concentrated on the most energy intensive industries. This could be partly dealt with either by reductions in corporate taxes or by tariffs at the border against products of those countries who do not protect the environment adequately by taxing energy.

Pollution permits

Pollution permits are another market approach to revenue raising to protect the environment. Theoretically, what happens with the pollution permits is as follows. Each company is arbitrarily and legally ascribed a notional level of pollution which it is allowed in a year. There is an incentive on the company to clean up because it can then sell its pollution permit, or more realistically, a percentage of that right to pollute, to another company which has chosen not to invest in clean-up. To trade in pollution permits only makes sense within the logic of conventional market economics.

The proponents of pollution permits argue that ultimately, there should be a global market in pollution permits. Thus, a developed country could buy from a developing country a proportion of its right to pollute. And *vice versa*, developing countries could buy the right to pollute from richer nations. But international trade in pollution permits begins to look ominously like an incentive to site polluting factories in developing countries. Relocating production in this way fails our 'keep it local' principle. In addition, trading in pollution merely enshrines the right to pollute, rather than emphasising prevention and a different kind of economy in the first place.

Pollution permit trading – within a framework of legislation to ensure specific environmental improvements by a set date, such as stabilizing carbon dioxide emission by 1995 – could be useful. It could provide those companies most able and willing to implement improvements with a financial incentive to do so quickly and allow companies that are unable to afford such changes immediately more time to adapt, or not to go out of business so rapidly. Ultimately, the people living near a plant or factory which is being allowed to pollute for a longer period by buying such a permit are unlikely to share in the enthusiasm for pollution permits trumpeted by the market economist. Their urgent need is to get rid of the pollution. We are wary about pollution permits if they allow polluters to carry on polluting, though as part of a range of measures to cut down on pollution, they could be useful. It is thought that they will be administratively extremely difficult even in the one country trying it at present, the USA, where it is part of an effort to reduce acid rain.[10] We wait to see how the US permit markets works out.

Depletion quotas

Depletion quotas would be even more effective than taxes, according to Herman Daly, senior environmental economist at the World Bank, in a recent book.[11] Depletion quotas set a limit on the amount of a resource which can be used or extracted, which is an important advantage over taxes because quotas *limit* aggregate throughput of the resource. Money would be generated by the auctioning of depletion quotas by the government, rather than by allocating them on non-market criteria. Daly also feels that funds recycled to the economy from taxes could increase economic output, for example through credit expansion or deficit spending, so that resource depletion takes place even though unit costs are rising because people can afford to pay the price. He concludes that:

> 'Finally it is quantity that affects the ecosystem not price, and therefore it is ecologically safer to let errors and unexpected shifts in demand result in price fluctuations rather than in quantity fluctuations. Hence quotas.'[12]

Why tax?

The debate about taxation's role in protecting the environment and in ensuring a decent quality of life needs to be broadened. In the last 15 years, taxes have been thought of as bad and fuelling some inefficient 'nanny' states. What needs to be reasserted is that taxes are socially necessary, but their effectiveness is determined by how they are raised and what they are used for. They should provide incentives to improve environmental standards and funds to restructure the economy in a sustainable and more equitable way and to enable society to do things that otherwise could not be achieved by individuals.

Taxes symbolize the relationship between citizen and state. The state – whether local or national or regional government – should serve the collective good. The free trade approach, in contrast, dismisses this potential, claiming taxes are undesirable. The New Protectionism challenges politicians to shift the tax structure to benefit the citizen, not just to be a burden, and to argue the case for taxes with conviction.

Protecting poorer countries

All of the innovations involved in the New Protectionism carry trade implications for the developing countries. Priority should be given to concrete measures which encourage and assist those countries to raise domestic environmental standards, and in so doing improve their long term environmental quality and economic security. These could take the form of the transfer of funds and expertise as well as phased timetables to allow for the necessary adjustments in poorer countries. In the EC, resources can be provided to help poorer EC countries and regions introduce improved environmental standards using the cohesion fund proposed in the Maastricht Treaty. On an international level, such a funding mechanism will have to be developed for poorer countries.

On a bilateral basis, one suggestion to protect forests, for example, is an import levy on unsustainably logged timber imports. The revenue from this would be repatriated and directed to improve sustainability in the forests concerned. At present, such moves would be GATT incompatible since countries are not allowed to use trade barriers to protect resources outside their own borders. The new GATT priorities we suggested in the last chapter would actively encourage such approaches. Multilateral commodity agreements, too, could also incorporate an 'environmental fund' jointly administered by the parties to the agreement to encourage internalization of environmental costs and direct financial investment towards sustainable production measures. Aid flows and debt relief geared to encouraging the kind of restructuring of the economy required by the New Protectionism will also have a pivotal role for poor countries in their transition to more self-reliant economies.

14.
Seven Misconceptions

We agree with President John F Kennedy's comment that 'the great enemy of truth is very often not the lie – deliberate, contrived and dishonest – but the myth – persistant, persuasive and unrealistic.'[1] In arguing for the New Protectionism, we have come across seven misconceptions, or false beliefs, which are thrown up against it. They are:

Free trade makes life better

Be careful. Living and working in the rich North of the world, as we do, it may seem that the whole world is full of goods and that most people can afford previously unimaginable possessions and comforts, but that is not the whole picture. Poverty grinds down the existence of billions of people. The social damage is also apparent. The hunger which already plagues around one fifth of humanity marches on. With the collapse of the Eastern Bloc, suddenly even the prospect of social disintegration in Europe does not look impossible. The social problems in the North (which pale into insignificance before the South's) are growing; the economic stagnation, the restructuring of the Cold War arms economy (which is looking for new wars to feed on[2]), the downturn in employment as firms replace people with new machines, all these are real. Above all, there is a loss of direction and confidence in many countries.

The proponents of trade liberalization could always argue that the world's economic cake has grown overall, and ignore global inequality. They could point to GATT's role in reducing tariffs as the motor force for growth, but others are not so sure tariff reduction has even caused the growth. Harry Shutt, former chief economist for the Fund for Research and Investment for the Development of Africa argues in his book *The Myth of Free Trade*, that trade liberalization was largely illusory, since the lowering of tariffs was everywhere offset by a far greater resort to 'market-distorting' state intervention than had ever been applied before the war. These interventions include tax incentives and subsidies to investment, military procurement programmes, subsidies to production costs and exports, and the underwriting of loans to the private sector by the government acting as 'lender of last resort'.[3]

What finally makes the argument that free trade improves life no longer sustainable is not just the seeming intractibility of the present recession but the impact of trade on the environment: the damage caused by increased transport, the increased use of non renewable resources and energy, the deforestation, the pollution and the damage to the climate. So, we reject the free trade package because we look at both sides of the coin. Getting goods into shops is a logistical triumph, but how long the ovation lasts can only be judged by the quality of production, the impact on equity and on the durability of the employment – the three 'Es' test.

New protectionists are luddites

Though it now has a perjorative and backward meaning, the Luddites were early 19th century English questioners of the introduction of new technology on farms and in mills. They were not against the new machines so much as against how they were being introduced – being used by owners to replace humans who then joined the paupers.[4]

Take it from us, we too are not against technology. The public is not won to the environmental cause by the promise of hairshirts. Nor are we desk-bound romantics who extol the virtues of digging ditches manually, when a mechanical digger means one can lean on the shovel and look at the view. But the scale of the impact of many new technologies brings into question whether they are being sensibly used and whether some of them are appropriate in the first place.

We can marvel at the power of an enormous 20th century dam or at the elegance of supersonic airliners, but are they the way to address the mass of humanity's needs? The World Bank project to fund Namada Dam in India, thankfully now halted due to relentless local and international opposition, was being promoted as a source of abundant electricity, yet it would have thrown 100,000 people off their land into penury. The supersonic Concorde may look beautiful but it is noisy, polluting and the ultimate in minority transport schemes, when local mass transit schemes are a far more pressing need for billions of people.

Another related criticism of New Protectionism is that our emphasis upon promoting more local and regional trade would mean a loss of the economies of scale. Should not consumers benefit from technology's higher productive capacities? It depends. Unit costs do rise if the economies of scale are lost, and a sudden transition to products from a locally diverse economy could push the price of products up. But in practice today, the introduction of microelectronic controlled production, and the small batch-production runs that are viable due to fast sales data retrieval (such as Electronic Point of Sale – EPOS – systems), has meant that the benefits of scale are reduced. In any case, any rise in narrow economic costs should be offset by the enormous social advantages obtained, notably from having people gainfully employed producing goods and services that people need.

New protectionism ignores market pricing

We are not against prices. For all their faults, no-one has come up with a better way to exchange goods and services; we are not against using prices as the mechanism for regulating markets – it just depends what prices reflect. Our concern is that markets are often rigged by those making the rules, and are concentrating fast in almost all important sectors – electronics, banks, cars, food. Freeing trade merely writes the dominant firms a blank cheque. There is no level playing field in international trade and, in any case, the playing field is a wholly inappropriate metaphor for what is, in fact, world politics, not a game. World politics are still dominated by US power when the level playing field runs all the way down from Washington.

The poor are generally penalized by hard-line free market policies. Prices go up, while wages are held down by the threat of competition with distant labour forces. Today, the UK government is making a positive virtue out of making the UK into a low wage haven, but a low wage economy does not ensure foreign investment.[5]

Prices do often disguise both the social conditions of the producer and the impact of the production process. The relative cheapness of imported hardwoods is because the price does not include tree replacement or care for the land or the people from where it came. A wealth of environmental studies has shown that the cost of protecting the environment for future generations is commonly underestimated.[6] Present, market economic theory does not reflect the real ecological and social costs of economic activity.

We believe that prices ought to incorporate the currently externalized costs of improved environmental or public health standards. This argument is beginning to be accepted, for example in agriculture, where evidence for ecologically appropriate land management practices to prevent damage to soil structures and nutrient loss and the threat to wildlife species is plentiful and public pressure strong. But even there practices are not yet changing fast enough. In other areas of the economy – such as steel or chemicals – the pressure and debate has hardly begun. Cost internalization is a major problem for economics in that it is difficult to ascribe agreed costs to activities. However, the process has to be begun.

New Protectionism undermines the nation state

On the contrary, it is existing trends which undermine the nation state. Rising political unease about the state of Western national economies is an opportunity to highlight one of the effects of a globalized economic order: a *decline* in national control, with less visibility and accountability – what in Euro-speak is termed 'transparency'. Due to the removal of barriers to international trade, a debate has now begun about the role and viability of the nation state.[7]

Our administrative model neither rejects nor blindly accepts the nation state. Everything depends upon what surrounds it and how its machinery is used. The best analogy we can come up with is one of those Russian dolls which contain ever smaller ones inside. In the name of free trade, power is oozing to the biggest, outside doll. We would like to see a reversal of the trend. Power is needed at all levels, but we would like the centre of gravity of power to be closer to the smaller doll than it is at present. Countervailing forces to the TNCs and superblocs are urgently required and we would like to see more local planning within national economies.

The Right sees a threat to its notion of national sovereignty in both regionalism and localism. The Left, which has for so long lionised internationalism out of a laudable antipathy to chauvinism, autarky and racism, has forgotten another tradition in its own political philosophy – to argue for more democratic control and for citizen's rights. We do not favour economic nationalism of the 'when Britain/USA/country X was Great' variety. Nor are we in favour of autarky, the retreat behind fortress walls, as in Pol Pot's Cambodia, or in Burma or Albania, ie total self-sufficiency without trade at all. Our vision for trade is to make it more local and diverse, more accountable and long term oriented.

Protectionism causes depressions

Not true. The cause of the 1930s' slump, for example, was very complex but a major role was played by the failures of governments of the time to stimulate the economy adequately and made worse by the old protectionist policies. To many modern free traders, the 1930s world depression, when tariff barriers were erected on a huge scale, is the worst example of protectionism. In fact, business cycles are integral to market economies. Old protectionism was a *response* to the slump of the 1930s, just as it is today when nation states try to protect their industries by imposing tariffs on imports. This exacerbated the slump, but did not cause it. Even a staunch free trader such as Professor Milton Friedman, of the University of of Chicago, accepts that state intervention did not cause the 1930s crash; his argument is that governments took the wrong turn in their attempts to manage the crisis.[8] Professor Jagdish Bhagwati, another free trader and a GATT advisor, writes:

> 'The Great Depression has been associated with beggar-my-neighbour policies of competitive exchange-rate depreciation and tariff escalation, each aimed at preserving and deflecting aggregate demand towards one's own industries at the expense of those of one's trading partners. Few believe that such policies caused the Depression; there are many more plausible candidates for the role of villain. But it is certainly arguable that tariff escalation deepened the Depression . . . the magnitude of the failure of tariffs, and indeed their seemingly counter productive results . . . helped to stack the cards in favour of the pro-trade forces, providing the ideological momentum for the liberal trade that persists to this date.'[9]

Just before World War II, Keynes and others explained how to cure the depression by injecting purchasing power into the economy. The problem, they said, was the lack of demand. People and banks with funds were not releasing them for investment while the economy was so depressed, which meant that business was unable to reflate the economy. According to Keynes, governments should manage prosperity through massive investment in public works. In fact, it was rearmament for the war which injected such purchasing power into the economy. No-one, except conceivably the armaments industry, wants to see that happen again.

Protectionism leads to racism and authoritarianism

This is nonsense. Protectionism does not inevitably lead to racism, authoritarianism and tight state controls.[10] Racism is at its height when the majority of people feel under financial pressure and are generally insecure. The rise of fascism and nazism in the 1930s began with the market's collapse and coincided with – but was not caused by – the rise of protectionism. Today, what should be called 'free market fascism' is growing on the back of another crisis in the markets. The association with racism is usually the argument against protectionism given by the Left, worried about protectionism generating nationalism and hence, via chauvinism, to racism. Alas, racism crosses all political boundaries.

There are contrary traditions at work on the Left concerning protectionism. On the one hand is the need to protect and defend the rights of working people and the underdog against uncontrolled capitalism, but on the other is a reflex internationalism which favours free trade thought. For us, the New Protectionism will provide the kind of security where racism withers, which allows for both protection of individuals against powerful trading forces and for more just global development. It positively celebrates cultural diversity and is therefore, again, opposed to racism. It aims for co-operation, rather than creeping cultural imperialism. The New Protectionism seeks to defend and extend democracy, arguing that current trade policies disenfranchise people. It seeks protection for all, not just the few.

New Protectionism is just the same as old protectionism

No, it is quite different and differs from the old protectionism in whom and what it seeks to protect. The old protectionism served the short term interests of the powerful elite and national companies; the New Protectionism seeks to protect the world's majority against the free trading elite. The old was committed to protecting narrow interests, the new protects the common interest. The old sought to preserve gross inequalities within and between states; the new seeks the reverse, arguing that today's challenges cross all geographical and social boundaries.[11]

We have to distinguish between the role protection played in the past and the role it could play in the future. As in the 1930s, today there is rising unemployment, stagnation of investment, growing international tension, loss of hope, rising support for extreme right-wing political groups in some countries, and a lack of a clear political and economic alternative. However, much has changed since the 1930s including: the collapse of the old imperial powers and of communism; the rise of modern, flexible-specialization systems of production; the emergence of the powerful new trade superblocs; the emergence of new service and manufacturing industries replacing old employment, often female jobs for male jobs; and the growing international environmental awareness. These and other changes make the world a completely different place today – one that requires a completely different set of policies, geared to providing prosperous but sustainable economies, in short the New Protectionism.

The case for the New Protectionism is not just a reaction to the present world recession. The arguments for a new economics, new trade policies and new urgent action to alter the world's gross inequities and environmentally damaging activities predate the present recession but learn from it, too. The New Protectionism is a response to longer term issues, principally the failure of conventional economics to deliver long term security, the global environmental crisis, and the plight of the poor. In the 1990s all around the world, pressure groups are beginning to educate themselves and their supporters about the implications of trade liberalization and the case for a change. This global coalition is emerging between NGOs committed to protect the environment, world development, welfare and the public interest, as well as organized labour.

Countdown to Protectionism

1992 and 1993 were not good years for free trade. Citizens in many countries had become decidedly restive and less aquiescent. Europe saw millions flocking to the 'No to Maastricht' cause during referenda in Denmark and France. Third World opposition to GATT grew, illustrated by the 'Home Rule Not GATT Rule' demands in India. But, perhaps most significant of all, were US polls showing that over 60 per cent were opposed to NAFTA, thus giving the campaign slogan 'Give NAFTA the SHAFTA' some real potential.

Giving NAFTA the SHAFTA

The US debate on NAFTA is so critical because it is probably only Congress that can scupper the treaty. The three countries have already signed an agreement. Indeed, Canada has already ratified NAFTA, but the ratification does not take effect until the pact is approved by the US Congress. Only Congress has the power and the level of scepticism to reject the treaty when it comes up for the vote in late 1993 or 1994. And if that happens, the Canadian and Mexican approvals fall.

Since 1989, the Mexican government and business groups have spent $25 million dollars to shape and ensure the enactment of NAFTA – the biggest foreign lobbying campaign on a specific issue ever seen in Washington.[1] Despite this and strong initial support for NAFTA from all the media and most commentators, the reality of the threats posed by the treaty to jobs and the environment rapidly dawned on the American people. A growing and ever stronger coalition of farmers, unions, consumer groups, environmentalists and even some business organizations emerged. The American Trade Council and the US Business and Industrial Council see NAFTA as a potential threat to small- and medium-sized US companies, less able to relocate to Mexico than big corporations. The Councils were worried that foreign companies will set up in Mexico to circumvent US trading laws.[2]

A coalition like this has not been seen in the US since the 1930s.[3] It has taken out adverts, lobbied lawmakers, mounted demonstrations and public information campaigns, and taken legislators on organized trips to Mexico.

Former Presidential candidate Ross Perot has also entered the fray. His organization, United We Stand, America (with an estimated membership of up to two million), is also campaigning against the treaty. Perot has testified before Congress against the treaty and in May 1993 he paid for a half hour 'infomercial' against NAFTA on prime-time TV.

Another success for NAFTA opponents occured when they won a case brought by the consumer group Public Citizen, on behalf of itself and two environment groups, the Sierra Club and Friends of the Earth. The ruling of federal judge Charles R. Richey in June 1993 ordered the Clinton administration to prepare an environmental impact statement on the NAFTA, before submitting the agreement to Congress. The judge ruled that 'such an impact statement is essential for providing the Congress and the public the information needed to assess the present and future environmental consequences of, as well as the alternatives, to the NAFTA'.[4] This is expected to result in further delay to the treaty's ratification timetable.

Should the ruling result in the final decision on NAFTA not taking place until 1994, then Congress will be faced with voting on an increasingly contentious issue during what is an election year for some members of Congress. Mexico is also holding an election in 1994 and a new set of US demands for stronger Mexican environmental action could create a political backlash against the treaty.[5] There is also the threat that Canada, with elections in late 1993, might vote in more opponents to the domestically unpopular treaty and try to change at least some of its provisions.[6]

GATT Uruguay Round threatened again

If NAFTA is eventually rejected by the US, or the vote is close, and if concerns about the effects on US jobs and the environment are heightened, then a conclusion of the GATT Uruguay Round also looks less likely.

Another consistent threat to the GATT is France. French opposition to the damaging effects of the new GATT on its agriculture was one of the main reasons why EC/US disagreements held up the Uruguay Round for so long. The Balladur government elected in 1993 is beset with problems over unemployment. Even the champagne workers joined the ranks of truckdrivers, fishermen and farmers in violent protest about job losses.[7] Farmers, who had demonstrated violently against GATT under the former socialist government, were again active after the election. They continued their protests about the bilateral Blair House agriculture agreement, hammered out between the US and EC in November 1992.

Governments get cold feet about free trade

1992 and 1993 saw growing scepticism that the GATT could deliver new employment and growth. Grassroots opposition to free trade agreements grew. By mid-1993, even political pundits and governments were expressing concern about the actual effects of trade liberalizing policies. Employment had become the big concern.

The new French Conservative government was particularly resistant to GATT's charms. With a French Presidential election due in 1995, trade policy was becoming central to the political jostling for postition. Prime Minister Edouard Balladur has already declared GATT a 'thundering god dispensing the lightning of free trade on the bowed heads of the people'.[8] The President of the French National Assembly, Phillippe Seguin (who led the opposition to the spring 1993 referendum on the EC's Maastricht Treaty in France), has asserted that the 'structural crisis' of the world economy justified GATT's 'pure and simple dissolution'.[9]

Political leaders of the USA, Japan and the rest of the EC all claim they are in favour of a quick signing of the Uruguay Round. Behind the rhetoric, political decisions move in a different direction. The US, for example, tightened limits on steel imports and government procurement bidding from the EC and demanded 'managed trade' with Japan. Japan – a country that tried to bar imports of US-made skis as unsuitable for Japanese snow![10] – is unlikely to give in to the Uruguay Round's demand to open up Japanese rice markets to imports, in particular from the US. Opposition to lifting barriers to rice imports was not restricted to the powerful Japanese agricultural lobby. Consumer groups, too, argued that rice imports would break Japan's tough pesticide residues standards. Imports would also make consumers dependent on external producers. Food self-reliance, they argued, is not just a goal for the Third World.

Boris Yeltsin cancelled a planned trip to the EC summit in June 1993 as a protest against European barriers to Russian steel and textiles, and the blocking by the US of uranium exports. Such measures even prompted the Foreign Minister Andrei Kozyrev, one of the most outspoken advocates of links with the West, to start talking about 'reasonable protectionism'.[11]

Unemployment figures, expected to reach a post-war high of 36 million in 1994, caused OECD countries to express fears over imports from cheap labour exporters from Asia. Even Jean-Claude Paye, the Secretary General of the OECD, was moved to talk of having some sympathy for 'piecemeal protectionism'.[12]

Public protectionism

The stage is therefore set for a major shift in public policy. The changes will be fundamental, will take years and will be painful. Change, however, is inevitable. We are optimistic that the growing opposition to the free trade package – whether at regional level, such as against the NAFTA or the EC's Maastricht Treaty, or globally agains the GATT – are evidence of wider understanding that free trade cannot answer the needs and challenge of the three 'Es' – economy, equity and the environment. Public protectionism should replace policies which favour only the powerful. Getting people to think of public protectionism as a practical alternative to the free trade orthodoxy has been what this book is about and is long overdue.

Glossary

ACDA	Arms Control and Disarmament Agency
APEC	Asia–Pacific Economic Co-operation
ASEAN	Association of South East Asian Nations
ATO	Alternative Trading Organisation
BSI	British Standards Institute
CACM	Central American Common Market
CFC	Chlorofluorocarbon
Codex	Codex Alimentarius Commission
CITES	Convention on the International Trade in Endangered Species
CUTS	Consumer Society and Unity Trust (India)
EAC	East African Community
EC	European Community
EEA	European Economic Area (EC + EFTA)
EFTA	European Free Trade Agreement
EPA	Environmental Protection Agency (USA)
EPZ	Export Processing Zone
ESI	Economic Strategy Institute (USA)
FAO	Food and Agriculture Organisation (UN)
FDA	Food and Drugs Administration (USA)
FIELD	Foundation of International Environmental Law and Development
FOE	Friends of the Earth
FTA	Free Trade Agreement (Canada–USA)
GATT	General Agreement on Tariffs and Trade
GEF	Global Environment Fund
GDP	Gross Domestic Product
GMP	Good Manufacturing Practice
GNP	Gross National Product
ICFTU	International Confederation of Free Trade Unions
IFAT	International Federation for Alternative Trade
ILO	International Labour Organisation
IOCU	International Organisation of Consumers Unions
IMF	International Monetary Fund
IPR	Intellectual Property Rights
ISO	International Standards Organization

ITO International Trade Organisation
JECFA Joint Expert Committee on Food Additives (WHO–FAO)
MAFF Ministry of Agriculture, Fisheries and Food (UK)
Mercosur Southern Cone Common Market Treaty (Latin America)
MFA Multifibre Arrangement
MIT Massachusetts Institute of Technology (USA)
MMPA Marine Mammal Protection Act (USA)
MTO Multilateral Trade Organisation
NFA National Food Alliance (UK)
NAFTA North American Free Trade Agreement (USA, Canada, Mexico)
NGO Non Governmental Organization
NHS National Health Service (UK)
NIC Newly Industrialized Country
OECD Organisation for Economic Co-operation and Development
OTA Office of Technology Assessment (USA)
PPS Purchasing Power Standard
QUANGO Quasi Autonomous Non Governmental Organizations
SAP Structural Adjustment Programme
TBT Technical Barriers to Trade (GATT)
TNC Transnational Corporation
TQM Total Quality Management
TRIM Trade-Related Investment Measure (GATT)
TRIP Trade-Related Intellectual Property Right (GATT)
UN United Nations
UNCED United Nations Conference on Environment and Development
UNCTAD United Nations Conference on Trade and Development
UNDP United Nations Development Programme
UNEP United Nations Environment Programme
UNICEF United Nations Children's Fund
USDA United States Department of Agriculture
WHO World Health Organisation (UN)
WRI World Resources Institute (USA)

References

Part One: Confronting the Myth

1. quoted in Holroyd, M, *Bernard Shaw; Volume 2: The pursuit of power 1898–1918*, Penguin, Harmondsworth, 1991, p 122.
2. Cuthbertson, J, 'US Free Trade with Mexico: Progress of self destruction', *The Social Contract*, fall, 1991, pp 7–11, quoted in Daly, H and Goodland, R, 'An ecological-economic assessment of deregulation of international commerce under GATT', World Bank (Environment Dept), Washington DC, Sep 1992, unpub.

Introduction

1. 'Don't green GATT: the dangers of mixing environmentalism with trade', *The Economist*, Dec 26 1992 – Jan 8 1993, pp 15–16; 'Trade and the Environment: the greening of protectionism', *The Economist*, Feb 27, 1993, pp 19–24.

1. The Challenge

1. UNDP, *Human Development Report*, UNDP, New York, 1992, quoted in Daly, H and Goodland, R, see Part One ref 2 above, p 16.
2. Madden, P, *A Raw Deal*, Christian Aid, London 1992; Watkins, K, *Fixing the Rules*, Catholic Institute for International Relations, London, 1992; Madely, J, *Trade and the Poor*, Intermediate Technology Publications, London, 1992; Hines, C *Green Protection: halting the four horsemen of the free trade apocalypse*, Earth Resources, London, 1990; Barratt Brown, M and Tiffin, P, *Short Changed: Africa and World Trade*, Pluto, London, 1992; Davidson, J, Myers, D and Chakraborty, M, *No Time to Waste*, Oxfam, Oxford, 1992; George, S, *The Debt Boomerang*, Pluto, London, 1991; Durning, A, *How much is enough?*, Earthscan, London, 1992.
3. Watkins, K, see ref 2, pp 12–13.
4. Kurien, J, 'Ruining the Commons: Coastal Overfishing and Fishworkers' Actions in South India', *The Ecologist*, vol 23, no 1, Jan/Feb 1993, pp 5–11.
5. Lara, F, 'Structural Adjustments and Trade Liberalization: Eating Away our Food Security', paper presented to Conference on International Trade and Food Security: Issues for the South, Protestant Academy of Mulheim/Ruhr, Germany, 1–3 May 1991, p 3.
6. BP, *BP Statistical Review of World Energy*, 1991, p 36.
7. UNDP, *Human Development Report 1992*, quoted in Oxfam, *Policy Dialogue*, no 9, Sep 1992.
8. Anderson, K and Blackhurst, R, *The Greening of World Trade Issues*, Harvester Wheatsheaf, Hemel Hempstead, 1992.

9. Durning, A, see ref 2, p 28.
10. Durning, A, see ref 2, p 50.
11. Gussow, J, Mary Schwartz Professorship Inaugural Lecture, Teachers College, New York; Durning, A, see ref 2, pp 44–45.
12. Galbraith, J K, *The Culture of Contentment*, Sinclair Stevenson, London, 1992.
13. Durning, A, see ref 2.
14. Prime Minister's deregulation initiative, launched 2 Feb 1993.
15. eg Coote, B, *The Trade Trap*, Oxfam, Oxford, 1992; Barratt Brown, M and Tiffen, P, see ref 2; Madeley, J, see ref 2.
16. Barratt Brown, M, *Fair Trade*, Zed Books, London, 1993.
17. Amin, S, *Delinking: towards a polycentric world*, Zed Books, London, 1990.
18. Amin, S, see ref 17; Barratt Brown, M, see ref 16, pp 46–49.
19. Barratt Brown, M, see ref 16, p 43.
20. Watkins, K, 'The foxes take over the hen house', *The Guardian*, Jul 17, 1992.

2. Reality and Myths of the Free Trade Package

1. Cohen, R, *Contested Domains: debates in international labour studies*, Zed Books, London, 1991, ch 8; see also, Barratt Brown, M, *Fair Trade*, Zed Books, London, 1993, ch 3.
2. ACDA, *World Military Expenditures and Arms Transfers* 1990 figures; and USDA, *World Grain Situation and Outlook*, Mar 1992, quoted in Brown, L et al, *Vital Signs*, Earthscan, London, 1992, pp 104–5.
3. GATT, *International Trade 90–91*, vol 11, Geneva, 1992.
4. French, H, 'Reconciling Trade and the Environment', in, Worldwatch Institute, *State of the World 1993*, Earthscan, London, 1993, p 157.
5. Ref 3, table 1.1.
6. See for example Gershuny, J, *After Industrial Society?: the Emerging Self-service Economy*, Macmillan, London, 1978.
7. Ref 3, chart 1.1.
8. Watkins, K, *Fixing the Rules*, Catholic Institute for International Relations, London, 1992, p 6.
9. GATT, *International Trade 90–91*, GATT, Geneva, 1992, quoted in Worldwatch Institute, *State of the World 1993*, Earthscan, London, 1992, p 161.
10. Ref 4, p 166.
11. Ref 8, pp 5&9.
12. Ref 3, Table 1.2.
13. Ref 3, Table 1.4.
14. See ref 3.
15. Ref 3, Table II.
16. Ref 3, Table 1.5.
17. Ref 3, Table 111.3.
18. Ref 3, Table 111.27.
19. Ref 3, Table 111.7.
20. Thomson, R, 'Japan's trade surplus surges to $107.06bn', *Financial Times*, 23 Jan 1993.
21. Smith, A, *Wealth of Nations*, 1776, quoted in Daly, H and Cobb, J, *For the Common Good*, Beacon Press, Boston, Mass, 1989, p 215.

22. Daly, H, and Goodland, R, 'An ecological-economic assessment of deregulation of International Commerce under GATT', World Bank (Environment Dept), Washington DC, Sep 1992, unpub, p 12.
23. Hancock, G, *Lords of Poverty*, Macmillan, London, 1989; George, S, *The Debt Boomerang*, Pluto, London, 1992; Mosley, P, Harrigan, J and Toye, J, *Aid and Power: the World Bank and Policy-based Lending*, vol 1, Routledge, London, 1991.
24. *The Ecologist*, FAO issue, vol 21, no 2, 1991.
25. Hayter, T, *The Creation of World Poverty*, Pluto, London, 1985; George, S, see ref 23; Madeley, J, *Trade and the Poor*, Intermediate Technology Publications, London, 1992; Barratt Brown, M and Tiffen, P, *Short Changed: Africa and World Trade*, Pluto, London, 1992.
26. Low, P, ed, *International Trade and the Environment*, World Bank Discussion Papers, no 159, Washington DC, 1992; Anderson, K and Blackhurst, R, eds, *The Greening of World Trade Issues*, Harvester Wheatsheaf, London, 1992.
27. Summers, L, foreword to Low, P, see ref 26, p iii.
28. Hearing of the Senate Finance Committee: confirmation of the US Trade Representative, 27 Jan 1989, quoted in Goldsmith, Sir J, 'Intensive Farming, the CAP and GATT', Caroline Walker Lecture, Royal Society, London, 16 Oct 1991, p 20.
29. Thurow, L, *Head to Head: the coming economic battle among Japan, Europe and America*, Nicholas Brealey Publishing, London, 1993, p 17.
30. Douthwaite, R, *The Growth Illusion*, Green Books, Bideford, 1992.
31. Reich, R, *The Work of Nations*, Vintage, New York, 1992.
32. Prowse, M, 'Report of its death an exaggeration', *Financial Times*, 8 Jan 1993.
33. From Keynes, J M, *National Self-Sufficiency*, in Moggeridge, D, ed, *The Collected Writings of John Maynard Keynes*, Macmillan and Cambridge University Press, London, vol 21, quoted in Daly, H, and Cobb, J, *For the Common Good*, Green Print, London, 1990, p 209.
34. Ref 33, p 216.
35. Ref 33, p 216.
36. Gandhi, M K, quoted in Goldsmith, E, *The Way*, Rider, London, p 323.
37. Seabrook, J, 'Still in the missionary position', *New Statesman and Society*, London, 5 Jun 1992, pp 12–13.

Part Two: The Powers Behind the Free Trade Package

1. Galbraith, J K, *The Culture of Contentment*, Sinclair Stevenson, London, 1992, p 53.

3. Transnational Corporations

1. Galbraith, J K, *The Culture of Contentment*, Sinclair Stevenson, London, 1992, p 53.
2. Cairncross, F, *Costing the Earth*, Business Books / The Economist Books, London, 1991.

3. Rockfeller, N, *The Rockfeller Report on the Americas*, Quadrangle Books, Chicago, 1963.
4. Watkins, K, *Fixing the Rules*, Catholic Institute for International Relations, London, 1992, p 9.
5. ILO, *Multinational Enterprises and Employment*, ILO, Geneva, 1988.
6. Daly, H and Goodland, R, 'An Ecological-Economic Assessment of Deregulation of International Commerce under GATT', World Bank (Environment Dept), Washington DC, Sept 1992, p 22, unpub.
7. Watkins, K, 'The foxes take over the hen house', *The Guardian*, London, 17 July 1992.
8. UN *World Investment Report 1992*, New York, 1992.
9. Dembo, D, Morehouse, W and Wykle, L, *Abuse of Power – Social Performance of Multinational Corporations*, New Horizons Press, New York, 1990, quoted in, Morehouse, W, 'GATT and the Right to be Human', paper for International Convention on People's Approach to GATT Negotiations, New Delhi, 18–20 Feb, 1983, p 4; *The Economist: A Survey of Multinationals*, Mar 27 1993, p 4.
10. Clairmonte, F, 'The Debacle of the Uruguay Round – an autopsy' *Third World Economics*, 16–31 Jan, 1991, p 11.
11. Barratt Brown, M, *Fair Trade*, Zed Books, London, 1993, Table 5, p 51.
12. Madden, P, *Raw Deal*, Christian Aid, London, p 46.
13. Tait, N, 'Why the Friesian Lady is feeling full of beans', *Financial Times*, 14 Jan 1993.
14. UN Centre on TNCs, *Transnational Corporations in Food and Beverage Processing*, UN, New York, 1981, chapter 1.
15. *Agrow*, no 112, London, Jun 1990.
16. Greenpeace, *The Environmental Impact of the Car*, Greenpeace International, Amsterdam, 1991, p 10.
17. Staple, G, 'Global Traffic Growth and the New Competition for "Offshore" Business', paper to World Telecommunications, Financial Times Conference, London, 1–2 Dec 1992, p 8.2.
18. ICFTU, 'The Challenge of Internationalism', background document to ICFTU conference on TNCs, Elsinore, Denmark, 1990.
19. Otter, J, 'Some Aspects of Environmental Management within a Chemical Corporation', in Koechlin, D and Muller, K, *Green Business Opportunities: the profit potential*, Financial Times/Pitman Publishing, London, 1992, pp 81–95.
20. Ref 12, p 56.
21. Ref 7.
22. Daly, H and Cobb, J, *For the Common Good*, Green Print, London, 1990, p 234.
23. Sklair, L, *Sociology of the Global System*, Harvester Wheatsheaf, London, 1991, pp 48–9.
24. Heller, R, 'The Big League', *High Life*, British Airways, Nov 1992.
25. *Financial Times*, FT500, Table: 500 Capitalisation by country, Feb 10, 1993, p 2.

4. The Superblocs

1. Eg Thurow, L, *Head to Head: the coming economic battle among Japan, Europe and America*, Nicholas Brealey Publishing, London, 1993.

2. Hashimoto, M, 'Facing an Era of Global Partnership: A View from Japan', and Akitt, J, 'International Trade: A View from the Americas', *Chemistry and Industry*, 16 Nov 1992, pp 862–5 and pp 867–871.
3. World Bank, *World Development Report 1993: Development and the Environment*, OUP, Oxford, Table 1, p 219.
4. see Sklair, L, *Sociology of the Global System*, Harvester Wheatsheaf, London, 1991; Amin, S, *Delinking: towards a polycentric world*, Zed Press, London, 1990, Barratt Brown, M, *Fair Trade*, Zed Books, London, 1993.
5. Janssen, D, 'Challenges of the European Renaissance', *Chemistry and Industry*, 16 Nov 1992, p 859.
6. Barratt Brown, M, see ref 4, Part One; Coote, B, *The Trade Trap*, Oxfam, Oxford, 1991; Jackson, B, *Poverty and the Planet*, World Development Movement, London, 1990.
7. Halvorsen, R, 'Trade Blocs: A View for Scandinavia', *Chemistry and Industry*, and Janssen, D, 'Challenges of the European Renaissance', *Chemistry and Industry*, 16 Nov 1992, pp 853–6 and pp 858–861.
8. Genetics Forum, 'Briefing on the biotechnology industry', forthcoming, London, 1993.
9. Hopkinson, N, *Completing the GATT Uruguay Round: Renewed Multilateralism or a World of Regional Trading Blocs*, Wilton Park Paper 61, HMSO, London, Aug 1992, p 1.
10. figures quoted in Dodwell, D, 'Protectionist wolf in sheep's clothing', *Financial Times*, 15 Dec 1992.
11. Dunne, N, 'Farmers in US exact a high price for Bush support', *Financial Times*, 16 Sep 16 1992; Reuter, *Financial Times*, 10 Sep 1992.
12. Dornbusch, R, 'Economic Focus', *The Economist*, 4 May 1991, p 89.
13. Wolf, M, 'The GATT makes its last stand', *Financial Times*, 20 Jan 1992; see also Wolf, M, *Global Implications of the European Community's Programme for Completing the Internal Market*, Lehrman Institute Policy Paper, Series on the US in the Global Economy, no 1, New York, 1992.
14. World Bank, *Global Economic Prospects and the Developing Countries 1992*, Washington DC, 1992, Table 2–13, quoted in Wolf, M 'How regional trading blocs can damage world trade', *Financial Times*, 13 Jul 1992.
15. figures from de Melo, J and Panagariya, A, *The New Regionalism in Trade Policy*, World Bank, Washington DC, 1992, p 85.
16. Martins, J, *Latinamerica Press*, 23 Jan 1992, p 2.
17. *Financial Times*, 13 Feb 1992, quoted in 'Trade Blocs do not make Free Trade fairer', report of IRENE study day, 11 Feb 1992, Amsterdam, *News from IRENE*, no 15/16, May 1992, p 22.
18. Marin, G, quoted in 'Trade Blocs do not make Free Trade fairer', ref 17, p 23.
19. Ref 15, pp 16–17.

5. GATT – A Charter for the Powerful

1. Daly, H and Goodland, R, 'An Ecological–Economic Assessment of Deregulation of International Commerce under GATT', World Bank (Environment Dept), Sep 1992, unpub.

2. For example: Watkins, K, *Fixing the Rules,* Catholic Institute for International Relations, London, 1992; Arden-Clarke, C, *The General Agreement on Tariffs and Trade, Environmental Protection and Sustainable Development,* WWF-International, Gland, June 1991; Raghavan, C, *Recolonisation: GATT, the Uruguay Round and the Third World,* Third World Network, Penang, and Zed Books, London, 1990; Clairmonte, F, 'The Debacle of the Uruguay Round – an autopsy', *Third World Economics,* 16–31 Jan 1991, pp 10–13; Madden, P, *Raw Deal: trade and the world's poor,* Christian Aid, 1992; FOE, *Fool's Gold,* FOE, London, 1992; Coote, B, *The Trade Trap,* Oxfam, Oxford, 1992; *The Ecologist,* special GATT issue, vol 20, no. 6.
3. GATT, *Draft Final Act Embodying the results of the Uruguay Round of Multilateral Trade Negotiations,* GATT, Geneva, MTN, TNC/W/FA, 20 Dec 1991.
4. Hopkinson, N, *Completing the GATT Uruguay Round: Renewed Multilateralism or a World of Regional Trading Blocks?*, Wilton Park Paper 61, HMSO, London, 1992, p 18.
5. Watkins, K, see ref 2, pp 19–20.
6. Open letter on the MTO, signed by 160 NGOs, see Dunne, N, 'Consumer protest at world trade plan', *Financial Times,* 11 Dec 1992, p 5.
7. Ref 3.
8. Watkins, K, see ref 2.
9. FOE, *Notes on the Proposal for a New Multilateral Trade Organisation (MTO),* London, Mar 1993, p 2.
10. 'Comparison of the Second and Third Revised Texts of the Draft Agreement Establishing the Multilateral Trade Organisation', GATT Secretariat, Geneva, 27 May 1992.
11. Action Aid *et al,* 'Notes on the Multilateral Trade Organisation (MTO) as proposed in Arthur Dunkel's Final Act, 1991', a briefing paper sent to all UK MPs by 10 UK environment, consumer and development NGOs, 25 Nov 1992.
12. Cameron, J and Ward, H, *The Multilateral Trade Organisation: a Legal and Environmental Assessment,* report from Foundation for International Environmental Law and Development (FIELD), Kings College London, for WWF International, Gland, May 1992.
13. See ref 6.
14. 'Senior OECD Official Plays Down Potential Gains From GATT Deal', Reuter, 1 Dec 1992, reprinted in *Trade News Bulletin,* 1 Dec 1992, vol 1, no 203, GATT News Summary.
15. Raghavan, C, see ref 2.
16. Arden-Clarke, C, 'Agriculture and Environment in the GATT: Integration or Collision', *Ecos,* vol 13, no 3, 1992, pp 9–14.
17. Ref 2.
18. Shiva, Vandana, personal communication concerning statement of 19 Sep 1991, New Delhi, India.
19. Sainath, P, 'Patent Folly', Indian School of Social Sciences, Bombay, 1992.
20. CUTS, *All About GATT – a consumer's perspective,* CUTS Calcutta and Jaipur, 1993.
21. GATT, *Focus,* 96, Jan–Feb 1993, p 8.
22. Ritchie, M, in *The Ecologist,* see ref 2.

23. GATT, *International Trade 90–91*, GATT, Geneva, 1992, vol 1, ch 3.
24. See the many publications by the Public Citizen Trade Watch Campaign, Washington DC, and by the Institute for Agriculture and Trade Policy, Minneapolis, such as *Trade News Bulletin*.
25. Dodwell, D, 'US film makers focus on Uruguay Round', *Financial Times*, 7 Jan 1993.
26. Williams, F, 'EC and US go for broke on cutting tariffs', *Financial Times*, 12 Jan 1993; Dodwell, D, 'Untried hands reach for global lever', *Financial Times*, 22 Jan 1993.
27. Ref 20 p 18.
28. Office of Technology Assessment, pp 5–6.
29. Figures quoted in Genetics Forum, 'Briefing on the biotechnology industry', forthcoming, London, 1993.
30. Ref 28, pp 50–64.
31. Vines, G, Guess what's coming to dinner?, *New Scientist*, 14 Nov 1992, pp 13–14.
32. Wilkie, T, 'Genetic patent on cancer mouse faces opposition', *Independent*, 13 Jan 1993.
33. Lang, T, 'Stop Press', *BBC Good Food*, Apr 1993.
34. Rifkin, J, *Biosphere Politics*, Harper Collins, London, 1991.
35. Shiva, V, *The Violence of the Green Revolution*, Zed Books, London and New Jersey and Third World Network, Penang, 1991.
36. 'KRRS activists storm MNC seeds firm', *Times of India* (Bangalore), Dec 30 1992.
37. SUNS, *SUNS Monitor*, 5 Mar 1993; 'Farmers threaten war on MNCs', *Pioneer*, March 4, 1993; also see Chetan, N, 'Farmers take on multinationals', *Down to Earth*, 31 Jan 1993.
38. George, S, *The Debt Boomerang*, Pluto, London, 1992.
39. Goldin, I, van der Mensbrugghe B, *Trade Liberalization: What's at stake?* OECD Development Centre, Paris, 1992; Brittan, Sir Leon, 'Free trade wears well in all weathers', *Independent*, 26 Mar 1993.
40. Bhagwati, J, on CNN, Inside Business, 29 Nov 1992, quoted in ESI, *The Uruguay Round and the United States: A Critical Analysis*, ESI, Washington DC, 1992, p 5.
41. ESI, see ref 40, Table 2.
42. Watkins, K, see ref 2, ch 6.

Part Three: The Effects of the Free Trade Package

1. Morris, D, 'Free Trade: The Great Destroyer', *The Ecologist*, vol 20, no 5, Sept/Oct 1990, pp 190–195.

6. On the Environment

1. Madeley, J, *Trade and the Poor*, Intermediate Technology Publications Institute, London, 1992, p 33.
2. French, H, 'Reconciling Trade and the Environment', in Worldwatch Institute, *State of the World 1993*, Earthscan, London, 1993, p 169.

3. 'Environmental Impact of Transport', in Ministerie van Volhuisvesting, *Re-usable versus disposable*, nr 1991/2, Publikatiereeks produktenbeleid, The Hague, 1992, Tables 1–5.
4. European Commission, '1992: The Environmental Dimension, Task Force Report on the Environment and the Internal Market', Brussels', nd., p v.
5. OECD, 'International lorry traffic transit through Austria', in OECD, *The State of the Environment*, OECD, Paris, 1991, p 209.
6. Jorgensen, et al, 1991, quoted in Greenpeace, *Green Fields, Grey Future: EC Agriculture Policy at the Crossroads*, Greenpeace, Amsterdam, 1992, p 17.
7. Figures quoted in Brunner, E, 'Fertilisers flooding the market', in London Food Commission, *Food Adulteration and How to Beat It*, Unwin Hyman, London, 1988, p 141.
8. 'Environment Strategies Europe, Identification and Analysis of Measures and Instruments Concerning Trade in Tropical Wood', report submitted to the European Commission, Sep 1992, p 2.
9. Ryan, J, 'Plywood vs People in Sarawak', *Worldwatch*, Jan/Feb 1991, cited in ref 2, p 162.
10. Ref 2, p 173.
11. Arden-Clarke, C, *The General Agreement on Tariffs and Trade, Environmental Protection and Sustainable Development*, WWF-International, Gland, Nov, 1991, p 15.
12. Vallette, J and Spaulding, H, *The International Trade in Wastes: A Greenpeace Inventory*, Greenpeace, Washington DC, 1990.
13. GATT – *International Trade 90–91*, GATT, Geneva, 1992, Ch 3.
14. Werksman, J, 'Trade Sanctions Under the Montreal Protocol', in *Review of European Community & International Environmental Law* (RECIEL), vol 1, issue 1, FIELD, London, 1992, p 71 in ref 2, p 174.
15. GATT arbitration panel ruling, 'United States – Restriction on Imports of Tuna: Report of the Panel', DS21/R, Geneva, Sep 1991.
16. Joint letter to House of Representatives from 21 environmental, conservation and animal protection organizations, on GATT and the Marine Mammal Protection Act, Washington DC, 13 Sep 1991.
17. Ref 11, p 29.
18. Shrybman, S, *Selling the Environment Short*, Canadian Environmental Law Association, Toronto, 1992.
19. OECD, 'Trade and the Environment: Issues Arising with Respect to the International Trading System', TD/TC(90)14, OECD, Paris, 1990.
20. GATT, 'Trade and the Environment' in *International Trade 90–91*, Geneva, 1992, Ch 3.
21. Arden-Clarke, C, WWF, personal communication, 30 Mar 1993.
22. *The State of the Environment in the European Community* COM (92) 23 Final, The Commission of the European Communities, 27 Mar 1992.
23. French, H, ref 2, p 172.
24. Hines, C, 'Greening Subsidiarity – A Step Towards The European Environmental Community', *London Public Policy Review*, Spring 1993, p 57.
25. 'Landmark EEC Court Case on Returnable Bottles Gives Boost to the Environment', *ENDS Report*, Sep 1988.

26. Fairlie, S, 'Long Distance, Short Life: Why Big Business Favours Recycling', *The Ecologist*, vol 22, no 6, Nov / Dec 1992, 276–283.
27. Ref 26, p 279.
28. Ref 26, p 282.
29. Caroll, S, *The Single European Dump*, Greenpeace International, Amsterdam, 1991.
30. Ref 2, 165.
31. *Europe Environment*, no 397 – 5 Nov, 1992, p 4.
32. Council of the EC, *Agreement on the European Economic Area*, Luxembourg, 1992.
33. Ref 32, p 44.
34. Hines, C, 'The green view of subsidiarity', *Financial Times*, 16 Sep, 1992.
35. quoted in Greenpeace International, '"Subsidiarity" Wont Save Maastricht Or the Environment', Press Briefing, Greenpeace International, 15 Oct, 1992.
36. Shrybman, S, 'The Costs of Economic Integration', *World Policy Journal*, New York, Winter 1991–92, New York.
37. Shrybman, S, see ref 18; Swenarchuk, M, 'Canada–US Free Trade Agreement: The Canadian Perspective' and Ritchie M, 'Canada–US Free Trade Agreement: The US Perspective' in RECIEL, see ref 14, pp 41–51; Alexander, C, and Stump, K, *The North American Free Trade Agreement and Energy Trade*, Greenpeace, Washington DC, 1992.
38. McQuaig, L, *The Quick and Dead: Brian Mulroney, Big Business and the Seduction of Canada*, Penguin Books, Toronto, 1992.
39. Ref 36, pp 93–110.
40. George, S, *The Debt Boomerang*, Pluto Press, London, 1992, p 26.
41. Fraser, D, 'Environment hit by too free trade', *Financial Times*, 2 July 1992.
42. Citizen Trade Watch/ Fair Trade Campaign, 'Talking Points, briefing on NAFTA', *Public Citizen*, Washington DC, 29 July 1992, pp 3–6.

7. On Work

1. Figures in Goodhart, D, 'Europe isn't working', *Financial Times*, 17 Dec 1992.
2. Ekins, P, Hillman, M and Hutchison, R, *Wealth Beyond Measure*, Gaia Books, London, 1992, pp 126–7; Girardet, H, *Cities: New directions for sustainable urban living*, Gaia Books, London, 1993, ch 3.
3. French, M, *The War Against Women*, Penguin, Harmondsworth, 1992, pp 28–9.
4. Figures produced for UN Conference on Women, Copenhagen, 1980, quoted in ref 3, p 24.
5. Figures quoted in Ekins *et al*, see ref 2, pp 122–3.
6. Goodhart, D and Balls, E, 'Unemployment in the UK', *Financial Times*, 18 Feb 1993, pp 8–9.
7. Thurow, L, *Head to Head: the coming economic battle among Japan, Europe and America*, Nicholas Brealey, London, 1992, pp 53 and 163.
8. UN, *World Urbanization Prospects 1990*, UN, Population Division, New York, 1991, Table A.4, line 1.
9. Ref 8, Table A.4, lines 2 & 3.
10. Population Concern, *Annual Report 1992*, p 3.
11. Harrison, P, *The Third Revolution: environment, population and a sustainable world*, IB Taurus, London, 1992.

12. Harrison, P, 'Getting beyond the question: does population growth cause environmental damage', in Action Aid, *Lifestyle Overload? Population and Environment in the Balance,* Development Report 5, Action Aid, Chard, 1992, p 8.
13. Hurtado, M, 'Population, economic development and environmental degradation', in Action Aid, see ref 12, p 18.
14. Ref 12, p 10.
15. Ayres, E, 'Automobile Production Drops', in Brown, L, Flavin, C and Kane, H, *Vital Signs*, Worldwatch Institute / Earthscan, London, 1992, p 70.
16. Murray, R, 'Benneton Britain', *Marxism Today*, Nov 1985, pp 28–32.
17. Hines, C and Searle, G, *Automatic Unemployment*, Earth Resources Research, London, 1979.
18. Schumacher, F, *Small is Beautiful*, Abacus, London, 1974.
19. Ref 18, p 163.
20. Gorz, A, *Critique of Economic Reason*, Verso, London, 1990; also Hewitt, P, *About Time: the revolution in work and family life,* Institute of Public Policy Research and Rivers Oram Press, London, 1993.
21. US Bureau of Labor Statistics, *International Comparisons of Hourly Compensation Costs for Production Workers in Manufacturing 1975–1990*, US Bureau of Labor report no 817, Nov 1991.
22. Trades Union Congress, *TUC Budget Submission 1992*, TUC, London, Feb 1992.
23. Figures from Eurostat database, quoted in *Industrial Relations Review Report, Pay and Benefits Bulletin*, no 287, 6 Sep 1991.
24. Lennon, P, 'Profits of doom on the border of blight', *The Guardian*, London, 21 Aug 1992, p 23.
25. Kochlin, T *et al*, 'Effect of the NAFTA on Investment, Employment and Wages in Mexico and the US', Skidmore College, New York, Feb 1991.
26. ESI, *NAFTA: Making It Better,* ESI, Washington DC, 1992, p 1.
27. Ref 26, p 4.
28. Quoted in George, S, *The Debt Boomerang*, Pluto, London, p 28.
29. Quoted in Center for Rural Affairs, 'Agreement reached in NAFTA', *GATT Tales*, Center for Rural Affairs, Nebraska, Aug 1992, pp 2–3.
30. Quoted in Richardson, D 'UK agriculture faces up to inevitability of change', *Financial Times*, 16 Feb 1993.
31. Ballinger, J, 'The New Free-Trade Heel', *Harper's Magazine*, USA, Aug, 1992, pp 46–7.
32. Robin Cohen, *Contested Domains: debates in International Labour Studies*, Zed Books, London, 1991.
33. ICFTU, 'The Challenge of Internationalisation', ICFTU, conference background paper, Elsinore, Denmark, 1990.

8. On Money Flows and Social Costs

1. World Bank, *World Development 1992: Development and the Environment*, OUP, Oxford, 1992, figure 4, p 11.
2. French, H, 'Reconciling Trade and the Environment', in Brown, L, *et al*, *State of the World 1993*, Worldwatch Institute / Earthscan, London, 1993, p 170.

3. UN Centre on TNCs, *World Investment Report 1991,* UN, 1992, p 36.
4. World Bank, *Debt Tables 1992–93*, Washington DC, 1992.
5. Dowden, R, 'Inside this building the officials are deciding what's best for Africa', *Independent on Sunday*, 28 Mar 1993 p 16.
6. Graph from ODI Briefing Paper, 1988, reproduced in Barratt Brown, M, *Fair Trade*, Zed Books, London, 1993, p 39.
7. Barratt Brown, see ref 7, p 36.
8. Coote, B, *The Trade Trap*, Oxfam, Oxford, 1992, ch 1.
9. Cheru, F, 'Structural Adjustment, Primary Resource Trade and Sustainable Development in Sub-Saharan Africa', *World Development*, vol 20, no 4, 1992, p 503.
10. Madeley, J, *Trade and the Poor* Intermediate Technology Publications, London, 1992, p 7.
11. Jackson, B, *Poverty and the Planet*, Penguin, Harmondsworth, 1990, ch 5.
12. George, S, *The Debt Boomerang*, Pluto, London, 1991.
13. Watkins, K, *Fixing the Rules*, Catholic Institute for International Relations, London, 1992, p 13.
14. UNICEF, *The State of the World's Children 1992,* Oxford, 1992, p 43.
15. Ref 13, pp 13–14.
16. Ref 12, pp 2–3.
17. Barrett Brown, M, personal communication, 28 Jan 1993.
18. Ref 9, p 497.
19. Quoted in 'Trade Blocs do not make Free Trade fairer', report on IRENE the study day, Amsterdam, 17 Feb 1992, *News from IRENE*, no 15/16, May 1992, p 20.
20. Ref 1.
21. Ref 9, p 501.
22. Pearce, F, 'Botswana: Enclosing for Beef', *The Ecologist*, vol 23, no 1, Jan/Feb 1993, p 26.
23. Ref 22, pp 25–29.
24. Ref 22, p 28.
25. Madden, P, *Raw Deal*, Christian Aid, London, 1992, p 22.
26. Europe Agence Internationale pour la Presse, 'UN/Multinationals: foreign direct investment in developing countries remains unequal, according to the UN report', no 6571, Luxembourg, 17 Jul 1992.
27. Hancock, G, *Lords of Poverty*, Macmillan, London, 1989.
28. Ref 27, p 192.
29. Ref 5.
30. Repetto, R, Dower, R, Jenkins, R and Geoghegan, J, *Green Fees*, WRI, Nov 1992; Jacobs, M, *The Green Economy*, Pluto Press, London, 1991; Daly, H and Cobb, J, *For the Common Good*, Green Print, London, 1990.
31. Ekins, P, Hillman, M and Hutchinson, R, *Wealth Beyond Measure*, Gaia Books, London, 1992; Daly, H, 'From Adjustment to Sustainable Development: the obstacle of free trade', Loyola Law School Conference, 29 Feb 1992; Ekins, P, 'Trade and Environment', *Integrated Environmental Management*, 1993 forthcoming; Ekins, P, 'Trade, Development and Environment', paper to FOE International Annual Conference, Madrid, 29 Oct 1992; Gee, D, 'An Economics for the Environmental Revolution', lecture to Economics Association, London, 2 Dec 1992.

32. Leggett, J, *Global Warming – The Greenpeace Report*, OUP, Oxford, 1989.
33. Godlee, F, 'Health implications of climatic change', *British Medical Journal*, 1991, vol 303, pp 1254–6.
34. Leggett, J, *Climate Change and the Insurance Industry-Solidarity among the Risk Community?*, Greenpeace, London, 1993.
35. Intergovernmental Panel on Climate Change, 'Policymakers' summary of the scientific assessment of climate change report to the IPCC from Working Group 1', Meteorological Office, Bracknell 1990, quoted in ref 33.
36. Greenpeace data; also *New Consumer*, Winter 1992.
37. 'Clinton Energy Tax Falls Short of CEC Proposal', *Energy, Economics and Climate Change*, Feb 1993, p 5.
38. Arden-Clarke, C, 'The General Agreement on Tariffs and Trade: Environmental Protection and Sustainable Development', WWF International, Gland, Nov 1991, p 13.
39. Hotten, R, 'Grinding steel down to size', *Independent on Sunday*, Business Section, 7 Mar 1993, p 6.
40. HM Treasury, *Public Expenditure Plans*, Cm 2219, HMSO, London, Jan 1993.
41. House of Commons Social Security Committee, *Low Income Statistics: Low Income Families 1979–1989*, HMSO, London, Dec 1992, Table 1.
42. Himmelstein, D, and Woolhandler, S, 'Cost without benefits: administrative waste in US health care', *New England Journal of Medicine*, vol 34, no 7, pp 41–5; also Schwefel, D, *et al*, *Indicators and trends in Health and Healthcare*, Spinger Verlag, Berlin, 1987.
43. Beveridge, Sir W, *Social Insurance and Allied Services*, HMSO, London, Nov 1942, para 8, p 6.
44. Clunies-Ross, T and Hildyard, N, *The Politics of Industrial Agriculture*, Earthscan, London, 1992.
45. UN, *World Urbanization Prospects 1990*, UN, New York, 1991, tables A.3 and A.4.
46. Goldsmith, Sir J, 'Intensive Farming, the CAP and GATT', the Caroline Walker Lecture, Royal Society, London, 16 Oct, 1991, p 20.
47. Ref 43, p 11.
48. MAFF and DAFS figures, quoted in SAFE Alliance, Briefing Paper, London, 3 Feb 1993.
49. *Ethical Consumer*, 'Special report on supermarkets', ECRA, Nov/Dec 1992, p 8.
50. Food from Britain, *Annual Report 1991–92*, p 6.
51. Fenelon, K, *Britain's Food Supplies*, Methuen, London, 1952, p 13.
52. UNICEF, *Food, Health and Care: the UNICEF vision and strategy for a world free from hunger and malnutrition*, UNICEF, New York, p 1.
53. Ref 51, p 29.
54. eg Roberts, I *et al*, *US grain policies and the world market*, Policy Monograph no 4, Australian Bureau of Agricultural and Resource Management (ABARE), Canberra, 1989.
55. United States General Accounting Office, *International Trade: Canada and Australia Rely Heavily on Wheat Boards to Market Grain*, Report to the Chairman, Subcommittee on Domestic and Foreign Marketing and Product Promotion,

Committee on Agriculture, Nutrition, and Forestry, US Senate, GAO/NSIAD-92-129, Washington DC, Jun 1992.

56. OECD, *Agricultural Policies, Markets and Trade: Monitoring and Outlook 1991*, Paris, 1991, ch 1–4.
57. Beveridge, W, *British Food Control*, Oxford, 1928; Le Gros Clarke, F and Titmuss, R, *Our Food Problem and its Relation to National Defenses*, Penguin, Harmondsworth, 1939.
58. Curry, D, *The Food War: the European Community and the Battle for World Food Markets*, European Democratic Group, London, 1982.
59. Burnett, J, *Plenty and Want*, Penguin, Harmondsworth, 1966.
60. Morris, David, 'Free Trade: the Great Destroyer', *The Ecologist*, vol 20, no 5, Sep/Oct 1990, p 191.

9. On Regulations and Standards

1. Keen, M, 'Agriculture faces the menace of environmentalism', *Financial Times*, 11 Sep 1992.
2. Quoted in Black, L, 'Nationalism back on the agenda', *The Independent*, Business section, 20 Jun 1992.
3. Lees, A and McVeigh, K, *An investigation of Pesticide pollution in drinking water in England and Wales*, FOE, London, November 1988; London Food Commission, *Food Adulteration and How to Beat It*, Unwin Hyman, London, 1988, ch 4 (pesticides) and 5 (fertilizers).
4. Figures quoted in Maddox, B, 'When profits land you in hot water', *Financial Times*, 20 Jan 1993.
5. Hurst, P, Hay, A and Dudley, N, *The Pesticide Handbook*, Journeyman Press, London, 1991, ch 6 and 7; Lang, T and Clutterbuck, C, *P is for Pesticides*, Ebury, London, 1991; Miller, M et al, *Green Fields, Grey Future*, Greenpeace International, Dec 1992.
6. Lees, A, and McVeigh, K, see ref 3.
7. Millstone, E and Lang, T, *Food Additives: look before you eat!*, Channel 4 and BBC Good Food, London, May 1992.
8. Hildyard, N, 'Maastricht: the Protectionism of Free Trade', *The Ecologist*, vol 23, no 2, Mar/Apr 1993, p 278.
9. Miller, M, 'Food Standards, Codex and GATT in seminar' IOCU proceedings of conference, *Food, International Trade and Quality Standards*, Oud Poelgeest, 14/15 May 1992, IOCU The Hague, 1992.
10. Millstone, E, 'Consumer protection policies in the EC: the quality of food', in Freeman, C *et al*, eds, *Technology and the Future of Europe*, Pinter, London, 1991, pp 330–343.
11. See ref 9.
12. Avery, N, Drake, M and Lang, T, *Cracking the Codex*, National Food Alliance *et al*, London, April 1993.
13. Philip James quoted in Lang, T, *Food Fit for the World?*, Safe Alliance, London, March 1992.
14. Quoted in Millstone, E, 'The character and operation of the WHO/FAO Joint Expert Committee on Food Additives: a critical review', unpublished paper for

T Lang's Codex project, University of Sussex Science Policy Research Unit, Brighton, 1992.

15. Ref 9, p 16.
16. eg 'hormones row causes fresh unease in EC', *Financial Times*, 7 Feb 1990.
17. Miller, M, Consumers Association, personal communication, July 1991.
18. *Financial Times*, 19 Jul, 1991.
19. MAFF News Release, 227/91.
20. *The Independent*, 31 Jul 1991.
21. Farm and Animal Welfare Council, *Report on the European Commission Proposals on the Transport of Animals*, FAWC Sep 1991.
22. Stevenson, P, 'The transport of live farm animals – an unacceptable trade', for Earthkind seminar, Horseguards Hotel, London, 28 Oct 1991.
23. RSPCA paper to Earthkind seminar, also broadcast by Face the Facts, BBC R4.
24. FAWC Report Press Notice, FAWC 3/91, 24 October 1991.
25. 'Food Poisoning: The Chicken Comes Home to Roost', in London Food Commission, see ref 4, ch 8.
26. Compassion in World Farming, *Agscene*, 106, spring 1992, p 4.
27. MAFF News Release, 36/93, 'MAFF strongly committed to deregulation says Gummer', 2 Feb 1993.
28. Balcombe, J, Strange, N, and Tate, G, *Wish You Were Here – How UK and Japanese-owned Organisations Manage Attendance*, The Industrial Society, London, Mar 1993.
29. Department of Health, Press Release, H93/574, 23 Feb 1993, p 2.
30. Otter, J, 'Some Aspects of Environmental Management Within a Chemical Corporation', in Koechlin, D and Mueller, K, eds, *Green Business Opportunities: the profit potential*, Financial Times / Pitman Publishing, London, 1992, p 91.
31. Rowling, N, *Commodities: how the world was taken to market*, Free Association Books and Channel 4, London, 1987, pp 81–4.
32. Barber, L, 'UK blocks funding for Brussels-backed HDTV strategy', *Financial Times*, 16 Dec, 1992.

10. On Citizens and Democracy

1. Morgan, K and Price, A, *Rebuilding our communities: a New Agenda for the Valleys*, a report sponsored by the Friedrich Ebert Foundation, for a conference, A New Agenda for the Valleys, Neath Town Hall, 12 Sep 1992.
2. Figures from European Policy Forum, *Accountability to the Public*, London, 1992; and Willman, J and Court, S, 'Resurgence of quangos defies Thatcherite initiative' and 'Patronage determines who serves at the top', *Financial Times*, 14 Jan, 1993.
3. Lang, T, 'Citizens or consumers?', *The Ecologist*, vol 21, no 4, Jul/Aug 1991, 154–5.
4. International Tourism, *Broadsheet* May–Jun 1992, Council for Education in World Citizenship, London.
5. Eber, S, ed, *Beyond the Green Horizon: principles for sustainable tourism*, WWF–UK, Godalming, Nov 1992.

6. Norberg-Hodge, H, *Ancient Futures*, Sierra Club Books, San Francisco, 1991.
7. World Bank, *World Development Report 1992*, OUP, Oxford, 1992, Table 28, lines 89 and 109.
8. Nader, R, *Unsafe at any speed*, Knightsbridge Publications, London, 1965.
9. Packard, V, *The Hidden Persuaders*, Penguin, London, 1960.
10. Adams, R, Carruthers, J and Hamil, S, *Changing Corporate Values*, Kogan Page, London, 1991; *Beyond Rhetoric*, FOE, London, 1990.
11. Cecchini, P, *The European Challenge 1992*, Wildwood House, London, 1988.
12. Black, A and Rayner, M, *Just read the label: understanding nutrition information in numeric, graphic and verbal formats*, HMSO, London, 1992.
13. Commission proposal for a Council Regulation on Novel Foods and Novel Food Ingredients, COM (92) 295 final – SYN 426, European Commission, Brussels, article 6 para 3.
14. Personal communication from Linda Bullard, Office of the Green MEPs, European Parliament, 1992.
15. Millstone, E and Abraham, J, *Additives: a guide for everyone*, Penguin, Harmondsworth, 1988.
16. Lang, T and Clutterbuck, C , *'P' is for Pesticides*, Ebury, London, 1991; also P label campaign launch, May 1991.
17. Food Advisory Committee, *Food Labelling*, FdAC report 10, HMSO, London, 1992.
18. Die Verbraucher Initiative, 'Comments on the proposal for an ordinance of the Council concerning a common system for the granting of an environmental logo', Bonn, 1990; Lewis, D, 'Doubts cast on claims for 'dolphin-friendly' tuna', *New Scientist*, 9 May 1992, p 10; FOE, 'Eco-Labelling', memorandum of Evidence to the House of Commons Environment Select Committee, London, May 1991; National Advisory Group on Eco-Labelling, *Giving Guidance to the Green Consumer – progress on an eco-labelling scheme for the UK*, Department of the Environment, London, 1991.
19. Davidson, M, *The Consumerist Manifesto: Advertising in postmodern times*, Routledge, London 1992, p 39.
20. Ref 19, p 23.
21. 'Landor Image Power Survey, 1990', quoted in Gellerstadt, L, 'The role of advertising in a market economy: the advertiser's perspective', DuPont de Nemoirs International, paper to CASIN seminar, Geneva, 26–27 Jan, 1993, p 2.
22. Longfield, J, 'Advertising and labelling: how much influence?', in National Consumer Council, *Your food, whose choice?*, HMSO, London, 1992, p 57–8.
23. Dibb, S, *Children: Advertisers Dream, Nutrition Nightmare?*, National Food Alliance, London, 1993, June.

Part Four: Protecting the Future

1. Daly, H and Goodland, R, 'An ecological-economic assessment of deregulation of international commerce under GATT', World Bank (Environment Dept) Washington DC, Sep 1992, unpub.

11. Trading Alternatives

1. Holdroyd, M, *Bernard Shaw, Volume 2: The Pursuit of Power 1898–1918,* Penguin, Harmondsworth, 1991, pp 121–6.
2. Barratt Brown, M, *Fair Trade*, Zed Books, London, 1993.
3. For further details contact the Fairtrade Foundation, c/o *New Consumer*, 52 Elswick Road, Newcastle upon Tyne, NE4 6JH.
4. Ref 2, p 193–5.
5. Jetter, M, 'Fair Trading Initiatives', briefing for the European Ecological Consumers Co-ordination, May 1992, unpublished, pp 3–4.
6. 'Multatuli' (Eduard Douwes Dekkar), *Max Havelaar or the Coffee Auctions of the Dutch Trading Company*, Penguin, Harmondsworth, (originally pub 1860) 1987.
7. Fair Trade Foundation, unpub, Newcastle, May 1992.
8. Johnson, V (ed), *Lifestyle Overload? Population and Environment in the Balance*, ActionAid Development Report No 5, 1992.
9. Madden, P, *A Raw Deal*, Christian Aid, London, 1992.
10. See ref 2, p 175.
11. Dodwell, D, 'EC banana plan 'grossly inefficient' says World Bank', *Financial Times*, 29 Sep 1992, p 7.
12. Cicada Films, 'Sex, drugs and dinner', introduced by Alexei Sayle, screened on BBC TV2, 16 May 1992.
13. Watson, R, 'The Single European Banana Market', *CAP tales,* Farmers Link, Norwich, Oct 1992, p 7.
14. Bull, D, *A growing problem*, Oxfam, Oxford, 1982.
15. Dinham,B, *The Pesticides Hazard*, The Pesticides Trust, Zed Books, London, 1993.
16. Coote, B, *The Trade Trap*, Oxfam, Oxford, 1992, p 152.
17. Ekins, P, *A New World Order: grass roots movement for Global Change*, Routledge, London, 1992; Getz, A, *Agriculture and community involvement*, Institute of Current World Affairs, Hanover, New Hampshire, 1992; also Soil Association, *Community Supported Agriculture*, Bristol, 1992.
18. Gussow, J, *Chicken Little, Tomato Sauce and Agriculture*, Bootstrap Press, New York, 1991, pp 96–104.
19. Festing, H. 'Consumer Groups in the UK and Overseas – Existing Models: A Report for the Creative Consumer Co-operative', New Consumer, Newcastle, 1992.
20. Redfern P, *The Story of the C.W.S. 1863–1913*, Co-operative Wholesale Society, Manchester, 1913.
21. Lang, T, 'Food Poverty and Health', Paper to Conference on Poverty, Glasgow Healthy City Project, Glasgow, 6 Nov 1992.

12. The New Protectionism

1. Cairncross, F, *Costing The Earth*, Business Books / The Economist, London, 1991, part II, ch 1.
2. Wagstyl, S, 'The child victims of India's slave trade', *Financial Times*, 19 Dec, 1992.

3. Kurien, J, 'Ruining the Commons: Coastal Overfishing and Fishworkers' Actions in South India', *The Ecologist*, vol 23, no 1, Jan/Feb 1993, pp 5–11.
4. 'Out of the Blue . . . and into the Brown', *Food Matters Worldwide*, Norwich, no 16, 1992.
5. Council of the EC *Agreement on the European Economic Area*, Luxembourg, 1992.
6. Daly, H and Cobb, R, *For the Common Good*, Green Print, London, 1990; on health, see Quick, A and Wilkinson, R, *Income and health: towards equality in health*, Socialist Health Association, 1991.
7. Quoted in Daly, H and Cobb, R, see ref 6, p 209.
8. President Franklin Roosevelt, speech in 1937 to US Congress, quoted in French, H, 'Reconciling Trade and the Environment', in Brown, *et al, State of the World 1993,* Worldwatch Institute/Earthscan, London, 1993, p 178.
9. Hines, C, 'The green view of subsidiarity', *Financial Times*, 16 September 1992.
10. Cooley, M, 'European Competitiveness in the 21st Century', FAST programme, European Commission, Brussels, 1990, quoted in Robins, N, *Reinventing Europe*, New Economics Foundation, London, December 1992, p 8.
11. Crabtree, T, McRobie, G and Roberts, A, *Towards A New Sector: Macro-Policies For Community Enterprise,* New Economics Foundation, London, 1992.
12. Wilkinson, D, 'The freedom to fail', *The Guardian,* 11 Dec 1992.
13. Gore, A, *Earth in the Balance: ecology and the human spirit*, Earthscan, London, 1992.
14. Durning, A, *How much is enough?: the consumer society and the future of the earth*, Earthscan, London, 1992.
15. Daly, H and Cobb, J, see ref 6.
16. Dinham, B, *The Pesticide Hazard: a global health and environment audit*, Zed Books, London, 1993.
17. World Bank, *World Development Report 1992,* OUP, Oxford, 1992, Table 30, line 89.
18. French, H, see ref 8, p 178.
19. Arden-Clarke, C, *South–North Terms of Trade, Environmental Protection and Sustainable Development*, WWF-International, Gland, Feb 1992, p 2.
20. Arden-Clarke, C, *The General Agreement on Tariffs and Trade, Environmental Protection and Sustainable Development*, WWF-International, Gland, June 1991.
21. French, H, see ref 8, p 178.
22. Hayter, T, *The Creation of World Poverty: an Alternative View to the Brandt Report*, Pluto Press, London, 1981.
23. Macneil, J, Winsemius, P, Yakushiji, T, *Beyond Interdependence: The Meshing of the World's Economy and the Earth's Ecology,* OUP, Oxford, 1991.
24. *See* Van Brakel, M and Buitenkamp, M, *Sustainable Netherlands: A perspective for changing northern lifestyles,* Discussion Paper, Friends of the Earth, Netherlands, Amsterdam, May 1992.

13. Paying for the Transition

1. World Bank, *World Development Report 1992*, OUP 1992, Table 11, pp 238–239.
2. Robins, N, *Reinventing Europe*, The New Economics Foundation, London, Dec 1992, p 9.

3. Repetto, R, *et al*, 'Green Fees: How a Tax Shift Can Work for the Environment and Economy, WRI Publications Brief', WRI, Washington DC, Nov 1992.
4. Von Weizsacker, E and Jesinghaus, J, *Ecological Tax Reform: a policy proposal for sustainable development*, Zed Books, London, 1992, p 9.
5. *Energy, Economics and Climate Change*, Cutter information Corp, Feb 1993, vol 3, no 2, p 2.
6. Congress of the United States, Congressional Budget Office, *Federal Taxation of Tobacco, Alcoholic Beverages, and Motor Fuels*, US Government Printing Office, Washington DC, Aug, 1990.
7. Repetto, R, see ref 3.
8. DRI European Energy Service, *The Economic Impact of a Package of EC Measures to Control CO_2 Emissions*, Final Report, Prepared for the Commission of the European Communities, November, 1991; Capros, P, 'Energy Pricing and Substitution in CO_2 Reduction Analysis, STOA workshop, European Parliament, 2 Feb 1993.
9. Jacobs, M, *Sustainable Development: Greening the Economy*, Fabian Tract 538, London, 1990, p 22.
10. Durr, B, 'A market made out of muck', *Financial Times*, 10 Jun 10 1992, p 14.
11. Daly, H, in Daly, H and Townsend, K, *Valuing the Earth*, MIT Press, Cambridge, 1993, pp 340–348.
12. Ref 10, p 341.

14. Seven Misconceptions

1. Kennedy, J F, quoted in *London Public Policy Review*, issue 1, 1993.
2. Smith, D, 'The Sixth Boomerang: Conflict and War', in George, S, *The Debt Boomerang*, Pluto Press, London, 1992, pp 136–167.
3. Shutt, H, *The Myth of Free Trade*, Blackwell, Oxford, 1985, pp 1–8.
4. Hobsbawm, E and Rude, G, *Captain Swing,* Penguin University Books, Harmondsworth, 1973.
5. Henke, D, 'Pay study rebuts Maastricht fear', *The Guardian,* 29 Mar 1993.
6. see Arden-Clarke, C, International trade, GATT and the environment, WWF Position Paper, Gland, 1992, May; Daly, H and Goodland, R, 'An ecological-economic assessment of deregulation of international commerce under GATT', World Bank Environment Dept, Washington DC, Sep 1992, unpub; George, S, *The Debt Boomerang*, Pluto, London, 1991, ch 1.
7. Reich, R, *The Work of Nations*, Vintage, New York, 1991.
8. Friedman, M and R, *Freedom to Choose*, Penguin, Harmondsworth, 1980, p 113–5.
9. Bhagwati, J, *Protectionism*, MIT Press, 1988, p 20.
10. Friedman, M and R, *Freedom to Choose*, Secker and Warburg, London, 1980.
11. Ekins, P, *New World Order: grassroots movements for Global Change,* Routledge, London, 1992; also see Lang, T, *Food Fit for the World?,* Sustainable Agriculture, Food and Environment (SAFE) Alliance, London and Public Health Alliance, Birmingham, 1992.

Countdown to Protectionism

1. Lewis, C and Ebrahim, M, 'Can Mexico and Big Business USA Buy NAFTA?', *The Nation,* 14 June 1993, p 826.

2. Ref 1, p 828.
3. Dawkins, K, *NAFTA: the new rules of corporate conquest,* Open Magazine pamphlet series, PO Box 2726, Westfield, NJ 07091, Jun 1993, p 20.
4. quoted in Public Citizen press release, Washington DC, 30 Jun 1993.
5. Behr, P, 'NAFTA Pact Jeopardized By Court', *Washington Post,* 1 Jul 1993.
6. Greenhouse, S, 'Judge in a Ruling That Could Delay Trade Pact', *New York Times,* 1 Jul 1993.
7. Allen-Mills, T, 'Bubbly with bouquet of burning rubber', *Sunday Times,* 4 Jul 1993, section 1, p 1.
8. Stelzer, I, 'G7 will send Clinton away empty-handed', *Sunday Times,* 4 Jul 1993, section 3, p 6.
9. Nundy, J, 'Euro-rebel lays claim for high office', *Independent,* 18 Jun 1993.
10. Ref 8.
11. Steele, J, 'West's honeymoon with Yeltsin's Russia is over', *The Guardian,* 5 Jul 1993, p 11.
12. Wolf, M, 'The sleeping giant awakes', *Financial Times,* 28 Jun 1993, p 15.

Index

Index

Index

Index

Index

Index

Tim Lang is Director of Parents for Safe Food, a consultant to the National Food Alliance GATT and food project, and chair of the Sustainable Agriculture, Food and Environment (SAFE) Alliance. He has worked widely in the consumer, environment and public health movements, and his former posts include Senior Lecturer at Manchester Polytechnic, Director of the London Food Commission, food policy advisor to the European Commissioner on the Environment, and Secretary of the Public Health Alliance. He was a founder member of the European Eco Consumers Coordination and of the Consumers Network on Trade. His research interests cover all aspects of food policy and he has written a number of books on the subject, including *Food Irradiation – The Facts* (Thorsons) and *P is for Pesticides* (Ebury Press).

Colin Hines has worked in the environmental movement for more than 20 years, campaigning on population, food, new technology and unemployment, nuclear proliferation, and most recently on the adverse environmental effects of international trade. He has been a lecturer at South Bank Polytechnic, a campaigner for Friends of the Earth, and a founder of the European Proliferation Information Centre (EPIC), and is on the board of Verification Technology Information Centre (VERTIC) and Earth Resources Research (ERR). He is co-author of *Agribusiness in Africa* and *Automatic Unemployment* (ERR), and is currently coordinator of Greenpeace International's Economic Unit.